2-21-2

D1604333

Beyond
Mortal Boundaries

By Annalee Skarin

Books by the same author:

CELESTIAL SONG OF CREATION

SECRETS OF ETERNITY

TO GOD THE GLORY

YE ARE GODS

MAN TRIUMPHANT

THE BOOK OF BOOKS

THE TEMPLE OF GOD

Library of Congress Catalogue Card No. 79-107347

ISBN: 0-87516-089-1

Distributed by:

DeVorss & Company
P.O. Box 550
Marina del Rey, California 90294

Printed in the United States of America

BEYOND MORTAL BOUNDARIES
By ANNALEE SKARIN

TABLE OF CONTENTS

PREFACE

Christ proclaimed, "I am come that ye might have life and have it more abundantly — even life eternal!"

Christ never spoke of death nor did He leave any teachings by which man could be prepared to die. He taught only Life! Life more abundant! Glorious, beautiful Life! Yes! He taught only the principles of Eternal Life!

He revealed "The Straight and Narrow Way that leads to LIFE ETERNAL, which so few find." At the same time He warned against the Broad Open Way which leads to destruction and which so many enter.

In the Book of Revelations are eight verses of flame which speak of the blessings and dynamic powers of those who would OVERCOME, even as He overcame.

Christ foretold of the time in which all distress and sorrows and evils would be OVERCOME and added, "And the last enemy to be OVERCOME IS DEATH!" He testified that if we believe on Him we need never die. Also he proclaimed, "If ye believe on me ye shall do all the works I do — and go on to do GREATER WORKS." These promises have never been fulfilled — or even considered.

And it must be here made known that God never planned death! He permitted it because of "the blindness of men's minds and the hardness of their hearts and because of the gross wickedness of unbelief."

Death is the dreary, back door entrance into the other world. It is the servant's entrance. But there is a great front door of glory for those who OVERCOME.

From the ancient record of Nicodemus, Chapter XVIII, verse 12, in the Lost Books of the Bible, is given this definite information. It was when Satan returned into Hell boasting that he had the Son of God crucified and hanging from a cross that the angel of Death answered in horror: "O Satan, prince of all evil, AUTHOR OF DEATH, and source of all pride, thou shouldst first have inquired into the evil crimes of Jesus of Nazareth, and then thou wouldst have found that he was guilty of no fault worthy of death." He even warned that Christ would be able to enter the realms of Hell and release all the prisoners from Hades, which He did, according to the record of St. Peter, in the Bible.

And it is true, "The wages of sin is death!" And from the ancient writings of the great ones comes this word: "Upon him who OVERCOMES ALL SIN, DEATH HAS NO CLAIM."

This book, "Beyond Mortal Boundaries," is the record which reveals the Way of Life Eternal — that "STRAIGHT AND NARROW WAY!" "And that Path is so simple and so easy a fool need not err therein." (Isaiah 35:8)

This record also reveals the glorious, triumphant march of man toward Godhood and the breath-taking wonder of his divine lineage, the dynamic race of Gods, his holy ancestry.

"We have had fathers of our flesh who corrected us and we gave them reverence; shall we not much rather be in subjection to the Father of Spirits and live?"

CHAPTER I

THE POWER OF THE PROMISES!

Oh, the marvel and the wonder of God's greatness! The unspeakable glory of His power! The breath-taking beauty of His love! And "the extent of His doings none can find out!"

These divinely directed books have been written under the hand of Almighty God. And they lie not! They have been given to prepare the children of men for the complete fulfilling of all the holy PROMISES given since time itself began.

This particular volume contains the final keys and the last unfolding of the directions and the powers along that divine road of fulfillment and of OVERCOMING. This record unfolds the method by which one may purchase the "gold tried in the fire that he might be rich indeed, and the white raiment" that he may literally become clothed in Light, that the shame of his nakedness will never appear.

Those who accept this record and fulfill its PROMISES will truly be "Born of the Spirit," as Christ explained to Nicodemus. To "be born of the Spirit" is the power of translation, which so few understand and so many deny. Those who have the faith to live by the higher laws will be "born of the Spirit" and will become translated beings and death will have no power to touch them. And "Everyone who is born of the Spirit will have the power to come and go as the wind and no one will know from whence he

7

came or whither he goeth." So declared Christ and His words cannot be broken.

And the Master declared: "The Father himself, which hath sent me hath borne witness of me. Ye have neither heard his voice at any time, nor seen his shape.

"And ye have not his word abiding in you; for whom he hath sent, him ye believe not.

"YOU search the scriptures; for in them ye think ye have eternal life: and they are they which testify of me.

"AND YE WILL NOT COME TO ME THAT YE MIGHT HAVE LIFE." So spoke Jesus to the multitude, as recorded in John 5:37-40.

In the thirty-ninth verse of the King James version of the Bible it reads thus: "Search the scripture: for in them ye think ye have eternal life: and they are they which test-ify of me." This is a *mis*translation. The word YOU was left out. But according to the original Greek writings, from which the above reference is quoted, it is not given as a command to search the scriptures but rather as a rebuke or an accusation, this constant searching of the scriptures.

And thousands down the ages and thousands today have searched or are searching the scriptures, thinking that in them they will find eternal life, while they ignore Christ completely with His continual outpouring, personal information and loving direction for the constant emergencies of life. It is in that personal contact with God, as one opens up his soul to be "taught of God" that all power lies. The great power to do the works which Christ did is not contained in the scriptures but in the living contact with God. And those who hold their minds continually within the pages of the Bible will become *word-bound* in their thinking and their lives will become as dried and brittle as parchment. It is these who have failed to go to Christ, in a love of devotion that will reveal the TRUTH and go beyond the dead letter of the law, that remain in their dead, orthodoxed conformity of unprogressiveness.

The tragedy of the thousands, as they have accepted of the mistranslation "to search the scriptures," is that they are living only by the letter of the law as various passages have appealed to their unopened, uninspired, unenlightened understandings. And their views become narrowed as they go forth to preach their own private doctrines with a fanatical, often self-righteous attitude of intolerance.

And there are those blessed, misguided ones who have overburdened the minds of their precious children with memorized verses and passages of scripture which the children comprehend not. Such over-zealous ones believe the road to glory is paved with dogmas and scriptural passages. They assume that the more passages of scripture one has stored in his brain the farther he will be able to ascend into the kingdom of heaven.

The most regrettable part of such erroneous conceptions is that those who believe thus have LIVED none of the things with which they have crammed their minds even while their souls and hearts are empty of everything except *quotations*.

Any individual who constantly quotes scriptures, which he has not PROVED by the living of them, and so obtained the powerful fulfilling of the PROMISES, is like a man who has eaten but has not digested or assimilated the food, then spews it out — as "VOMIT" "to defile the banquet tables of the Lord," as Isaiah proclaimed. Unlived scriptures is as unacceptable as undigested food, spewed out. It is not only defiling but an insult to those who are invited to partake of it. These spewed-out, hashed-over words that have not been digested or lived, are a mockery. And from this time forth they will be totally unacceptable, for those who profess to carry the powers and authority of God will be required to *prove* their claim by doing the works which Christ Did — and GREATER WORKS. "For *my kingdom is not in word, but in* POWER saith the Lord."

Yes, "YOU search the scriptures; for in them ye think ye have eternal life: and they are they which testify of me. AND YE WILL NOT COME TO ME THAT YE MIGHT HAVE LIFE!" The great command is to learn to go to Christ who will forever pour out the LIVING WORD of His enlightening power to all who will seek for it or who request instruction. The living, eternal invitation is to: "Come unto *me*," (Not to the scriptures) "all ye who labor and are heavy laden" (with mortality and its earthly burdens) "and I will give you rest;" ("which rest is the fulness of my glory!" This is according to the fullness of this divine spiritual PROMISE.) "Take my yoke upon you (for my yoke is love) and my burden is Light!" It is the great Light of Jesus Christ which He offers to share with any who will only ask or who will go to Him, the great LIVING CHRIST with their burdens.

This near-sightedness to the scriptures was a failing of mortals even in the days of Jesus Christ upon the earth. He told how the letter killeth, that little written letter of the word. But "THE SPIRIT GIVETH LIFE!" Or that contact with Christ, which maketh alive all things.

In those ancient days they kept their eyes so centered upon the letter of the law they failed to behold Jesus Christ, the Son of the Living God — and so they crucified Him.

Here is Paul's explanation of it as given in the second chapter of Galatians and the sixteenth verse, which is as follows: *"Knowing that a man is not justified by the works of the law,* BUT BY FAITH IN JESUS CHRIST, *even we have believed in Jesus and not by the works of the law*s FOR BY THE WORKS OF THE LAW SHALL NO FLESH BE JUSTIFIED."

Then in verse twenty-one of the same chapter, Paul adds: "I do not frustrate the grace of God: for if righteousness come by the law, then Christ died in vain."

Also in Galatians, chapter three and verses ten to thirteen, Paul continues: "For as many as are of the works of the law are under the curse: for it is written, Cursed is every one that continueth not in all things which are written in the book of the law TO DO THEM.

"BUT THAT NO MAN IS JUSTIFIED BY THE LAW IN THE SIGHT OF GOD, it is evident: FOR THE JUST SHALL LIVE BY FAITH.

"And *the law is not of faith*: but the man that doeth them shall live in them.

"CHRIST HATH REDEEMED US FROM THE CURSE OF THE LAW."

Then in verse nineteen, Paul adds: "Wherefore serveth the law? It was added because of transgression, till the seed would come to whom the promise was made."

Paul then explained that: *"Abraham lived under the glory of* the PROMISES, BY FAITH.' It was four hundred thirty years later that the laws were added because of the wickedness and transgressions of the people. And the law is: that those who are wicked must live under the CURSE of the law.

The wicked not only must live under the curse of the law *they must be judged by the law. They must be ruled by the law* instead of by LOVE and FAITH and TRUTH, which comes under the direct contact with God. When Christ came it was again granted unto man to leave the law and to live according to the power of the PROMISES by FAITH. And again man failed to accept the PROMISES in their literal meaning or to exercise the FAITH TO PROVE or fulfill them.

The scriptures are to be used to PROVE and to verify all instructions received and to establish TRUTH, for no newly revealed *truth* will ever contradict the Bible. But the Bible does not contain ALL of God's words, nor can it bind God down to eternal silence for much of it can only be fully comprehended by a continual outflowing of the divine Spirit of God.

"AND THEY ARE CALLED GODS UNTO WHOM THE WORD OF GOD COMES!" This does not refer to the scriptures, remember. There are milions to whom the Bible has come who are wicked, unbelievers, disobedient, or fanatical and sometimes sanctimoniously self-righteous and without the tiniest ability to love. "The WORD" that is referred to is the LIVING WORD which is that divine contact with God at all times.

This WORD is best explained by the inspired writer of the Odes of Solomon, contained in the Lost Books of the Bible, as follows: "And from it (THE WORD) came love and concord; and they spake one to the other whatever was theirs; and they were penetrated by the WORD:

"And they knew Him who made them, because they were in concord; for *the mouth of the* MOST HIGH *spake to them;* and His explanation ran by means of it:

"FOR THE DWELLING PLACE OF THE WORD IS MAN: AND ITS TRUTH IS LOVE.

"Blessed are they who by the means thereof have understood everything, and have KNOWN THE LORD IN HIS TRUTH! Hallelujah!"

These books which God has commanded me to write, have been written under the direction of God, to reveal the great, dynamic PROMISES OF THE ALMIGHTY! There are no new revelations in this work — no new PROMISES. These books only contain the PROMISES which God has given down the ages. And at a casual, unthinking glance there will be those who might proclaim them to be the most beautiful Fairy Tales ever written. But this is not so. Every *promise* quoted in these books is one of the ETERNAL PROMISES given by GOD HIMSELF, or by His Beloved Son, Jesus Christ, or by some divinely chosen prophet. None of these *promises* has been made by me. I was only appointed to hold a giant magnifying glass over them to make them apparent, yes, so that "ALL MEN MIGHT BE LEFT WITHOUT EX-CUSE." These are God's PROMISES and He will fulfill them unto all those who BE-LIVE.

Too many have sat back with their hands folded awaiting Christ's glorious coming to fulfill all PROMISES for them. These mistaken. ones, who have become the blind followers. of the blind, will be the ones who will have no oil in their lamps when He does appear. Christ left these words behind for man's guidance, "If ye believe in me YE SHALL DO THE WORKS WHICH I DID AND GO ON TO GREAT-ER WORKS!" *Every professing Christian is required to exercise Faith in the* PROMISES until he is able to do ALL the works which Christ did — then go beyond them. And "Without FAITH it is impossible to please God."

Those who do accept the PROMISES of God and who begin to LIVE by them, THROUGH FAITH, are no longer under the law. Such as can reach beyond the law unto His divine PROMISES, AND live by them, become *the true followers of the Lord Jesus Christ* for they go to Him for fulfillment as they accept *every promise* ever given and LIVE according to these dynamic, breathtaking PROMISES, by Faith, even as Abraham did.

It is not by the law or by quibbling over obscure passages of scripture that one is justified or exalted. It is only by fulfilling the PROMISES as one LIVES by FAITH that he can possibly be glorified and exalted above earthly mortality.

This Spirit of understanding, or of revelation, if so you choose to designate it, or the ability to be taught of God, or to receive that power to have "The Word of God come to you, that you might be called Gods" is something which any humble, searching soul may receive. "The Spirit of Revelation is in connection with these blessings. A person (any person) may profit by noticing the first intimation of the Spirit of Revelation; for instance, when you feel pure intelligence flowing into you, it may give you sudden strokes of ideas, so that by noticing it, you find it fulfilled the same day or soon; (i.e.) those things that were presented unto your minds by the Spirit of God WILL COME TO PASS: and thus by learning the Spirit of God, and understanding it, you may grow into the principle of revelation, UNTIL YOU BECOME PERFECT IN CHRIST JESUS." This can only be achieved as one opens up his soul so that the LIVING POWER OF GOD can instruct him personally.

The following gives a perfect analysis of man's capacity to be taught of God. "We consider that God has created man with a mind capable of instruction, and *a faculty which may be enlarged in proportion to the heed and diligence given to the light communicated from heaven to the intellect* and that the nearer man approaches perfection the clearer are his views, and the greater his enjoyments, till he has OVERCOME the evils of his life and lost every desire for sin; and like the ancients, arrives at the point of faith where he is wrapped in the power and glory of his Maker and is caught up to dwell with Him. But we consider that this is a station at which no man ever arrived in a moment; he must have been instructed by proper degrees, until his mind is capable in some measure of comprehending the propriety, justice, equality and consistency of the same."

"And they were called Gods unto whom the word of God came. And the scriptures cannot be broken," so said Jesus Christ as He reaffirmed the ancient scriptures before Him, that they might become ALIVE in the hearts of the children of men. "Lay hold of the *Promises!*" LIVE by them! *Prove them!* "For nothing is impossible to him who believes!" Such is the PROMISE!

Chapter II

POWER UNLIMITED

Christ gave the glorious, beautiful PROMISE that if one lived the TWO FIRST AND GREAT COMMANDMENTS he would have fulfilled ALL THE LAWS AND KEPT ALL THE COMMANDMENTS AND WOULD NO LONGER BE UNDER THE LAW.

Again, quoting from Galatians, chapter five, verse eighteen, Paul informs us: "BUT IF YE ARE LED BY THE SPIRIT, YE ARE NOT UNDER THE LAW!"

In first John, chapter four and verses seven and eight, this is given: "Beloved, let us love one another, for love is of God; and EVERY ONE THAT LOVETH IS BORN OF GOD, AND KNOWETH GOD. HE that loveth not knoweth not God, for God is love!" Yes. He that loveth not knoweth not God though he be a walking concordance of every passage of scripture ever given.

Now, again I am commanded to unfold the First and Great Commandment and the fulness of its power and glory. This particular scripture has been referred to several times in these books. But never before has the complete unveiling been opened with all the breath-taking powers and blessings revealed in their fulness. It is man who benefits from fulfilling this perfect law. And it is man who is exalted and glorified by its released, almost incomprehensible, wondrous blessings. And the time IS NOW!

16

This First and Great Commandment does most assuredly fulfill ALL the laws as it opens wide the gates of glory. It perfects any individual who will only put it to the test and begin to live by it, instead of just quoting it, or by nodding his head in approval at the mention of it.

Within this revelation, by Jesus Christ, is contained the power of translation which is the overcoming of death. It contains the divine power of the unspeakable promise given by Christ to Nicodemus, that "Every one who is born of the Spirit can come and go as the wind (whenever there is a need or an assignment which requires it;) and no man will know from whence he came or whither he goeth."

The strangest thing is that this First Great Commandment has been with man from the beginning and has been ignored in the ages past as completely as it has been ignored in our present day. It was given eight times by Moses — AND IGNORED. So it has remained down the centuries, an unproved, unglorified string of words, without power. (Note the following references: Lev. 19:18, 34; Deut. 6:5; 10:19; 11:1, 13, 22; 19:9; 30:6). Why have those who have continually searched the scripture never beheld these numerous references to a law or invitation so divine and so powerful?

It is by the fulfilling of this One great law or divine invitation to approach the throne of God, that ALL the laws of righteousness are fulfilled and ALL power bestowed.

This time, as it is quoted, the full power of its revealing glory will unfold to him who can take hold of THE PROMISES AND ACCEPT THEM, by FAITH.

The wonder of God's unfolding is almost unspeakable. And with deepest love I invite you to venture with me into the sacred precincts of your heart.

As one concentrates his energies on loving God with *all* his heart — the great, living heart-center (not just the heart organ) he will find that holy center of peace, "The peace that passeth understanding." This is a heavenly place to enter into, even for only a few minutes, in these days of hectic, wild, anguished living.

As one enters that heart center with all the love he can possibly generate flowing out from him, he will realize it is a realm of unfolding, breathtaking power. Within this divine heart center is contained the "Holy of Holies" of his own inner soul, in which he can commune with God. This is the place of "Holy Communion!" It is "the secret place of the Most High!" Here one can close the door to the whole outside world and its conditions of strife and know that he is being bathed in a purity of Light and Love such as he has never before known. He discovers his own great center of love and thus he can open up within himself "The fountains of living Waters," which Christ promised. They could also be designated "the fountains of eternal youth."

As one continues to enter into this sacred precinct of his own heart he will realize that as he sends out love *the love of God* will begin to be poured out through him. And this "love of God, which is shed forth through the hearts of the children of men, is the "FRUIT OF THE TREE OF LIFE!" He will know that *he can partake of that Fruit every day of his life* and those divine life-forces will increase within himself. He will be able to exchange an aging, worn-out, sickly body for one vibrant and alive. And in his increasing devotion his heretofore hardened, blinded heart will melt in a love so graciously tender he will know, that in Spirit, he is kneeling at the very throne of God. And God is shedding out His love through him.

As one sends love through his heart he discovers that this love, which he releases, contains that which is required "to buy the gold tried in the fire," mentioned in Revelations 3:18.

This precious gold which man is invited to purchase can only be obtained through the released love of his own heart. This gold will make one rich indeed. This is the gold of which "Christ is the Refiner, as He sits with His fan in His hand." (Mat. 3:12 & Luke 3:17). As the Refiner occasionally leans over and fans away the vapors from that molten cauldron of ore he will be able to see his own face reflected in that precious gold when it is completely purified. Then it is that one becomes so perfected he will be able to behold the face of Christ as that veil or those vapors are cleared away.

And as the heart is fully opened and purified, through love, one is offering God the only sacrifice that would be henceforth acceptable — the sacrifice of *an open or broken heart*. And only through a contrite, humble spirit can this sacrifice be offered.

This molten gold also has another purpose. This is the gold bought from God that not only makes one rich, not with physical, material riches, but with the riches of unspeakable power. This is not the riches which the rich man may boast of saying, "Behold, I am rich and have need of nothing; and knowest not that thou art poor and wretched and miserable and blind and naked." Behold, saith God, "I counsel thee to buy of me the gold that is tried in the fire that thou mayest be rich."

It is into this pool of liquid, molten gold that one can ray out his desires in their pure perfect patterns and they will be reflected out into the universe to bring the return of all that is desired or requested. This sacred, rayed-out pattern, held out by the mind of man, has the efficacy to gather the *"substance of things hoped for"* into tangible form. And thus all things will be added, as promised. Such a one will have every request and desire fulfilled. "As one seeks this sacred Kingdom within, all else will be added." This is the wealth not subject to moth or rust or thieves. This is the great power of creation that will create from *"The substance of things hoped for"* every desirable condition and thing. And not only the physical desires and needs are provided but those divine yearnings of the soul can be fully accomplished.

Love God with ALL your heart? Yes. Try it! Love Him with ALL the strength of your heart and feel the power of that love bring its full measure of plenty and happiness and fulfillment into your life. "And he who asks *anything* AND DOUBTS NOT IN HIS HEART shall have whatsoever he asks." Doubting disturbs the smooth surface of that pool of gold and it becomes like "waves of the sea, driven by the wind and tossed; and let not that man think he shall receive anything of the Lord."

Few indeed have accepted the PROMISES or sought to fulfill them. And none have sought to PROVE the powers of fulfilling that first commandment which was reaffirmed by the Lord Jesus Christ Himself.

As one takes upon himself the responsibility of fulfilling this dynamic invitation of love, he will learn of its unspeakable power and everlasting glory. But this responsibility must be assumed by each individual as he selects to PROVE it. It is not something to be used once a week or once a month or once a year — or once in a lifetime. This is a melody that will grow into a divine symphony of eternal power and unfolding as it is practiced constantly until it becomes a very part of one's life — or until one becomes the love!

Glory? This is glory unspeakable in the fulness of its sublime power. "Therefore *purify yourselves.*" Yes. "Live the principles of truth — and most important, love with every cell and fibre of your being until love is established within you to such an extent you actually become the love. "For he who would interpret the wonders of the Lord will be dissolved and will become that which he interprets." "Live these things and you will KNOW FOR YOURSELF AND YOU WILL NEED NONE TO TEACH YOU, FOR GOD HIMSELF WILL BE YOUR TEACHER."

Love with ALL your heart! Love with ALL the *strength* of your heart! Use your full strength to send out and perfect your own outflowing gift of love and love will flow back to you increased and multiplied and glorified.

So many reach out their empty, hungry hands clutching for any small crumb of love. These starved, unhappy ones know not the meaning of love or of the method of releasing it or of receiving it. The whole secret of receiving love is in learning to give out love. Love attracts and multiplies itself. Love draws friends and multitudes and becomes an enlarging magnet of glorious outpouring, healing perfection. It is endless, boundless and powerful in its tender release. It is the glory of God in action in the lives of men.

This great, powerful love of divine perfection is not self-love, which so many possess. Self-love is stifling and most destructive if it does not include one's neighbors and the whole world and the Creator thereof. Love must flow out in order to be increased and returned.

Love heals! Love blesses! Love restores and perfects all things! Love is as limitless as the universe as one seeks to bless others with it. Love overcomes the ugly little mortal self that is always trying to take and to receive and yet never gives. The strident little mortal self with its self-seeking and self-acclaim is dissolved before the releasing of one's own fountains of love. As one continually practices love, love unfeigned, "and prays with ALL the energy of heart to be possessed of it he will eventually be born of love — or born of God.

This released love of the heart contains the power and the blessings for anyone who will look beyond the words into the very heart of its powers and begin to take hold of its everlasting, divine promises, through faith.

The dross in the original ore is the mortal self with its selfish vibrations of desired credits and acclaim blocking its way. It is the physical, mortal weaknesses that are cloaked in the covering of pride and hypocrisy that veil the wondrous glory of this path of fulfillment.

As one perfects love within himself the dross is burned away and "Christ, the refiner of pure gold," rejoices in the revealed vision of perfection which finally stands forth purified and prepared for use.

CHAPTER III

THE LIMITLESS GLORY OF LOVE'S
RENEWING POWER

As one learns to love God with ALL his soul, he soon trains every cell and fibre and atom of his entire being to accept love until his whole being becomes the very essence of pure, divine love. One can so command his soul to receive this love, flowing through his own heart, that his physical body will be changed and he will become literally the very fulness of that divine love of God.

As one spiritualizes his physical body in this manner he cannot grow old or ugly or die. He cannot be ill or experience pain for these things will be transmuted or "done away in him." These negative conditions, these physical harassments are *overcome* in him and he fulfills the words and the promise which states: "He who overcomes the evils of his life and loses every desire for sin * * * will be wrapped in the power and glory of his Maker and will be caught up to dwell with Him." This is the power of *overcoming* made manifest. It is the glory of translation. And those who deny these things know nothing of God or His divine powers or of His eternal PROMISES. "For nothing is impossible to him who believes!" This comprehension of the power of love and of learning to send it through the entire body is part of the divine method of *OVERCOMING* mortality with its sordid conditions and grim penalties.

23

At this point one has not only been able to buy the gold tried in the fire he is invited to "Buy the white raiment that he might be clothed, that the shame of his nakedness will never appear" — or the shame of his physical, mortal weaknesses.

It is quite possible, through this exerted effort of sending out love, through every living cell of the mortal body, to transform those cells of flesh into Spirit. Then one can take on the glory of the Spirit as he becomes clothed in Light, or in that precious "White raiment," promised by God. And every haggard blotch of age and mortality, every wrinkle of ugliness, every mark that has been engraved upon the body through dislikes, hateful thoughts. jealous, greedy or selfish thoughts can be erased and the shame of their physical imprint will never appear or become apparent.

This is the process of Translation. It is done thought by thought, cell by cell, as one completely spiritualizes his entire being and becomes clothed in Light. Thus one can be transformed into a vibrant being, clothed or arrayed in the "White raiment" or in the beautiful power and Light of immortality. For "Man can evolve from the man kingdom into the God Kingdom."

Anyone can do it! Just love with ALL your soul and prove it!

"Live the laws and you will KNOW!" Use your strength to practice and fulfill and so prove the unspeakable power of His perfection and of His promises! "For if you do as He says, then is He bound! And if you do not as He says then you have no PROMISE!"

———

Now, we must take another step along this road of *overcoming*, which, in itself, is a road of utter glory!

This step can be taken in perfect stride along with the two foregoing ones. They are really one and the same for one cannot possibly take one of them without taking the others unless he desires to fall flat on his face and refuses to pick himself up and go on to full mastery.

"Love God with ALL your mind!" This phrase is backed up by many quotations from the ends of the earth. For instance, "Think no evil" "Let your mind and lips lose the power to hurt and wound and your voice will be heard among the Gods!" Or, "Think only the most beautiful things possible!" Or, "Think as God thinks!" Or, as Paul declared, "Let the same mind be in you which was also in Christ Jesus, who being in the form of God thought it not robbery to be equal with God."

Then there is the great and glorious promise contained in the following: "And if your *minds* become *single* to the glory of God your whole bodies shall be filled with Light, and there shall be no darkness in you. And that body which is filled with Light comprehends all things!" And the promise is that God will unveil His face to such a one.

This contains the unspoken promise given in the purifying of the gold as the dross in the crucible of man is relinquished and purified or drained away so that Christ can behold His face in that reflected pool of molten purity. And the individual, thus purified, is able to behold the face of Christ. It is the same promise and the method of receiving it is the same — the perfecting of love.

As one loves God with ALL his mind he will give up or relinquish his own little narrowed, bigoted ideas for he will outgrow them completely as he outgrew the toys of childhood. And he will feel a renovating process begin to take place in the dark caverns of his subconscious. This realm of the subconscious mind is where every discord, every hurt, real or imagined, has been stashed away to corrode and stagnate in the sewer level of the brain. All the shameful, hidden, sneaky, unworthy actions, every selfish, undesirable motive, despicable shadow of jealousy, every inferior trait is stored into the depths of those dark recesses of the mind. Every undesirable memory, every weak, hateful trait of character is smouldering there to be hidden from the eyes of the world. But they have NOT BEEN OVERCOME. They have been accepted and nourished and fed on the vitality and strength of the individual who harbors them or who has ignorantly permitted their existence to continue beneath the covering of his own blindness.

These are the realms the psychiatrists are trying to heal by their often harmful delving as they open these Pandora boxes of evils.

It must be acknowledged that there are these levels of hidden, negative memories and guilts that can destroy one's mind—and life. And there are those individuals who dwell constantly in the sewer levels of their minds. These have become overpowered and overwhelmed by the darkness of their own creating. They are unwholesome and repellent. They permit themselves to become sewer rats as they dwell mentally upon all the evils of life, seething in their self-pity, their hatreds, their imagined wrongs and the burden of their own dismays. They are to be doubly pitied as they seek for love, not by earning it, but by trying to force it from others. These dwell only in the dark hallways of the *past*.

Love returns to him who gives it out. One does not possess love by pretending he has it as he makes excuses for all his lacks. And often these unloved and unlovable ones believe they are disliked because of their greater righteousness. And they do not realize that actually they have no claim whatsoever upon righteousness as they justify their undesirable state. They dwell in the realm where all their individual faults and weaknesses and contaminated dislikes are hoarded.

No person who gives out real love—"the love unfeigned"—is ever friendless or unwanted or alone. Anyone who loves with a great, unselfish devotion will as automatically draw people to him as the sun draws the faces of the flowers upward to his rays.

And as one begins to concentrate on loving God with ALL his mind these negative, discordant, selfish fears and self-pity of destruction are OVERCOME. This is the OVER-COMING of the darkness mentioned in the great promise of glory, which is as follows: And "If your minds become single to the glory of God you will be filled with Light and there shall be NO DARKNESS IN YOU; and that individual who is filled with Light shall comprehend all things" —And God will unveil His face unto him."

This overcoming of the nether regions of the mind is the first victory to the one who begins to practice loving God with *all* his mind. This is also how one "OVERCOMES THE EVILS OF HIS LIFE, and loses every desire for sin; and arrives at the point of faith where he is caught up in the power and glory of his Maker."

This is the OVERCOMING! This is redemption! This is glorification! And this can be so complete that none of the gross iniquities of the past "will ever come in remembrance before the Lord." What a supreme promise of everlasting, merciful beauty! As the dark evils and sordid memories are overcome, by love and light, so that they will never come in remembrance before the Lord, one can be assured that they will also be blotted out of his own memory by his own great OVERCOMING. To such there is no judgment. To such the glorified law of mercy becomes the full essence of his divine existence.

As these traits of darkness are overcome so that the memory of them will be forever blotted out in a glorifying radiance of Light and Love he will be lifted beyond the physical law of death. The Tree of Life is only guarded from mortal man "so that he cannot partake of the fruit thereof and LIVE FOREVER IN HIS SINS." When sin is overcome then can one have free access to that divine Tree and partake forever of its Fruits insomuch that he cannot die.

This is the full purpose and the sacred PROMISE given to those who OVERCOME. And to him who overcomes there is no bar of judgment, in which his sins and secret thoughts will be revealed or displayed before the eyes of the entire creation. This is indeed MERCY. And this divine, glorious gift can only be claimed by one who OVERCOMES the evils of his life — the darkness of the sewer system in his subconscious mind—and it becomes purified thereby.

Those who die because of their failure to overcome, while in this life, carry the vibrations of all the evils and darkness, the dislikes and the self-pitying corrosion of the past with them into the world beyond. And by the darkness of these evils and the dreary vibrations of their unconquered negations they will be retarded in their progress in the realms beyond. And these vibrations of one's own failures remain with him for those in the entire universe to look upon.

To him who OVERCOMES, death has no claim. He cannot die, for having *overcome* all the evils of his life, death has to back down for it is the last enemy to be *overcome* in any individual's life if he fulfills the laws of its *overcoming*.

And if such a valiant one is called to serve in even the highest realm of Light he can step across, unhampered and without restraint and with perfect ease. The rays of retarding darkness have been so transformed into Light they bring the added power of their transformation into a brilliance of everlasting radiance.

These are the powers and the wonders opened to anyone who will take hold of the fulness of that First and Great Commandment and apply its dynamic powers in their lives. There is no individual on the earth who can claim a monopoly upon these gifts and stupendous powers.

And each individual has the freedom of his own desiring to select or reject this unspeakable glory of *overcoming*. There are no weaknesses, no inferior traits, no evil in this world or in any individual's life that cannot be *overcome*. The method is so simple even a child can fulfill the PROMISES. For God will grant wisdom to anyone who asks. He will grant wisdom and help to every living soul who desires them that he might comprehend the gracious glory of such possibilities, and so receive the power to prove the laws or PROMISES BY LIVING THEM.

It is when LOVE can be poured down into that "lowdown" "maybe" area of doubt and fear and anguish and self-pity and hatred that the precious subconscious mind will be renovated, purified and transformed. Then the powers of its unused potentialities will come into perfect functioning. It is in the subconscious that the power to learn, to memorize and to store eternal truth abides. This part of the mind is also where one has the ability to master any task, skill or art. This part of the mind is where the sacred Holy Ghost or (Divine Helper) functions from. This divine power of unfolding is also the Revealer of Truth and is the ETERNAL WITNESS OF TRUTH.

This divine gift has never really been permitted to function in its fulness because it has been crowded out by the evil, negative thinking of men. When the subconscious is cleansed by love and filled with Light and of joy and gratitude then the amazing powers of Almighty God are henceforth released into the life of the individual.

We have here revealed the first step in the practice of learning to love God with ALL the mind, for LOVE casts out all fear — and all darkness and negation and evil.

Now, comes the second step.

There is also the conscious mind that flutters and fluctuates between indecision and its outside strivings. This part of the brain must also be held in calmness and control as it is held in the awareness of released love. This is the realm of complete awareness. It is a condition of superb alertness, of undeadened perfect control.

As one learns to "Think only the most beautiful things possible," the most gracious and powerful thoughts possible, then love will become the indwelling glory and holiness of its functioning. Then can the individual's thoughts and pure desires be immediately dropped or reflected into that perfected pool of purified gold, within the heart center, to create the reality of the most glorious hopes and dreams possible to maintain. This is the perfection of receiving the great wealth — the power to have "all else added".

In this enlightened stage of progress one truly "walks in glory and becomes clothed in Light!" His whole existence takes on meaning and purpose and such happiness as few on this earth have ever dreamed of.

This precious mind is the one that comes into perfect

control and dwells in full power in the great eternal NOW! The subconscious is of the past until renovated and cleansed of all the evil and negative harborings. The conscious mind controls the ever-living PRESENT—THE ETERNAL NOW in a joy of ever unfolding perfection.

And when the subconscious and the conscious mind are thus renovated and purified they join forces with the great superconscious or divine mind and become united with eternal Light. HIS MIND BECOMES SINGLE or At-One! Such a one will become powerful! "He will comprehend all things! He will be filled with Light and there will be no darkness in him!"

THIS IS THE OVERCOMING—this complete relinquishment of the darkness and the fears and the evils of one's mortal life.

This perfect condition is best described in the breathtaking PROMISE revealed in the following: "And if your *minds* (not mind) become SINGLE to God (or become united and work together as one powerful, synchronized unit) you shall be filled with Light and comprehend all things; and there shall be no darkness in you! And God will unveil His face unto you." And when that happens you will no longer be a mere mortal for the gift of Eternal Life will be yours.

This Superconscious mind is the great spiritual mind which is used by God. It is the God-mind within the individual. It is the glorified place of complete union or AT-ONE-MENT or the place of ATONEMENT, in which a man can become ONE with God, as Christ so earnestly prayed for.

As one practices "thinking only the most beautiful things possible," he is preparing himself to abide continually in that realm of Spiritual power. This is the realm which belongs to the OVERCOMER. It is the realm that contains all the powers of heaven. And these powers were meant to be brought forth by man and used.

These great powers are revealed as follows: "Therefore it is given to abide in you: the record of heaven; the Comforter; the peaceable things of immortal glory; the truth of all things; that which QUICKENETH ALL THINGS, which MAKETH ALIVE ALL THINGS; that which KNOWETH ALL THINGS, and HATH ALL POWER, according to wisdom, mercy, truth, justice and judgment."

According to the divine *wisdom* of God is this power available to man. And according to HIS *mercy* He has placed such an infallible fountain of power within the reach of man. And according to His great TRUTH He has placed the record, or memory of heaven within the scope of our minds as well as the comprehension of ALL THINGS, or ALL TRUTH. We have not been placed on a lost, "lone and dreary world" without any access to truth and Light and the power of God. For according to the JUSTICE of God we have been granted an access to that which can QUICKEN us and MAKE ALIVE our bodies. And accordingly we will be JUDGED by the use we make of such dynamic powers of eternity.

These almost incomprehensible powers *are* given to abide in man. They are in the realm of the great superconscious mind, which man has more or less rejected and left unused as he has often dwelt, in his ignorance, in the lowest realms of his thinking area.

This higher or spiritual or superconscious mind is available for man's use at all times. But it is only when we have united our other two minds, the conscious and the subconscious minds, with that divine one, after they have been cleansed and purified, that we can reach the AT-ONE-MENT, Or receive the full degree of Christ's Atonement.

In practicing constantly the privilege of learning "to think only the most beautiful things possible" one soon learns to abide in that higher spiritual realm of his own divine self. He learns to rejoice and to use those fabulous powers which God, in His great mercy, has given to abide in man "that he might subdue all things."

As the three minds are thus united and become SINGLE or become cleansed and united as one single unit of functioning one truly *becomes filled with Light and comprehends all things* for he then opens the record of heaven, which is given to abide in him, for the subconscious realm will have been cleansed and so it will function in the purest power of its possibilities, which are breathtaking. And the conscious mind, filled with that Celestial Song of everlasting glory will exalt the body into a state of spiritualized perfection, knowingly and consciously. And thus all power will be bestowed upon the individual who will begin to develop the hidden glories of his own dynamic being, as a son of God.

These truths can be PROVED by anyone who is willing to give up his old ways of thinking and feeling and begin to live by the "higher laws of perfection, even as the Father in Heaven is perfect."

This superconscious mind is the great spiritual mind which is used by God. It is the God-mind within the individual. It is the glorified place of complete union or At-one-ment or the place or condition of ATONEMENT, in which man can become one with God as Christ so earnestly prayed for — and gave His life to reveal.

"If your *minds* become SINGLE and are purified so that they can function as one, then all things are possible."

The minds can only be perfected, purified and united through the great love as one uses his conscious mind to direct this perfecting. And the conscious mind is most quickly brought to its fulfilling by the perfecting of the great Celestial Song of Praise and Love and Gratitude in a continuous melody of joyous release.

As one loves with ALL his mind he has OVERCOME the very possibility of remaining a repulsive, discordant person, clothed in bigotry, or of becoming such an individual. Such a one could not possibly lose his memory, or alertness or become senile. With his mind linked with the mind of God "he will comprehend ALL THINGS AND ALL THINGS WILL BECOME SUBJECT UNTO HIM!"

As one practices this great love in order to fulfill ALL laws and ALL commandments and release the unspeakable powers of divine love into his life he will be able to love with all his strength. This can be practiced in two ways. One can love God with *all* the strength of his heart, *all* the strength of his soul and *all* the strength of his mind. This will be accomplished automatically through practice. But if one practices loving with his heart, then with his soul, then with his mind and draws the love forth in a deep concentration of his entire strength he will feel for a moment of dynamic wonder the blending of the powers of his entire being leaping into a great thrill of fulfilling. He will feel, in that moment, such an amazing power surge through his entire being he will know that God is God. He will feel in that instant his entire soul being co-ordinated in one great, dynamic glow of Lighted power.

This will be only an instantaneous experience at first, but as it is practiced it increases in length of time until it becomes an established vibration in the life of that individual.

CHAPTER IV

THE ETERNAL POWER OF ALMIGHTY GOD

With the foregoing information established the realms of Light can be opened wide to the understandings of the righteous that they might truly be filled with Light and comprehend all things, "THROUGH FAITH IN THE PROMISES!"

"And again, verily I say unto you, and I say it that you may chase darkness from among you;

"He that is ordained of God and sent forth, the same is appointed to be the greatest, notwithstanding he is the least and the servant of all.

"Wherefore, he is possessor of all things; for all things are subject unto him, both in heaven and on earth, the life and the Light, the Spirit and the Power, sent forth by the will of the Father through Jesus Christ, his Son.

"But no man is possessor of all things except he be purified and cleansed from all sin.

"And if you are purified and cleansed from all sin, ye shall ask whatsoever you will in the name of Jesus and it shall be done."

In this almost unspeakable PROMISE is given the information that one must be *ordained of God* (not man) and be SENT FORTH by the power of God and under His direction.

The world is filled with those who lay claim to such divine calling but have only assumed such authority as God has

35

enlightened them occasionally in their dire needs or earnest searchings.

To be ordained of God and to be sent forth by God is to be directed by God in every instance and in every word. This can only be fulfilled in the fulness as it was with Christ, Who proclaimed, "I speak no word except my Father commands it." And the Father can only direct the one who has united his three minds in the power of divine love until they become ONE—or SINGLE.

And in that holy ordination and unit the individual *is "appointed to be the greatest, notwithstanding he is the least, and the servant of all."* This seemingy contradictory statement was first declared of John the Baptist and needs an explanation.

It is most easily understood by those who have fulfilled the divine calling and received that sacred ordination. No one having such a holy calling of greatness upon his shoulders could ever boast of it. Nor could he acclaim his superiority or greatness.

With the power of God upon him he would become the very least in his own selflessness and sublime degree of devotion and loving humility. He would become the least in his own opinion and the very servant of all in his great love. He could never lift his voice to bear witness of himself or entertain, for an instant, even a desire to do so. Like Christ, he would realize that he could never become an insufferable braggart, but as Christ, would say, "I do not bear witness of myself." But the very power of his calling would bear witness of him. As long as anyone boasts of his higher place or qualifications or self-importance and self-righteousness he is denying the holiness of such a calling as he seeks to exalt himself, "even above the throne of God."

Those who boast of all their personal experiences, as they seek to hold themselves in the limelight, can never receive the anointing of God or of greatness for it is impossible for them to take the lowest seats, to become "the least and the servant of all," until they are invited down. Thus the humiliation becomes often quite devastating as their pride is crumbled. And often such crumbling includes the individual and he is revealed as nothing.

And so it is necessary to explain just what the power and the anointing of God entails.

As one begins to take hold of the great and mighty PROMISES of God, by first his exerted faith in seeking to *live the promises,* he will soon grow into the KNOWLEDGE of their power. And KNOWLEDGE IS POWER!

Thus, as one learns to love God with ALL his mind, instead of himself, the darkness of that treacherous, subconscious mind is cleansed and renovated. This caverned basement of accumulated selfishness and self-justification and the evils and the hypocritical self-righteousness is faced and cast out as the garbage which it is. And as the self-pity is eliminated, then there can be "NO DARKNESS IN HIM." And he becomes filled with Light and "truly comprehends all things" even his own past failings.

These are the PROMISES of fulfillment. And as one comprehends ALL things he is given the understanding to use the powers of Light and glory under the divine, minute direction of God.

And as one is "filled with Light," he is born of the Spirit, even as Christ explained to Nicodemus, as recorded in John, chapter three, verses five to eight, as follows: "The wind bloweth where it listeth, and thou hearest the sound thereof, but canst not tell from whence it cometh and whither it'

goeth: *so is everyone that is born of the Spirit.*" EVERYONE
WHO IS BORN OF THE SPIRIT is able to come and go,
by the power of God, to whatsoever locality or destination
he is sent forth in his higher service of actually becoming the *"greatest,"* as PROMISED and fulfilled by his own
faith and humility.

Now, I must quote the whole reference of this dynamic
revelation, as Christ patiently explained it to Nicodemus,
who came to him by night to inquire of Him concerning the
unheard of power which continually bore witness of Christ's
greatness.

"Rabbi, we know that thou art a teacher come from God:
for no man can do the miracles that thou doest, except
God be with him.

"Jesus answered and said unto him, Verily, verily, I say
unto thee, Except a man be born again, he cannot see the
Kingdom of God.

"Nicodemus saith unto him, How can a man be born when
he is old? Can he enter the second time into his mother's
womb, and be born?

"Jesus answered, Verily, verily, I say unto thee, Except a
man be born of the water and of the Spirit, he cannot enter
into the Kingdom of God."

Then Christ explained fully and clearly the question of
re-entering the mother's womb. "THAT WHICH IS BORN
OF THE FLESH (or from a woman's womb) IS FLESH:
AND THAT WHICH IS BORN OF THE SPIRIT IS
SPIRIT.

"Marvel not that I said unto thee, Ye must be born again."

Then He gives the eternal PROMISE of the POWER
OF GOD bearing witness of *everyone* who is born of the
Spirit. Such would not only have the power to do all the

marvelous works and perform the mighty miracles, of which Nicodemus came to inquire, he would be able to fulfill the following almighty *promise*: "THE WIND BLOWETH WHERE IT LISTETH, AND THOU HEAREST THE SOUND THEREOF, BUT CANST NOT TELL WHENCE IT GOETH: SO IS EVERY ONE THAT IS BORN OF THE SPIRIT!

"Nicodemus answered and said unto him. How can these things be?" Or, how is it done?

And Christ's answer holds out a mild rebuke as he said unto him: "Art thou a master in Israel, and knowest not these things?" And today there are thousands such as Nicodemus who claim to have received the baptism of the Spirit and like Nicodemus know nothing about It or the laws and the powers pertaining to It. And these professing ones could be asked today, "Art thou a professed minister or preacher in a church and knowest not these things?" Or, "Art thou a professed believer in Christ's teachings and knowest not these things?" Or, "Art thou a High Priest in Israel and knowest not these things, yet claim to be born of the Spirit?"

Then Christ said to Nicodemus, "If I have told you EARTHLY THINGS, and ye believe not, how shall ye believe, if I TELL YOU HEAVENLY THINGS?"

This divine power of translation, for such it is, this power to be able to come and go as the wind, and to be able to do the miracles, of which Nicodemus came to inquire about, ARE EARTHLY THINGS! They belong to this earth, for it is here that they must be applied. And since no man has sought to take hold of these dynamic truths and unspeakable powers he is not prepared in any way to comprehend "THE HEAVENLY THINGS!" So said Christ to Nicodemus.

Yet, since this power to be born of the Spirit, so that one might be able to be transported physically from one place to another, as one becomes the servant of all, is supposed to be fulfilled right here on this earth, why has there been such gross wickedness of unbelief and such blindness among the professing Christian world?

These laws, which Christ explained belong to mortality that those who ask, desire and reach might evolve from the man or mortal kingdom into the God Kingdom. The PROMISE IS that EVERYONE who fulfills the laws of these dynamic powers shall receive those powers. THIS IS THE LAW!

As one learns to love God with ALL the strength of his heart, his soul and his mind he automatically moves into these powers naturally and beautifully, even as an embryoed infant grows into the full pattern of itself.

The greater powers and the divine fulfillment belong to the living of that First and Greatest of ALL Commandments. As love is developed and perfected within a human being he outgrows his confining walls of humanity and evolves or is born into the Spiritual condition required for this birth, of which Christ spoke. As love is developed and perfected one is truly born of God—"For God is love." As one blends his entire being into the vibrations of praise and love and gratitude he will be born of the Spirit because he will become spiritualized. And the mortal takes on immortality without ever needing to taste of death. Through OVERCOMING ALL things, death also is OVERCOME.

Christ told Nicodemus in no uncertain words: "That which is born of the flesh is flesh!" In other words, that which is formed in the mother's wonb and born of the flesh IS

FLESH! It is not Spirit. But, "THAT WHICH IS BORN OF THE SPIRIT IS SPIRIT."

How is a child formed and brought forth from its mother's womb?

The fetus or infant seed begins to draw its sustenance and food, to build its flesh and to complete its form, by drawing its nourishment into its being through its navel. The mother does not push that food into the child. She could not possibly do so. That embryonic infant has intelligence and the power to use its instinctive knowledge to draw its supply of material to feed its cells, its bones, its marrow, and its various tissues as this life substance is proportioned out for the perfect fulfilling of the pattern contained within itself. And when that pattern is filled full or fulfilled that child is born into this world. IT IS BORN OF THE FLESH! AND ITS BODY IS FLESH!

However, that infant had a spirit form before the flesh was conceived or created. This spirit body, which existed before the foundations of the world, thus becomes clothed in a mortal frame.

Then, in order to reach perfection it is necessary for the physical body, formed of material, earthly atoms, to now blend so completely into the spiritual form that the Spirit becomes predominant and the flesh takes on immortality. The spiritual perfection of this entire being of man can only be accomplished by loving God with ALL the heart, with all one's intelligence and entire being. Then that which was born of the flesh becomes completely spiritualized and made perfect. This is Man's true heritage.

This spiritual birth or transformation belongs to those who desire to reach a higher status than mere, grubby mortality. This spiritual birth is accomplished when the physical, mortal body of flesh becomes enhanced and quickened by the spirit being perfected and brought forth to rule and reign, "He whose right it is to reign!" When the physical form has been thus filled with the spirit it becomes spiritualized and that individual will be given all the gifts and powers of heaven. He will be able to "come and go as the wind and no one will know from whence he came or whither he goeth!"

As one begins to open his heart to the love of God he begins in that moment to draw on the divine, spiritual supply of nourishment required to bring forth and invigorate this new, indestructible body of eternal Light. The heart begins to draw this love, through one's own great living heart center, and it is then distributed out through the tissues of his own being. And he begins to love God with ALL his soul, which is every cell and atom of his physical body and his spirit. As soon as one begins to LIVE this greatest of all COMANDMENTS he swiftly learns of the dynamic power it contains and the blessings which are enfolded within it. Thus "It is given to abide in you that which quickeneth all things and which maketh alive all things." In loving one draws the love of God into his own heart and out through it to feed his entire being. As he continues to draw upon this source his supply of Spiritual nourishment increases according to his need. And his need will increase with his own divine growth.

And "The fruit of the tree of life is the love of God, which is shed forth through the hearts of the children of men." This is the source of the "Life more abundant." It is also the source of the "Life Eternal!" And within it is contained the power to be *born of the Spirit* that one can fulfill the PROMISES which have been awaiting those who "ask and seek and knock."

THE ETERNAL POWER OF ALMIGHTY GOD

As one "Begins to live this greatest of all laws" he learns of its power! And he himself is the one who receives the blessing. As one sends out love he draws the love of God into his own being — through his own heart — and into the living cells of his entire body, until his higher Spiritual body is full formed and he is then born of the Spirit. This is the law — and this is the PROMISE. "And he shall come and go as the wind and no one will know from whence he came or whither he goeth. So is EVERYONE who is born of the spirit."

This holy, spiritual food, which is required for the complete formation and fulfilling of one's entire being, is drawn from the great love of God. One will be born of God when he has perfected the power of love. As one begins to exert the energies of his heart to draw love into himself he will soon discover that the fountains of Living Water are opened up within him to supply his every need. And this divine heart-center of Living Water or of great love is just behind the navel. And so the spiritual body is formed in like manner to the physical one, and the nourishment is drawn through the umbilical cord connected to the very center of the soul. The spiritual food itself is drawn in through the high vibrations of released love and gladness and thanksgiving. As one takes hold of this supply with his mind he begins to grow into "THE LIFE MORE ABUNDANT!" As one uses these laws of fulfillment he automatically advances into a stage beyond mortality. "He does literally *evolve* from the man kingdom into the God Kingdom," with all the power of heaven bestowed upon him.

Among the ancient Egyptians, those who inhabited the land along the Nile before it was overrun by the dark race, there were those who knew of the laws of the "TWICE

BORN!" These ancient teachers of Light were the ones who built the Great Pyramid and those magnificent temples of old, not the tombs, but the temples. And the special ones who were permitted to receive of this sacred ordinance, were those who were willing to give their lives to a higher service and completely to God. After such a relinquishment of their own desires for wealth and fame and luxuries they went through a long period of training or preparation and purification. When they were completely prepared they were taken into one of those sacred temples for their ordination and were sent into the Fourth Dimension. This ordinance was never written down nor publicly revealed. But those who received it were never the same again. They were holy and anointed—and POWERFUL! The Great Pyramid secretes such a temple, deep within its bosom, where such divine ordinances were performed. There were also other holy temples where this most sacred ritual could be achieved.

The ancient masters of India also knew of the power of the "Twice Born Ones!" And there are a few who still do.

For the first time in the history of the world these divine, sacred, unspeakable truths of infinite power are now being revealed. And anyone can receive the splendor of their fulfilling if so be he desires to PROVE them by "LIVING THE LAWS PERTAINING TO THEM."

Those who keep that "First and Great Commandment" could not possibly fail to fulfill the Second One. As one's mind is trained to LOVE "His mind and lips automatically lose the power to hurt and wound. Then he advances to the point where his voice can be heard among the Gods," for he will have overcome mortality.

Generate the vibrations of love and joy and happiness and you will be feeding upon the spiritual food of Gods and will be able "to buy the white raiment and will be clothed in Spirit and in Light" as you mature into your own Spiritual perfection.

Every divine vibration of love and praise and joyous gratitude is that exotic spiritual food of the Father being drawn into the mortal body to develop the Spirit in its completed fulness as it is perfected and spiritualized; and like Christ and John the Baptist, one will "grow and wax strong" spiritually; and eventually he will be born into a higher type of being. He will become divine and radiate graciousness and love and beauty as he becomes POWERFUL.

As one renovates his subconscious mind and purifies it for a higher, divine functioning he steps into a new advancement of divine preparation. One can behold the tragedy of the darkness and will realize that the desolation of the subconscious is a selected condition which many mortals choose to exist in because they learn to "love the darkness rather than the light." As this condition is comprehended the darkness and the evils can be OVERCOME and he becomes filled with Light and will comprehend all things."

As one learns to love God with ALL the strength of his heart and ALL the strength of his soul and ALL the strength of his mind until his three minds become united or "*single* to the glory of God," he moves into the promised powers. They belong with the fulfilling of that Greatest of all Commandments ever given to man. And to man is the glory and the power when he takes hold of it to PROVE it.

As the love is developed and perfected one is truly born of God, "for God is love", and "He who is born of God cannot commit sin." (I John 3:9).

As one blends his entire being into the vibrations of praise and love and gratitude he will be born of the Spirit and will receive the gift of translation or the power to come and go as the wind to whatsoever area or place God directs him. He will be able to travel with the speed of thought and under complete control as he holds his goal and the sacredness of his assignment in his conscious mind. This is power — the power to become the least, though he is the greatest, and the servant of all. In this type of high, perfected service one puts aside all desires for personal glory and acclaim and becomes selfless in the very wonder of pure love and deepest humility.

This birth of the Spirit must also be considered from another angle. So the question arises, how is an infant born? First it must fulfill the measure of its growth and forming. When the measure or pattern of that tiny body is fulfilled the child is born.

So it is with the birth of the Spirit. As a man gathers the elements of the Spirit into his being by constant devotion of love and praise and gratitude he will be formed or clothed in Light. He matures into the completed pattern of the fulness of Spirit as the glorious design of himself is prepared to come forth, full formed. He becomes literally clothed in Spirit.

"I counsel thee to buy of me the white raiment that thou mayest be clothed and that the shame of thy nakedness do not appear." In this spiritual raiment one becomes clothed in Spirit and the shame of his mortality is exalted into the translated condition in which the great OVERCOMING achieves all things.

These are the higher laws of God, which still pertain to this earth. And everyone can fulfill them who desires to do so. For the first time in the history of the world they are fully revealed and made so plain a fool need not err therein.

These great and mighty truths are the PROMISES of Almighty God, held out to be accepted by the mere exercising of Faith. And all that is required at first is just enough faith to try to PROVE them by LIVING them. In this slight effort Faith will become knowledge. And so it is that each individual may grow into the *power of proving and fulfilling* these stupendous laws for himself. And the powers thereof are limitless and eternal.

These powers are all yours to use and to glorify and to be glorified by as you take hold of them!

But only those can take hold of them "Whose names were written in the Lamb's Book of Life from the foundation of the world." For only those whose names are engraved upon that most holy of all records will have either the desire or the understanding to even seek such divine fulfillment.

Know this: That divine, holy "Lamb's Book of Life" was not written and inscribed with names *before the foundations of the earth,* because some Supreme Being has such a hobby. If your name was placed in that sacred record it was because you existed at that time and had earned so great an honor and privilege. It was not that this record of names was gathered out of nowhere and then centuries later men and women were created just to bring forth individuals to fill those names. Those names were written in that immemorial time of eons agone because we were there and had earned that honor. We existed and the privilege of having our names engraved upon so sacred a document was a reward of great honor.

And, according to the scriptures, there were those whose names were not written in that "Lamb's Book of Life," but who were also permitted to make their abode upon this planet.

Those who proclaim that I am hereby expressing a belief in reincarnation err greatly and are without either vision or understanding. They know not the Truth. Neither could they understand Truth if it were placed before them in a language a babe could not ignore or deny.

And I must add this bit of information here, for there will not be another place in this record to receive it. There are many who seek to glorify the stepping stones of their individual paths of advancement as they are directed, according to their own hungering, into the great Truth. In thus seeking to glorify their individual pathways they, too, err. Often that which they worship as their sacred stepping stones, believing that no one can possibly reach any degree of enlightenment unless he travels each step they trod, will eventually learn that most of their cherished stepping stones were only stumbling blocks. Those who have been held back or in any way retarded because of orthodoxed conformity or dogmatic sectarianism have traveled much of their way into Truth over stumbling blocks, not stepping stones.

Chapter V

"ALL THINGS WILL BECOME SUBJECT UNTO YOU!"

Now it is necessary to go back to the scripture mentioned in chapter three, which is as follows: "He that is ordained of God and sent forth, the same is appointed to be the greatest, *notwithstanding he is the least and the servant of all.*

"Wherefore, he is possessor of all things; for ALL THINGS ARE SUBJECT UNTO HIM, BOTH IN HEAVEN AND ON EARTH, THE LIFE AND THE LIGHT, THE SPIRIT AND THE POWER, sent forth by the will of the Father through Jesus Christ, His Son."

Take these marvelous words of PROMISE into your mind for they are POWER! Look at them! Hold them forth for your spiritual understanding to gaze upon. Behold them clearly and you will never again be able to sleep in a dull, dead unalertness.

Mortality itself is a sleepy, unanimated condition of drab existence. It is an unawakened state of unaliveness. And millions upon millions are accepting this condtion without questioning the dreariness of its utter desolation. This acceptance is a complete compliance with all the conditions of this "lone and dreary world!" Those who accept mere mortality are not only willingly abiding in the dreariness but are actually adding to it by their own acceptance of it.

49

Many dislike this life, and are completely dissatisfied with it. But their dissatisfaction finds release in trying to change the world to fit into their own discontentment. They work blindly upon the world and their surroundings instead of upon themselves. It is only through oneself that one can obtain the vision and the power and the goodness to help lift the world into a higher condition. The power to help is accomplished only by one's own OVERCOMING. Otherwise one is but adding to the misery and decadence and evils which already exist.

And there are many who sit in their dark, dreary realms of the subconscious and in their accumulated misery weep about their overwhelming sorrows and afflictions as they secretly hope for death or continually express their desire to die. These uninformed ones believe that death will release them from all responsibility and from every unhappy condition. And in this they are greatly mistaken. Anyone who does not have the vision and understanding to rejoice in the dynamic, glorious gift of life "is without hope. And he who is without hope must needs be in despair. And despair cometh because of iniquity." This condition can only come when one has relinquished all contact with the divine, ceased to make any effort to extract himself from the swamps of his own accepted darkness.

Life is such a glorious, sacred privilege, such a divine opportunity, such a dynamic wonder that anyone who does not appreciate it will fall into those dark realms of his own subconscious desolation — and abide there. He will remain a failure and an increasingly repulsive person until and unless he begins to cast out the darkness from him. His darkness is right within himself. It is not on the outside, for to every human being was given the power to "overcome the evils of his life," "To have dominion over the earth" and every condition upon it as he exerts himself to use the power of his dominion and divine heritage. And if one dies in the realms of that darkness he will take that darkness with him into the next world. And it is a thousand times more difficult to escape it in that condition than it is right here in the glorious, ever-present NOW. This is the time of OVERCOMING! This is the opportunity to rise above the evils and the vicissitudes and to transmute them into everlasting power.

Death will not make anyone happy who has not earned or merited happiness in this life. The scripture states that those who are filthy will be filthy still and "those who are unhappy will be unhappy still and those who are holy let them be holy still." Or, as it is given in the twelfth chapter of Daniel, verse two, as follows: "And many of them that sleep in the dust of the earth shall awake, some to everlasting life, and some to shame and *everlasting* contempt."

Death does not change anyone. Death only takes from one the great opportunity to OVERCOME — the darkness — the negation and the evils of life.

A desiring for death is a condition of self-pity which takes full control as one permits himself to wallow in the darkness of his own subconscious realms of accumulated evils.

Only those who OVERCOME have any PROMISE!

As death is left behind and the desire to revel in the stench from which a desire to die originated one can begin to grow into the great PROMISES OF JESUS CHRIST. Christ stressed throughout his earthly ministry that "He who believes on me need never die!" Continually was He announcing that He came so "That they might have LIFE and HAVE IT MORE ABUNDANTLY! EVEN LIFE ETERNAL!"

What is this life more abundant? Life more abundant is a state of living vibrancy, not dead, repulsive decadence. The "life more abundant" is an inner ecstasy! It is a condition of exultation, such as the writer of the Odes of Solomon describes. It is a condition of singing thankfulness, a joy in the great gift of being privileged to live upon this beautiful earth. It is a singing gratitude that flows out in a spontaneous glory to increase every blessing and multiply every quality of appreciation. And only he who has developed the gift of appreciation or thankfulness can possibly know joy.

As one begins to look about him and seeks to develop even a tiny degree of gratitude and appreciation for his blessings, no matter how meager they are, those blessings will begin to increase and the darkness will begin to diminish. Then it is that one's blessings begin to multiply; and the darkness will begin to be cast from him and the vibrating glory of that "Life more abundant" will begin to manifest in his life. If one will but continue he will be given the power to OVERCOME the darkness and the evils of his life and every desire for sin, which is often just the weakness of wallowing in the darkness.

All suicides dwell in that sewer realm of their own subconscious brains. All criminals abide there and all mental patients and those addicted to the use of narcotics.

The great and mighty ones are those who *overcome* that realm of desolating darkness and evil. It is the failures who willingly abide in the horror chambers of their own subterranean realms of accumulated dross who permit themselves to become lost.

No person can possibly remain in such vile conditions of evil who will begin to develop the gift of appreciation for his precious gift of life and who will only offer up thanks to God for an endowment so divinely beautiful.

As one begins to take hold of the holy gift of Life and to thank God for it he will begin to create the Christ vibrations of Light and to not only draw those unspeakable forces to him, but to send them out to help heal and benefit a world. And the "Life more abundant" will begin to fill his entire being as it flows out from him. Such will have the power to draw upon that holy supply of spiritual nourishment so that he cannot possibly die, still-born in the womb of eternity.

As one's gift of appreciation and gratitude increases he will become ever more vibrant. Those who have the "Life more abundant" continually vibrate with life — joyous, glorious life! The very gift of life flows to them in an ever increasing splendor of breathtaking, glorious renewal and endless beauty. They are radiant!

It is only after one has learned to appreciate the wonder and the power and the precious glory of so priceless a gift as Life that "The Life more abundant" or the divine gift of *Life will become subject unto him!*" He will be able to take hold of its fabulous powers and to increase them within himself. And like the writer of those Precious Odes of Solomon, in the Lost Books of the Bible, he will proclaim: "I cast out darkness and clothed myself in Light. And I acquired a body free from sorrow, or affliction, or pain!"

The writer of those sacred Odes arrived at such a condition. He overcame death and he was translated. And so can every individual on this earth who will seek to fulfill the laws pertaining to such dynamic possibilities. This is being born of the Spirit!

Anyone who brings forth the promised glory of "The Life more abundant" and who will continue to abide in it will KNOW that he will have that gift of life under his command, that it will become subject unto him. This state of supreme wonder is accomplished through the perfecting of love and appreciation or thankfulness. And after he has opened his understanding or become filled with Light so that he can comprehend the magnificence of the gift no man will ever be able to take his life from him. And then one can fully lay claim to immortality. "He has evolved from the man kingdom into the God Kingdom." And this is possible and can be accomplished by any individual who will only begin to exercise his powers to BELIEVE, for this is Faith in action.

As one takes hold of that precious "Gift of Life" it will most assuredly become SUBJECT UNTO HIM. This is the promise and God cannot lie. This is every man's heritage as a child of God unless he forfeits it by relinquishing his rights to the powers of darkness. Christ always asked those He was requested to restore to health, "Wouldst thou be healed?" "Do you really desire to be healed, or do you enjoy the attention you get from being ill? Do you wish to stand up straight and tall and free from physical handicaps?" Many do not, though they would never admit it.

Then, too, came this warning from the divine Son of God after he had healed some of their afflictions, "Go thy way and sin no more lest a worse thing befall thee."

Christ was seeking to teach mankind that they were to rise above their trials and vicissitudes and evils by the very attitudes which they carried and by their *overcoming* of the darkness.

And as one can literally take hold of the precious "gift of LIFE" until he is actually in command so can he take hold of the divine gift or element of LIGHT and it will also become subject unto him! For such is the PROMISE to those who cast out the darkness.

The divine gift of LIGHT, which includes joy and happiness and a divine understanding, comes only to those who have lifted themselves from the gutter levels of their subconscious minds and who chase darkness from among them. Then such become purified as the dark realms of their subconscious minds are exalted into the full functioning of power. To such the Light is a living factor of eternal, constant beauty. "And it becomes SUBJECT unto them!" In this condition one can call forth this holy, supreme LIGHT of Christ in every dismaying condition, in every emergency or need or devastating calamity and they can be transmuted instantly into power and blessings.

It is within each man's realm and power to be able to command that "LIGHT TO STAND FORTH!" And if he has sought to fulfill the laws of righteousness THAT LIGHT WILL OBEY for "IT WILL HAVE BECOME SUBJECT UNTO HIM!" And God lies not!

The Light becomes subject unto one who uses it knowingly and brings it forth, banishing the darkness of all vicissitudes and dismays as they are transformed into conditions of power and joy. Yes, "ALL THINGS WILL BECOME SUBJECT UNTO HIM, both in heaven and on earth!" THIS IS THE PROMISE!

Next is the promise that "THE SPIRIT WILL BECOME SUBJECT UNTO HIM!" These words contain almost un-

thinkable glory as one takes hold of them and receives the
fulness of that holy, divine PROMISE by the exercise of his
faith. Every individual on this earth can PROVE THE
TRUTH OF THESE PROMISES, by faith and by LIVING
the laws pertaining to them.

The Spirit is expressed in vibrations even as love is. And
there are those who mistakenly believe that the Spirit of
God can only be made manifest through unseemly behavior,
such as shouting, or in physical, uncontrolled contortions.
When John baptized in the River Jordan there were no such
undignified manifestations. Christ must always be used as
the pattern and example and He expressed only majesty
upon every occasion.

When one understands the Spirit and Its powers and
grows into Its greatness he knows that It can only be expressed perfectly through the control of his own exerted
majesty. One can only be BORN OF THE SPIRIT when
he has earned such a holy privilege by having fulfilled the
law of his own perfecting. The gift of the Spirit can NEV-
ER BE GRANTED PERMANENTLY to anyone who ex-
presses It in uncontrolled hysteria or in any way less than
majesty. The divine Holy Spirit, in action, is the expression
of all that is holy and Godlike in Its unfolding of everlasting splendor and breath-taking glory. Those who thus
express themselves have NOT BEEN BORN OF THE
SPIRIT no matter what their claims. They could not possibly be. They have only had a flash of divine inspiration
to help open their understandings to the fulness of the holy
powers of the Spirit of God. And many, believing they have
received the great fulness go forth to demonstrate their
own contact with God. They do not understand in the least

the powers or the promises which go with this Birth of the Spirit.

When one has been truly born of the Spirit, by fulfilling all the laws of its divine coming forth, then will THE SPIRIT BECOME SUBJECT UNTO HIM — not he to the spirit. And in the Spirit and power of Almighty God he will attain complete control, even as an infant learns to control and bring into subjection his tiny physical body of flesh. And in this control the Spirit obeys the individual and he can be carried forth to whatsoever place or field of service he is called. *"He can come and go as the wind and no one will know from whence he came or whither he goeth.* Such is the power of *everyone* who is born of the Spirit."

This is majesty! And this is power! And this belongs to those who learn to hold themselves under control as they feel the Spirit of God beginning to be released upon them.

This is the fulness of the breathtaking PROMISE that "ALL THINGS SHALL BECOME SUBJECT UNTO HIM!" It will be fulfilled to all who lay claim to it by the exertion of their own FAITH in the PROMISE and by *living* the laws pertaining to it. Thus: "all things do become subject unto him: the Life and the Light, and the Spirit — AND THE POWER!"

This is the POWER of which it is now necessary to speak.

The stupendous, breath-taking PROMISE of being able to have the POWER subject unto one is glory almost unspeakable. The POWER will be his to control the vibrations, hurled at him from without, in a majesty of divine love, such as Christ used at his trial and crucifixion. And *it is possible!* It is beautifully possible! Hereby do the heavens bear witness of this POSSIBILITY for these *promises* were given by 'God Himself and He is a God of truth. His words cannot return unto Him unfulfilled" or "Void!" as long as there is an individual upon the earth who will exercise the FAITH to live by the laws pertaining thereto — and so PROVE them.

Those disturbing, intensified vibrations of hate, resentment, evil, envy, jealousy or any other evil thoughts which are sent to one from the outside must be dissipated by one's own out-flowing love. As one accomplishes this he will receive the divine power to control his own released vibrations, which are the most deadly ones, "For it is what goeth out of a man that defiles him." It is his own vibrations of discords and evils which are the most defiling of all.

As one comprehends this power and uses it aright he can hold and control his vibrations always by that released Song of Celestial Glory — the love and the praise and the gratitude of his own joyous, singing heart. And thus the POWER of Almighty God will become *subject* unto any man who exerts the Faith to PROVE the PROMISES!

One must grow into the use of this stupendous power as he permits himself to "be tested and tried in all things." This power cannot possibly be entrusted to anyone who has not been *proved.* Those desirous of obtaining such limitless potency and dynamic force, without being able to control their own reactions, might, in an unguarded moment of anger, hurl out such negative vibrations they would annihilate and destroy. Only in purest love can this POWER become subject unto one. It is a two-edged sword when used amiss. It will not only destroy those to whom it is directed in negative wrath, it will destroy the individual wielding it in anger. Thus this divine force of almost incomprehensible potency can only be entrusted to those who have perfected love. Love only can be entrusted with the control of this POWER.

Therefore the *power becomes subject* only to those who have earned the right to use it by learning to control the vibrancy of their own lives in a balance of perfect, divine, Christ-like love. And this is a goal anyone can achieve who desires it and begins to work upon themselves, instead of upon others. It can be achieved through the practice and the LIVING of that First and Great Commandment. This is the easiest, most direct method of accomplishment in fulfilling any of those marvelous *promises* given by God to man.

As love is perfected and the Light is increased within one the glorious radiance of Light will take over and *one will be able to comprehend all things.* This *is* power! This is the state one reaches when he has purified his two lower minds and brought them into At-one-ment with the divine, superconscious mind — and they become ONE in functioning, in comprehension and in their limitless unity of divine achieving. One who sets his heart upon this desired goal will achieve or reach it. And such a one will have the POWER to do *all* the works which Christ did — AND GO ON TO THE GREATER WORKS!

He who purifies himself and casts out all darkness and negation so that he is prepared to "be *ordained of God* and sent forth will have all things become subject unto him, both in heaven and on earth!" And as the Spirit becomes subject unto an individual he becomes filled with the Spirit of the Lord and will automatically become refined and magnificent in his perfect control. The Holy Spirit is a refining glory when permitted to function fully under restrained mastery. Such a one will become a joy and a pleasure to associate with for he will take on divine majesty. The Spirit of the Lord carries with it the true culture of Divinity.

In this higher advancement there are no unseemly actions or loud shouting. There could not possibly be. As this is understood and the individual brings the Spirit into subjection, instead of being subject to It, he finds that all the holy, divine POWER of eternity is his to use, in love and blessing and healing and wisdom. Such a one "evolves from the man kingdom into the God Kingdom!"

One cannot possibly begin to do THE WORKS WHICH CHRIST DID without taking on the divine majesty of the Son of the Living God! Act always as you think Christ would act and no unseemly behavior could possibly be tolerated in your life. Begin to live as He lived and you will grow into the perfection which He is!

THESE ARE THE PROMISES!

CHAPTER VI

THE TREE OF LIFE!

It is time, at last, for the great, sacred Tree of Life to bud, to blossom and to leaf out with the foliage that will be used for the healing of the nations. This tree is beautiful beyond all others. And as it begins to bear its life-giving fruit it will be for the glory of God and for the joy and benefit and happiness of man.

This Tree has been dormant for ages and centuries. And NOW it is again coming into its appointed season of fruitage.

Glory be to God for a day so great!

This precious Tree is the Tree of which Christ declared Himself to be the vine and man the branches. God is the husbandman to prune away undesirable, rejected traits and weaknesses through tests and trials. "We must be tested and tried in all things." We must *prove* our worth. We must be able to bring forth the precious, divine fruit, which is within our sacred natures to produce. And the privilege is so breathtaking it is almost overwhelming, when comprehended.

Of all the worlds which God created *this one* is the most wicked. It is the most rebellious — not the earth, but those who inhabit it. Yet all the other worlds envy us. For this is the school for Gods. Upon this wicked, polluted, beautiful world it is possible to achieve in one sixty-year life span all the testings and trials necessary to prove one's worth for

all eternity. Those who come out of the fires of such testings are great indeed and their glory will be eternal. All the
other worlds envy us such an opportunity as is ours. On
milder worlds, without the evils and the conflicts and vicissitudes and continual temptations it would take a thousand
years to achieve what can be accomplished in one short, life-
span upon this wonderful little world. The very privilege
of being permitted to dwell upon this "lone and dreary
world" is one of the greatest opportunities that could be
granted.

Here upon this earth is the greatest opportunity to serve.
Here upon this earth is the greatest opportunity to OVER-
COME! Here upon this benighted little world is the great-
est opportunity to be PROVED and GLORIFIED.

Each person who permits or develops and brings forth
that great Christ Light or the Spirit of Love will be given
the glorious life-energy and substance of Christ's holy essence of perfection and the power to begin to produce the
Fruits that will be everlasting. These are the fruits of sharing, in which each man assumes, to a certain degree, the
privilege of becoming "his brother's keeper," which law
was rejected by Cain and all the ungodly since that period
of time. To be one's brother's keeper does not mean that
one's brother or neighbor is to be coddled or waited upon.
It does mean, however, that we love our brother as we love
ourselves — that we guard his interests as we guard our
own. In this love it would be impossible to cheat anyone.
We would be willing to protect our neighbor's life with our
own life, if necessary. And there is no greater love than this.
And this is the Fruit of the Tree of Life!

And since man is given the divine privilege of being a
branch upon that precious Tree of Life, man also has the

ability to subsist upon its fruits. And "THE LOVE OF GOD IS THE FRUIT OF THE TREE OF LIFE as it is shed forth through the hearts of the children of men." Bring forth this perfect love or fruit and it will be impossible to die, for death will be overcome. The fruit of this divine Tree of Life is yours to partake of always. And as this love of God is shed forth through your own heart you will have opened within you "THE FOUNTAINS OF LIVING WATER."

Yes, Christ is the Vine of that precious Tree. But man is the branches. And it is man also who is required to hold forth those precious "leaves for the healing of the nations." These leaves contain the healing balm for the hates of the world and for the lacks of mankind. These leaves hold the power of healing the selfishness and the greeds and envies and the viciousness. These leaves contain the power for healing and for the binding up of the wounds of those who have broken themselves and been wounded upon the fields of their battles. And it must be remembered that the nations are made up of individuals. Send love out to enfold and bless individuals and the healing will commence.

America has continually sought to bind up the wounds of those whom it has been forced to fight and conquered. It has held out a helping hand and shared its own life food with nations in need. It has been a noble and a great nation. But sometimes it has acted unwisely as it has turned its giving into a system of buying friendships. Friendships can never be bought for the feeling of obligation often breeds a resentment that seethes forth in new misunderstandings.

Yet this role America has assumed from the beginning of its history. The holding forth of those precious leaves of healing will find a glory of fulfillment as the nations of the earth are chastened and humbled by the hand of God. For such is in the plan. And in His rebuke there will come the humility and the appreciation and the power to be healed. Then every precious leaf of peace, as held out, not only from the awakened nations, but from the loving hands of individuals, will be most gratefully and joyously accepted. And the healing will come.

Blessed are those who begin to hold forth these sacred leaves of love and healing. This is the outpouring of a love such as this world has never known as it flows forth through the opened, human hearts that are exalted into the divine fulfillment of their own perfection.

It must be here explained that love is released through a human heart as vibrations. Vibrations are the expression of love as they are released through a soul reaching toward perfection. Hate is also released through vibrations. But the vibrations of hate are destructive and deadly and it is because of these negative, hate-filled vibrations that this world has reached the measure of its own accumulated wickedness — and God must take a hand to save it from annihilation.

Love is a living essence of power. It is released from human hearts in a vibrancy of such living glory, if only mortal eyes were conditioned to behold it, that would instantly change the world. But since these vibrations are felt, rather then seen, the process of receiving is slowed down.

Remember always: *"The love of God that is shed forth through the hearts of the children of men* IS THE FRUIT OF THE TREE OF LIFE!" And it is the released vibrations of pure perfection as one opens up his heart to receive of its powerful gift — the gift of Eternal Life.

Learn to open up your heart to the vibrations of this released love of God and you cannot possibly grow old or ugly or die. This Fruit is the source of Life and the power of it. And it is the Spiritual food, of which Christ spoke. And it is the released vibrations of God's eternal, unfailing love.

This glorious information cannot be contradicted except by the most wicked of men. And it cannot possibly be disproved, not even by the most depraved of human beings.

But, IT CAN BE PROVED! It can be proved by any individual who desires to make the effort to see if God's PROMISES can be fulfilled by the LIVING of the laws pertaining to them. And any who will LIVE the laws shall KNOW of their Truth and of their power.

Do you wish to overcome death? Then partake of the Fruit of the Tree of Life and become a branch of that precious Tree as its fruits are offered out to the world, through you.

Or are you one of those of whom the inspired writer of the Odes of Solomon was speaking when he stated: "Whatever I did not know TRUTH MADE CLEAR TO ME, *all the poisons of error, and the plagues of death* which THEY THINK TO BE SWEETNESS!" If you can look beyond that dismal heritage of death with the intelligence and the power to BELIEVE sufficiently then you will begin to LIVE the laws required for the great transition and you can have immortality WITHOUT DYING. "You will evolve from the man kingdom into the God Kingdom" without tasting death. So is God's PROMISE. "It is the wages of SIN which is death!" And "If ye do as I say then am I bound," declared God; "But if you do not as I say then you have no PROMISE!"

It is most simple to *prove* this one great and mighty PROMISE, "that there shall be no more death." And the words that: "Death is the last enemy to be OVERCOME in any man's life." It is in the living of the First and Great Commandment that the requirements are fulfilled and perfected.

Love God with ALL your heart and the hard seals of UNBELIEF will melt and the "love of God can begin to be shed forth through it!" Often these seals upon the heart are but the selected conformity which freezes one into an unprogressiveness of dead and lifeless dogmas, with the love of God shut out.

As anyone begins to develop the first little whisper of love his heart will begin to open and expand. It is then that God can begin to shed forth *His great love* through that opened heart in a fountain of vibrant, living life.

First, that holy gift of everlasting life will become his and he will "Acquire a body free from sorrows or affliction or pain" and death will be OVERCOME in that individual, for he, having OVERCOME ALL THE OTHER EVILS OF HIS LIFE, the darkness, the envy, the jealousies, the fears and hates and greeds will have but that one enemy left—DEATH. And in the OVERCOMING of the evils of his life one becomes the master and the gift of Life becomes subject unto him. And death will have no claim!

As one begins to give out love, which is the fruit of the Tree of Life, he will also be able to partake of that Fruit freely himself. And as he absorbs that divine power of its holy essence and substance he will have the power to hold that fruit forth to his own loved ones and friends and then to go on to hold it out for the healing and the eternal blessing of a world. Eventually, death will be banished from the earth and "there will be no more tears, or weeping, or sorrow for these former things will be done away."

THE TREE OF LIFE!

There is in the record of Daniel a description of this work. It is in Daniel, chapter twelve, verses eight to ten, as follows: "And I heard, but I understood not: then said I, O my Lord, what shall be the end of these things?

"And he said, Go thy way, Daniel: for the words are closed up and sealed till THE TIME OF THE END (which is now).

"Many shall be purified, and made white, and tried; but the wicked shall do wickedly: and none of the wicked shall understand; BUT THE WISE SHALL UNDERSTAND."

Then in verse three of the same chapter, it states: "And they that be wise shall shine forth as the brightness of the firmament; and they that turn many to righteousness as the stars for ever and ever!"

This work "is the preparation, wherewith, I design to prepare mine apostles to PRUNE MY VINEYARD FOR THE LAST TIME THAT I MAY BRING TO PASS MY STRANGE ACT, THAT I MAY POUR OUT MY SPIRIT UPON ALL FLESH.

"Behold, verily I say unto you, that there are many who have been ordained among you, whom I have called BUT FEW OF THEM ARE CHOSEN.

"And they who are not chosen have sinned a very grievous sin in that *they are walking in darkness at noonday.*"

Light has been poured out without measure and they walk in the darkness of their sealed minds and their unenlightened understandings because they refuse to ask God concerning anything, thinking they already possess all truth. And in this they do err greatly. And their darkness is increasing.

To return to the former quotation it reveals: "What I have said unto you must needs be, THAT ALL MEN MAY BE LEFT WITHOUT EXCUSE:

"That wise men and rulers may hear and know that which they have considered." The only thing that has not been considered is the possibility that man can fulfill the PROMISES given by God, that man "can be perfect even as the Father in heaven is perfect," that every professing Christian is expected "To do the works which Christ did— and go on to greater works", and that man *can* OVER-COME all things, *even death.*

Again, to continue with the above quotation: "That I may proceed to bring to pass my act, my strange act, and perform my work, my strange work, that men may discern between the righteous and the wicked, saith your God."

Or as Isaiah declared: "For the Lord shall rise up as in Mount Perazim, he shall be wroth as in the Valley of Gibeon, that he may do his work, his strange work: and bring to pass his act, his strange act." (Isa. 28:21)

God's apostles and his leaders are truly prepared and ARE going forth TO PRUNE HIS VINEYARD FOR THE LAST TIME. And in that pruning they are gathering the tares into bundles to be destroyed by "the overflowing scourge." This work of pruning it is itself most strange, for it is more or less in reverse since it is to themselves they are gathering the tares and the worthless branches. This pruning is for the gathering into bundles and groups those who "Are willing and desirous of TRUSTING WHOLLY IN THE ARM OF FLESH!" Instead of going to God to learn of His will, there are those who rely solely upon the word of their leaders and their pastors and their bishops, or apostles or chosen authorities. These are the ones who are satisfied with learning only ABOUT GOD instead of following the strict command that they *"seek Him early and diligently* that they might KNOW HIM, instead of just *knowing about Him.*

It is those who love God with ALL their hearts, with ALL their souls and with ALL their minds and who are LIVING the higher laws of righteousness, who are being pruned off, according to the belief of the leaders, while the reverse is true. They are but gathering the weak and the unsaintly unto themselves into the bundles which are to be destroyed. And very shortly "ALL MEN WILL BE ABLE TO DISCERN BETWEEN THE RIGHTEOUS AND THE WICKED, SAITH YOUR GOD."

Those who are willing to sacrifice themselves to PROVE their love for God and their belief in His words and in His PROMISES will be clothed in the white raiment of power —and nothing will be impossible to them.

Thus is the last pruning being performed as the righteous are being segregated from the wicked. The wicked are those who love and serve their appointed or chosen leaders. The righteous are those who love and serve God, even to the complete relinquishing of their most cherished possessions, even their memberships in churches—or their very lives, if necessary.

Chapter VII

THE KEYS OF THE KINGDOM

In most organizations there are the "dos" and the "don'ts" that are often so over-stressed they blot out the road of glory completely. The pots and the pans of the Hebrews have finally so filled their lives there is little time or opportunity left for worship. Others so emphasize food taboos they forget all the Spiritual glory and blessings of our loving Father. Some believe that lovely apparel or beautiful jewelry is an abomination and a transgression, not realizing that God created all beautiful things. The only ugly things upon this earth are the things men's hands have brought forth. And since woman was God's crowning creation, she was intended to be the most beautiful of all — not in pride or vanity but in a sacredness of tribute her loveliness was to be offered for the divine glory of God, like the perfection of a flower, the song of a bird, the indescribable beauty of a perfect day.

As one accepts the higher laws of love and devotion and joy and praise and gratitude he does not need to be clubbed over the head in order to give up his errors and weaknesses and immaturities. It would be like taking a child and beating it to make it outgrow its desire for dolls, for roller skates, for bicycles or for any other childhood attachment. A child will automatically outgrow the things of childhood if left to mature properly and with love.

Parents who pound their small children, or their older ones, into churches and conformities, thinking they are saving their children's souls, assuming they are guiding them into heaven, often find out, too late, that they have driven their precious ones into hell and lost them, mayhap, forever. They have lost their love at least. When children DO LOVE their parents it is the most precious gift possible to receive. But it must be earned. Remember, "LOVE CAN NEVER BE FORCED." Love must be won and held through a respect and an appreciation of the child's rights also. "Children, obey your parents" has been emphasized down the centuries. But there is another great law rarely looked at and seldom, if ever, considered. This most important one is: "PARENTS, PROVOKE NOT YOUR CHILDREN TO WRATH!" (Eph. 6:4).

Cherish this law! And LIVE it!

As one steps into this higher work he gives up nothing except the ugliness within himself. He gradually relinquishes his own weaknesses, dislikes, hates, prides, selfishness, his desire for self-acclaim, his greeds and his lusts. And these automatically drop away as his feet tread the divine Highway of the Gods in the pathway of his own *overcoming*. This is not a pathway of stress or of torture. It is a pathway of discipline, it is true, but it is a joyous path of divine discipleship as one moves onward and upward with increasing power and understanding and everlasting happiness.

Automatically, one releases his own inferior traits as he develops new and more noble ones. He does not need anyone to stand over him with a club or even an accusing finger pointed at him. He outgrows his unworthy traits and leaves them behind like old rags. And no man can be his accuser. Each individual stands alone with God, and is accountable to God only. If one fails to *overcome* then he is only failing himself. And that too is his privilege. But he who succeeds benefits a whole world.

It is utterly impossible for anyone to start on this journey of holiness and keep going without these divine, holy principles of love and perfection becoming a very part of himself. They embed themselves into his entire being like an inner cloak of glory and can never again be cast off or discarded.

And no one can continue to travel this road of holiness ,of love, of devotion or of reaching for the fulfillment of perfection without eventually reaching its glorious ending. It is impossible for anyone to keep going AND NOT GET THERE!

Those who often have the most difficulty in traveling this Highway of Holiness are not so much the sinners as the self-righteous. These may be the ones who have developed too much personal ego in their own method of service, as they continue to relate their own experiences, as though they were in some manner, far superior to others. Because God has directed them upon occasions they assume it was because they were more favored of God. This is possible, but that favor is lost in any self-acclaim. It is easier to give up any trait or condition or thing than the little *self*, with this boasting trait. These precious ones believe they are glorifying God in the retelling of each personal experience of their lives. Instead they are only dragging along their own stairways. They are completely over-burdened with this heavy load—AND WITH THE PAST. These often have great difficulty in stepping across into the realms of LIGHT and POWER. Their pathway is blocked by themselves.

God bless such mistaken ones. They usually insist that they are only "letting their Light shine forth!" They realize not that they have developed no light as yet. They comprehend not the real meaning of "LIGHT!"

The command is: "Let your LIGHT so shine that others *seeing your good* WORKS might glorify the Father which is in heaven!" It does not say, "Let your experiences be shouted forth that others *hearing* your WORDS may glorify the Father which is in heaven."

As one sends out LIGHT he must have learned to comprehend and to release Light. And no individual is filled with Light until his eyes become single to the glory of God! One learns to send out Light, the great Light, through casting the darkness from him and developing eyes single to the glory of God instead of to his own. Then it is possible for one to be so filled with Light it will flow forth through him to heal and to bless all with whom he comes in contact. He will never need to bear witness of that Light. It will bear witness of him. This is accomplished through loving humility — not for self, but for God.

"God's Kingdom is not in WORD *but in* POWER!"

These blessed ones will take longer, perhaps, to reach the great fulfilling than others. But they too will make it in time as that little, grubby, mortal self wears itself out and humbles itself in a devotion that sings in an ever increasing you within the purified heart.

And now, there is this bit of information I am instructed to share as this divine road of holiness is opened wide. In Hebrews, the eleventh chapter and the fifth verse, it states: "By faith Enoch was translated that he should not see death; and was not found because God translated him: for *before the translation he had this testimony that he pleased God.*"

As one accepts these higher laws of PROMISE and "lays hold of them as the *best gifts*" he begins to live according to their fulfilling, by *faith!*" And as he continues he will reach the point where God will bear witness to his soul, *"That He* (God) *is pleased with him!"* This is not that self-righteous feeling of an inferior person being pleased with himself. This is the divine, holy touch of God's hand upon him as the sacred glory of this unspeakable blessing is released deep into the soul of the individual with a completeness that is so perfect and so divine there can be no more doubting or evil—or too much delay. As one gathers this LAST great PROMISE, in the joy of his own final quickening, the assurance within increases and love and praise and ecstasy fills his entire soul.

This sacred witness from God is most necessary for each individual to receive and only God can give it. And it is fulfilled by the fulfilling of the law—that divine law of love and devotion and increasing joyous praise and gratitude.

Daily that inner assurance will increase as one evolves into the fulness of the PROMISE and he, at some unexpected moment, yet in a complete state of awareness "will be wrapped in the power and the glory of his Maker and will be caught up to dwell with Him!"

Or, as stated before, one may request the privilege of returning to earth that he might be permitted to serve here where the need is so great and the laborers so few — AND the time so short!

Whatever your request, or whatever the desire or the desires of your heart, they will be fulfilled according to the fulness of your own sanctified hope. And, whenever your fulfillment is accomplished and "your calling and election is made sure" or is completed, there will be those before you who will be there to welcome you as the hosts of heaven rejoice over your achievement, for it will be a blessing to the entire world. God bless you great and noble ones! And may your graduation be fulfilled speedily!

"And *all* the sons of God shouted for joy and the morning stars sang together" over the anticipated wonder of the promise contained in the laying of the foundations of the earth. We were therein PROMISED that we were to possess this beautiful planet as our future abode or school room of progress. It was a world in which we would learn to handle tangible things and receive denser bodies than we had ever known, and would be given the opportunity to be tested and tried in all things and so PROVE ourselves worthy or unworthy of greater honors and opportunities.

As we, the Spirit children of our Almighty Sire, became clothed in flesh, with our memories of the past veiled, God gave out many PROMISES that drifted out across space and time as snatches of melody rippling over the ocean of eternity. And sometimes, even now, our souls catch some haunting refrain, some hope forgotten, some special promise pending — and we stand lost in silent, expectant waiting—waiting for we know not what.

And later it was those of great faith, those divinely inspired ones, those ancient, holy prophets or the chosen sons who put those divine PROMISES INTO WORDS, under God's minute direction. And so all those great and mighty PROMISES, given forth before ever earth began, became the heritage of man. These eternal PROMISES are even now man's to reject or ignore or to accept and to PROVE!

And the following words of TRUTH came drifting across the ages to be heard by those of open, questing minds and to be recorded thus: "Behold, when ye shall rend the veil of unbelief which doth cause you to remain in your awful state of wickedness, and hardness of heart, and blindness of mind, then shall THE GREAT AND MARVELOUS THINGS THAT HAVE BEEN HID UP FROM THE FOUNDATION OF THE WORLD FROM YOU * * * be made manifest!"

What were those "Great and Marvelous things that were hid up from the foundation of the world because of our awful state of wickedness, our hardness of heart and our blindness of mind?"

Those "great and marvelous things" were the great and mighty PROMISES of God as they were either buried or submerged between the words and the passages of scripture. And because of the hardness of men's hearts and the blindness of their minds and because of the gross wickedness of UNBELIEF those sacred PROMISES have lain buried under the dust of ancient verbiage — and ignored.

It is true that "God hath chosen the foolish things of the world to confound the wise: and God hath chosen the weak things of the world to confound the things which are mighty!" (I. Cor. 1:27)

And it was I, the most weak, the most foolish and the most lowly of all His children, whom God chose to catch the wondrous melodies contained within those hidden PROMISES. At first, I would only lift my head momentarily from the deep sleep of the centuries as my intellect would catch a glorious phrase of some divine refrain, which those around me seemed to hear not.

It was as I lifted my head to listen and opened my ears to hear and to ponder on words, that none seemed to see in all their searching, that God increased my hearing and my power to see. And gradually those sacred, almost silent melodies became a Celestial Chorus of divine, magnificent, breath-taking glory!

God's PROMISES began to stand out in letters of living flame as they sang of the greatness of the Almighty and of His desire to exalt His children above the drabness of mortality. Those PROMISES increased and magnified and became a symphony, revealing fully "THE GREAT AND MARVELOUS THINGS THAT HAD BEEN HID UP FROM THE FOUNDATION OF THE WORLD, because of the great wickedness of UNBELIEF, the hardness of our hearts and the orthodoxed blindness of our minds!"

As each PROMISE became apparent it was revealed to be but a part of a great symphony of eternal glory, held out for the contemplation and acceptance of man.

These PROMISES were not of mortality, or of earth, or of death! These PROMISES marked a path of utter glory, leading back into the divine, Holy Presence of God—with death and sorrow *overcome*—with eternal triumph the reward and God's welcoming arms waiting to enfold any who would rend that VEIL OF UNBELIEF and follow through.

And when the Path is fully revealed and the separated melodies are gathered into the great Chorus of Eternal Glory, they are ONE. It is composed of the divine PROMISES of Almighty God, gathered into a blinding, exalting triumph— the triumph of each individual *overcomer,* who will only begin to take hold of the PROMISES, and live them. Within the Celestial Concert of this Almighty rendition of God's WORD is the glory of each man's *overcoming* as he *rends the veil of unbelief* and accepts the PROMISES of "The great and Marvelous things which have been hid up from the foundation of the world!"

As each phase or portion of the whole divine symphony was revealed, first as separate PROMISES, they were finally gathered into my heart as the divine musical composition of pure perfection. And I was commanded to write the divine TRUTHS of those eternal PROMISES of God into these books for all the world to read and understand.

None of these TRUTHS are new! Nor was I the one to reveal them. They have been with men from before the foundations of the world. But they have been hidden from the eyes of man's understanding because of the blindness of the minds of men and because of the hardness of their hearts and because of the state of their awful wickedness of UNBELIEF.

And now, these "great and marvelous TRUTHS" have at last been brought out of their obscurity with a giant magnifying lens being placed over them, so that "ALL MEN MIGHT BE LEFT WITHOUT EXCUSE!"

Each holy PROMISE, given by God in the ages past, has been made clear and apparent as God's finger has pointed out each hidden, heretofore unthought-of, secret pledge of God. And each of the almost unspeakable PROMISES contained in these records is backed by God Himself.

They are His PROMISES!

It is time for man to let the hardness of his heart be melted through the cultivation of love as he develops the desire and the faith to fulfill each holy promise given by God. And there is no possible way in which an individual can so please God as to begin to desire His precious PROMISES to be fulfilled. It is only in the power of such appreciation that any gift can be fully received and the joy of its bestowal fulfilled.

It is as one ceases to be a blind follower of the blind and begins to go to God for the confirmation of His Promises that one's mind will be opened to comprehend the "great and marvelous" Truths, which were hidden up from the eyes of the millions who have plodded their weary, mortal ways to the grave. This dreary road could have been by-passed at any time in the past ages if man had only rent the veil of *unbelief* and laid hold of the PROMISES.

These Almighty Promises are to assist one in fulfilling every divine suggestion, that he "might become perfect, even as his Father in heaven is perfect"—that he might again enter into the "Kingdom of Heaven, wherein all else is added"— And the fact that death can be overcome along with sin and sorrow and affliction is made plain and apparent. Henceforth all men will be left without excuse for the Path is made so clear even a fool need not err therein.

As each individual catches the divine refrain, contained within each single promise, he is opening his soul to comprehend. And as he begins to interpret the wonders of these PROMISES and apply them in his own life he will be dissolved and will become that which he seeks to interpret. So *promised God* through His chosen writer of the Odes of Solomon. Yes! Seek to interpret the divine love of God— "And you will be dissolved and will become that love!" Yes! Become this love and your mortal form will become translated into its higher spiritual functioning as you "evolve from the man kingdom into the God Kingdom!"

LIVE THE LAWS AND YOU WILL KNOW OF THEIR POWER! Live the PROMISES and *you will become all that is* PROMISED!

And now, the final key of fulfilling I am instructed to unfold.

God has proclaimed: *"My words cannot return unto me void or unfulfilled!"*

God released His Holy PROMISES and sent them forth to fill time and space with their eternal power of Almighty blessing. But because of the hardness of men's hearts and the blindness of their minds, which has caused them to remain in their awful STATE OF WICKEDNESS AND UNBELIEF, the glory and the power of His WORDS and PROMISES remained closed. But as man opens his eyes to see and his ears to hear his mind will also be opened so that he will be able to comprehend and to enter the realms of eternal Light.

And since God's words cannot possibly RETURN UNTO HIM VOID OR UNFULFILLED all that is required is for any individual who catches the meaning of even one of those holy PROMIESE, or all of them for that matter, to hold them forth for God's fulfilling. Such a one will REND THE VEIL OF UNBELIEF through his own desire to PROVE or fulfill the PROMISE his own heart lays hold of.

And as the individual holds a PROMISE, or PROMISES forth for God to fulfill they have to be fulfilled. They cannot possibly be held forth to God and be ignored by Him. Since God's *words* cannot be returned to Him VOID OR UNFULFILLED it is time that man begins to understand that it is only man himself who can lay hold of those PROMISES and *return them to God. It is man who must return God's* WORDS unto Him for fulfillment.

Any individual who lays hold of any PROMISE or PROMISES and returns them to God, as he kneels before His throne, or before the altar within himself, The Father is bound to return such requests unto him "OPENLY," or out into the open in tangible manifestation — or FUL-

FILLED. No PROMISE of God can be rejected or left unaccomplished if man will but exercise his faith even in the slightest degree. All that is required is for man to carry the desired PROMISE of his yearning heart to that inner altar of God and hold it forth, without wavering, or doubting in his heart.

As any individual accepts of God's PROMISES, through such *faith* and desire, God is bound! "If ye do as I say then am I bound! But if ye do not as I say then ye have no PROMISE!" Yes! "Lay hold of the PROMISES OF ALMIGHTY GOD" through the faith of your own desiring, and God will be required to fulfill His PROMISES — for they *cannot return unto Him unfulfilled or void!* And only man can return these PROMISES TO GOD! And in this requesting man has the right to DEMAND OF GOD the acknowledgement and the fulfilling of His WORD. And God must answer!

There is no loophole! There is no flaw in God's plan! There is no excuse for God to fail and no excuse whatsoever for man to go on, *locked behind the great, black veil of* UNBELIEF!

God *cannot* fail! God will not fail! And it is time for man to awaken to the fullness of his own possibilities and responsibilities and requirements as "he lays hold of the Best Gifts!" The very best! And lives according to the PROMISES and by Faith holds them forth for God's fulfilling.

"God will not be mocked!" Neither will God mock His children with unattainable PROMISES; Every PROMISE ever given holds locked within it the germ or seed of its own fulfillment! Rend the veil of *unbelief* and behold the glorified vision of God's Almighty power made manifest as all things are perfected unto you.

"He that *overcometh* shall inherit all things; and I will be his God, and he shall be my son.

"But the FEARFUL, and UNBELIEVING, and the abominable, and murderers, and whoremongers, and sorcerers, and idolaters, and all liars, shall have their part in the lake which burneth with fire and brimstone: which is the second death." (Rev. 21:7-9).

"Perfect love casteth out all fear!" But there are churches and organizations and groups that have only been able to imprison and hold the minds of their followers in subjection through FEAR — fear of being deceived, fear of their own inadequacy to judge intelligently — fear of evil — fear of every ray of light as they are trained to abide in the darkness and trust wholly in the arm of flesh.

Fear is a deadly thing. It is without love! It is without understanding! It is without Faith! And those whose minds have been blighted and warped and sealed by fear do not even Trust God to have the power to answer their prayers or to be capable of revealing His own great Truths to them!

Fear, according to the foregoing scripture, is the first of the deadly sins. Unbelief is the second. Murderers and whoremongers and sorcerers and idolaters and liars follow.

To travel the road of glory into the realms of Light — and to PROVE the teachings of Almighty God and to receive the glorious fulfillment of those almost unspeakable PROMISES—one must rend that veil of FEAR, of UNBELIEF, of darkness and step forth, in FAITH! One must have the power to BELIEVE for that is the first requisite to gaining knowledge and enlightenment — and POWER!

The higher realm belongs to those who can lay claim to it, through FAITH and courage and love and a joy of increasing ecstasy as they lay hold of eternal Light and it becomes subject unto them.

To be cautious is good. To be fearful is damnation!

"Trust in God with all your heart and lean not to your own understanding!"

"O Lord, I have trusted in Thee, I will trust in thee forever. I will not put my trust in the arm of flesh; for I know that cursed is he that putteth his trust in the arm of flesh. Yea, cursed is he that putteth his trust in man or maketh flesh his arm."

Chapter VIII

"THE POWER TO COME AND GO AS THE WIND!"

"As many as are led by the Spirit of God, they are the sons of God." (Rom. 8:14)

"They are known as gods unto whom the word of God comes." When one has rent the veil of unbelief, *overcoming* the hardness of his heart, and has opened his eyes so that they are no longer half closed in blindness, "that he might have eyes to see," then he will be prepared to "be taught of God," and will no longer be just a plodding, grubby mortal with his vision focused only upon the earth and the things and conditions thereof. He will have opened up his soul, through faith, to the extent that God's minute instructions and powerful, loving wisdom will direct him in every act of his life. And his life will become powerful! He will begin to do the WORKS which Christ did — and then GO ON TO THE GREATER WORKS! This is the eternal *promise* of God to those who truly believe, not just profess to believe.

The attaining of this divine contact with God contains the power *promised* — the power to "be born of the Spirit," not just in words or in self-righteous phrases or in false acclamations, But in ACTUAL FACT! And that one "will be able to come and go as the wind and no one will know from whence he came or whither he goeth!" This is the power Christ had and used as he disappeared out of the midst of those who sought to lay hold of him upon various

84

occasions, seeking to force their wills upon Him. And this is the power He used as He walked upon the Sea of Galilee.

"And he who is *thankful in* ALL THINGS *shall be made glorious!*" To be made glorious one would have developed the Song of Praising love and gratitude until his whole being would have fulfilled all the laws of righteousness. He would have filled the measure of his own Spiritual pattern and would be born of the Spirit and receive the almost incomprehensible power thereof. And from there on his growth would be much more speedy and perfect than the slow maturing of an infant born of the flesh. He would be able also to step across ages and eons of plodding as "his mind and lips would lose the power to hurt and wound!" And so his voice would be heard among the Gods because he would be admitted into their presence as a member of their divine, progressive glory.

Such are the *promises!*

"When you cast the darkness from among you, you will be ordained of God, and will be sent forth to be the greatest, notwithstanding you are the least and the servant of all. And all things will become subject unto you, both in heaven and on earth, the Life and the Light; the Spirit and the Power, sent forth by the Will of the Father, through Jesus Christ, His Son!" And in the fulfilling of this *promise* one is given an assurance of receiving all the powers possible to receive — the very powers of heaven and of earth. But because of the gross wickedness of unbelief and the hardness of men's hearts and the blindness of their minds they have failed utterly to even look at "the great and marvelous things which God has held waiting since the foundations of the world." And the only reason these mighty things have been hid is because man himself has been too fearful and too unbelieving to even look!

But the *promise* is, that when man would "REND THE VEIL OF UNBELIEF *which has caused him to remain in his awful state of wickedness"* — then the great powers of these *promises* will be made manifest in the lives of the children of men.

Yes! "The nearer man approaches perfection (through his own *overcoming*) the clearer are his views and the greater are his enjoyments, till he *overcomes* the evils of his life (the temptations, the vicissitudes, the darkness, the fears and even the calamities, misfortunes and dismays) and loses every desire for sin, and like the ancients, he will arrive at the point of faith where he will be wrapped in the power and glory of his Maker and will be caught up to dwell with Him!"

Just words? Oh, NO! PROMISES! *Promises* so great they have blinded men with their glory insomuch that they have been enfolded in the dark veil of unbelief and held there for centuries. And because of the blindness of men's eyes and the hardness of their hearts these dynamic blessings have remained unfulfilled.

God has left the following divine invitations awaiting man's acceptance of them: "Seek me diligently and you shall find Me!" "Seek me early and you shall find Me!"

There are over sixty references in the Holy Scriptures which hold forth that everlasting *promise* that they might KNOW God. This does not mean just to *know* ABOUT Him. It means to KNOW HIM! And "This is LIFE ETERNAL THAT THEY MIGHT KNOW THEE, the only True and living God and Jesus Christ whom thou hast sent!"

Then there is the *promise* that he who would pray continually without ceasing: yea, "unto such it shall be given to KNOW the mysteries of God; yea, unto such it shall be given to reveal things which never have been revealed!" "And they shall comprehend all things!"

Almost the same exact *promise* is given in these words: "And if your eyes be single to my glory your whole bodies shall be filled with Light and there shall be no darkness in you. And *that body which is filled with Light shall comprehend all things* — and I WILL UNVEIL MY FACE UNTO HIM!" Which, fulfilled is Life eternal!

With these dynamic, glorious *promises* waiting down the centuries for fulfillment how is it possible that man could have been so blind he could not see them? How could his heart have been so hard he could not test them or even accept them? By his own unbelief man has woven that dark, dismal, unholy veil of evil and doubt and gross UNBELIEF that has caused him to remain in his awful state of wickedness and darkness and despair.

There is none of these *promises* recorded here, or the many that have not been included, that if accepted and lived, will not prepare one to receive that glorious birth of the Spirit, which all churches claim and none have received.

With that Birth of the Spirit one's entire being becomes so filled with the Spirit of the Almighty it is thereafter a permanent factor in his life. This being born of the Spirit is not just a fragmentary or temporary experience to be recalled in memory or spoken words for the remainder of one's life. This retelling is but carrying one's stairway with him. This is not the Birth of the Spirit. The birth of the Spirit is a gift and contains even more than the ability to "be able to come and go as the wind — and no one will know

from whence he came or whither he goeth!" The bestowal
of this power is very great indeed for if one IS "Born of
the Spirit" he will also receive the gift of translation. Being
Born of the Spirit IS the power of translation! They are one
and the same thing! And this power contains the understanding and ability to serve to one's fullest capacity of love,
wheresoever he may be directed by God. Such will become
a servant in the hands of God in very deed. And he will be
able to GO FORTH AND DO THE WORKS WHICH
CHRIST DID, instead of just talking about them.

He will also have the power to go on and DO THE
GREATER WORKS, which Christ *promised!* "He will do
greater works than these because I go unto my Father!" It
was necessary for Christ to go unto His Father that His
greater assignment to contact and send out His power and
blessings and enlightenment to ALL who would only ask
or seek for His help might become a fact. "And lo, I am
with you always, even unto the ends of the world!"

As an individual is Born of the Spirit, or receives of the
power of translation, the privilege, if so be he desires, will
be granted to continue to serve right here on this earth
where the opportunity to do all the works which Christ did,
while here on earth, and the greater works will become his
privilege to accomplish and fulfill.

Those of great faith and great love will be permitted to
remain on this earthly plane, though they will no longer be
of it. "They will be able to step to and fro" but their services will be to help suffering mankind. These *overcoming*
ones are only required to "go to the Father," that they
might receive their most holy ordination to be sent forth,
for "They will be ordained of God and sent forth to become
the greatest, notwithstanding they are the least and become

the servant of all." These will have the power, as they are born of the Spirit and are ordained of God, to "be able to come and go as the wind" and no one will know from what assignment they came or to what assignment they will go.

Such is in the plan of God! Such has been in the plan even from the beginning of time. "These are the great and marvelous THINGS that have been hid up from the foundations of the world because of the hardness of the hearts of the children of men, and the blindness of their eyes and because of the gross wickedness of UNBELIEF!"

Accept any one of the great *promises* of Almighty God, or ALL of them and live by them and you will KNOW of their POWER for the power they contain will become your own for you will be born of the Spirit — or become a translated being with a higher calling placed upon you as you go forth in the joy and the power of eternal glory to serve!

In closing I shall quote only a fraction of the *promises* contained in the Holy Scriptures, regarding the power to overcome death.

Remember: "The wages of sin is death!" "And the gift of God is LIFE ETERNAL!" Then glance for a moment into the record of the LOST BOOKS OF THE BIBLE, to Nicodemus, chapter XVIII, verse twelve which states; "O Satan, prince of all evil, AUTHOR OF DEATH, AND source of all pride," etc. God did not ordain death. He permitted it! Satan ordained and has manipulated it from the beginning.

"In the way of righteousness is LIFE; and in the pathway thereof is no death." (Prov. 12:28)

"The law of the wise is a fountain of life, to depart from the snares of death." (Prov. 14:27)

"Verily, I say unto you, THERE BE SOME STANDING HERE, WHICH SHALL NOT TASTE DEATH, TILL THEY SEE THE SON OF MAN COMING IN HIS KINGDOM." (Matt. 16:28; Mark 9:1; Luke 9:27).

"Verily, verily I say unto you, He that heareth my word, and believeth on Him that sent me, hath everlasting Life, and shall not come into condemnation; but IS passed from death into LIFE." (John 5:24).

This *hearing of His Word* is the opening up of one's heart so that "one may be taught of God" in every emergency as God directs that individual *personally* in the pathway of his own *overcoming* and calling.

Those who have not yet learned to be taught of God are frequently jumping off the deep end into the mysteries which have not become completely opened to their understandings, by God's Personal instruction. They begin to focus their attention upon the great possibility of translation without understanding in the least the cleansing of themselves that they might attain unto the PROMISE to be "born of the Spirit."

Translation is not the fullness of the resurrected state. Translation is that which Christ received upon the Mount of Transfiguration. It is not the resurrected state, but it holds all the powers of "BEING BORN OF THE SPIRIT."

After the experience on the Mount of Transfiguration Christ had the power to disappear or appear upon occasion and the power that no one could take his life from Him. He could relinquish it, which He later did WILLINGLY. But no one could take it from Him. He could lay His life down and He could take it up again, according to His word. But when Christ came forth from the tomb He had received the full powers and the glory of the RESURRECTION.

To those who have *overcome* their impatience, their impurities and their every desire and inclination for sin and selfishness and self-acclaim, the gift of translation will be granted and they will "be able to come and go as the wind and no one will know from whence they came or whither they have gone." And when they have finished their ministry upon this earth or at the coming of Jesus Christ in His glory, "They will be changed in the twinkling of an eye from mortality into immortality." The translated ones are not subject to death or to aging or to suffering and can "Come and go as the wind," to whatsoever assignment may be theirs at the moment — AND THEY TAKE THEIR BODIES WITH THEM, though they can become invisible to those who are upon a lower vibration or plane.

During the Millennium all will be taught these higher laws, for they are the laws of the Millennium. AND THERE WILL BE NO MORE DEATH — FOR DEATH IS THE LAST ENEMY TO BE OVERCOME in every individual's life.

The admonition is not to worry about the dynamic power of translation or to be impatient concerning your receiving it. Be only concerned about the condition of your own heart and the power of its releasing love. Love alone is the key. Therefore the admonition is to be watchful of your thoughts and the caliber of the vibrations which you release. Cleanse yourself of all darkness and of the evils of negative, hateful, fearful, lustful or jealous thoughts and the memory of those negative conditions which you have harbored, unwittingly in the temple of your soul.

And again, the *promise* is: "If you will chase darkness from among you, you will be ordained of God, and sent forth to become the greatest, notwithstanding you are the least" — and the humble, loving servant of all.

"God's WORD cannot return unto Him void or unfulfilled!" This is the law of eternity! It cannot be changed for it is irrevocable! It cannot possibly be revoked, not even by God because He established it at the dawn of creation! And His WORD is His PROMISES to man! And it is man, as he opens his eyes and his heart to BELIEVE, who has the power to return these PROMISES TO GOD for fulfillment! This is the plan and the pattern and the glory as man steps forth to fullfill his part in the divine system of glorious accomplishment! It is only man who can return God's *promises* to Him! And when man holds those *promises* forth God must fullfill them! This too is His PROMISE!

Take any one of God's most holy *promises,* or ALL of them, and hold them upon the altar of your own soul, that Sacred Holy of Holies, the Secret Place of the Most High — your very own heart-center, and there hold them forth *"without wavering"* or *"without doubting* in your heart!" And they will have to be fulfilled. The law of the fulfilling of God's *promises* is perfect! It cannot fail! And nothing in existence can hold back the power of those divine and holy *promises* except man's desolating UNBELIEF as he continues to exist in the darkness of his own blindness and in the hardness of his own heart. It is impossible to even contact the power of God let alone return His divine *promises* to Him as long as one's heart remains in that hardened condition of UNBELIEF and while his eyes refuse to look or his mind to investigate. Often that deadly evil of FEAR, which is the first of the great crimes, holds one's mind in bondage to the past ages of darkness and dead dogmas.

Herbert Spencer said: "There is a principle which is a bar against all information, which is proof against all argument, and which cannot fail to keep a man in everlasting ignorance. That principle is condemnation before investigation."

As one opens up his eyes to *see* and his heart to *believe* and his mind to investigate, nothing in existence will remain impossible if he will pray for understanding as he makes his search. THIS IS THE LAW! This is the law of the great unveiling of TRUTH!

"Rend the veil of unbelief that the great and marvelous things which have been hid up from the foundation of the world," might be confirmed and fulfilled in you! Do not let it matter to you what others have done or have not done — or what they are doing. ALL THINGS ARE POSSIBLE TO YOU — IF YOU WILL ONLY BELIEVE!

And God be with you in your great unfolding! His angels will attend you as the Light of Christ is brought forth in you! And ever as you open up the doors of your own soul to rejoice those heavenly angels will rejoice with you and will begin to be glorified in Light! And as you progress you will forever glorify the pathway for those who follow and it will become the great Highway of Transparent Gold.

CHAPTER IX

"ALL THAT THE FATHER HAS IS YOURS."

"To look back is vicious!" To abide in the hallway of memories is dwelling ignorantly or willingly in the dark realm of mortality and accepting grubby mortality with all its ugliness, vicissitudes and its sufferings and despairs.

Every returning thought to the past, whether to individuals or happenings, is but sealing the past and mortality more firmly upon the consciousness of your subconscious mind.

Leave the past behind enfolded in your awakened love and blessings. Then release it with joy.

Take up your abode in the great, eternal NOW, which is the threshold entering into the limitless realms of the ETERNAL, the divine realm of endless POWER and ever-lasting beauty.

Let every thought be upon the purification of yourself as you begin to transform yourself into a regal person through praise and love and gratitude. Worship God and adore Him and give thanks in a joy of increasing happiness.

As you place God upon His throne and hold Him there in singing devotion you will find that you have only been placing a crown of glory upon your own head. You will find yourself established in His Presence — one of His praising ones, glorified and exalted beyond dismays or sorrows or tears.

Love and praise God. This is the road of sanctification.

Let none of the dark memories of the past enter your mind without enfolding them in forgiveness and love and blessing as you perfect them in the healing Light of Christ. Thus you can glorify the past and release yourself from mortality. And you, too, will become cleansed and purified.

This information contains the holiness and the power of the complete purification of yourself, your past and of the world. It is the Celestial melody which anyone can easily master who desires to overcome mortality. All that is required is for one to open up his mind to BELIEVE and then conform his life to the living of these simple laws of glory as he develops the POWER TO PROVE EVERY WORD GOD EVER GAVE AND EVERY PROMISE HE EVER MADE.

"LIVE THESE THINGS AND YOU WILL KNOW OF THEIR TRUTH!"

Oh, the glory and the wonder of the Truths of God! And the mercy of His unfolding is as limitless as eternity and as boundless as man's capacity to test and to prove all things.

"It is given to abide in you: the record of heaven; the COMFORTER; the peaceable things of immortal glory; the truth of all things; that which QUICKENETH all things, which MAKETH ALIVE all things; that which KNOWETH all things, and hath ALL POWER"

It is definitely true that the Divine, Holy Comforter is given to abide in man, along with all the foregoing, dynamic powers of heaven. For "all that the Father has is yours."

The very abode of that Divine Comforter, or Holy Helper is in the subconscious mind where all facts and knowledge are stored.

As one purifies the abode or realm of that Powerful, Divine Assistant he cleanses his subconscious mind and renovates it. Then this Holy Helper, or Holy Ghost, as the scriptures call it, can function in Its dynamic fulness. "It will bring all things past to your remembrance." It will assist you in achieving any assignment or glorify any accomplishment. It will bring culture and refinement and perfection into your life. It is impossible for anyone to master any skill or art without the help of this Divine Helper. It alone can bring mastery or proficiency or perfection into any achievement from the playing of a musical instrument to the driving of a car or the manipulation of any piece of office equipment or the operating of any piece of machinery.

It is the Divine, Holy Helper that takes care of the inner functioning of the physical body. And when It is crowded out of Its abode by the evils of desolate, bitter memories and life's corroding stench of self-pity, dislikes, hates or bitterness the body begins to age and to sicken — and to die. It is also within the power of this Divine, Holy Helper to QUICKEN and to renew or TO MAKE ALIVE the physical body. This Holy Spirit, this Divine Helper will lend its full cooperation, if only one is aware of Its willingness to assist and permits It to do so. This is Its purpose and the power of Its functioning. Only man must acknowledge It and accept of Its assistance. It must be consciously included in all one's undertakings and projects and even in the ordinary tasks of daily living if one's life is to go smoothly and be always under perfect control.

Call this Divine, Holy Helper by NAME. Give it a NAME, a wondrous, loving, personal Name. Speak to It as though It were your most intimate, loving associate. Then make your requests or desires known and rely upon Its help, fully and completely without doubting. And always give It thanks for the assistance rendered.

Speak to It thus as you rejoice in Its ability to hear you and Its desire to serve: "Beloved Helper, quicken and renew me in mind and body and soul. I am seeking to purify the realm in which You abide in me. As I do I ask humbly for your help. Help me to cleanse my mind of all darkness, filling it only with Love and Light and beauty and perfection and with everlasting joy!"

Speak to It often thus. And rejoice in the power of Its fulfilling accomplishments. When you are trying to recall some word or phrase or fact, ask It to assist you. And soon you will become completely aware of Its reality.

This is how the darkness can be completely overcome and be forever eliminated.

Always be firm in making your requests, not domineering, just firm and grateful and filled with praise and thanks and love. And rejoice always.

Invite the Divine, Holy Helper to be your constant companion and watch yourself grow into a new, dynamic being of glorious love and increasing abilities and stupendous achievements. Talk to this Divine, Holy Helper and take It into your confidence. And always remember to thank It for Its help. And you will soon KNOW that you walk with God for He will draw near to you as you draw near to Him through the invited companionship of His Holy Helper, which He has given to abide in you.

This inner knowledge of closeness of the Divine Helper, this Sacred Holy Ghost, is a part of the "GREAT TRUTH!" It is also the witness of Jesus Christ and will always bear witness of Him.

"KNOW THE TRUTH" — the full Truth, "and the Truth will make you free — and you *shall* be free indeed!"

And now I quote from the record of Moroni, an ancient

prophet who received and fulfilled the great law of translation.

Moroni 7:13-19: "But behold, that which is of God inviteth and enticeth to do good continually; wherefore, everything which inviteth and enticeth to do good, and to love God, and to serve him, is inspired of God.

"Wherefore, take heed, my beloved brethren, that ye do not judge that which is evil to be of God, or that which is good and of God to be of the devil.

"For behold, my brethren, it is given unto you to judge, that ye may know good from evil; and the way to judge is as plain, that ye may know with a perfect knowledge, as the daylight is from the dark night.

"For behold, The Spirit of Christ is given to every man, that he may know good from evil; wherefore, I show unto you the way to judge; for everything which inviteth to do good, and to persuade to believe in Christ, is sent forth by the power and gift of Christ; wherefore ye may know with a perfect knowledge it is of God.

"But whatsoever thing persuadeth men to do evil, and believe not in Christ, and deny him, and serve not God, then ye may know with a perfect knowledge it is of the devil; for after this manner doth the devil work, for he persuadeth no man to do good, no, not one; neither do his angels; neither do they who subject themselves unto him.

"And now, my brethren, seeing that ye know the light by which ye may judge, which light is the light of Christ, see that ye do not judge wrongfully; for with that same judgment which ye judge ye shall also be judged.

"Wherefore, I beseech of you, brethren, that ye should search diligently in the light of Christ that ye may know good from evil; and if ye will lay hold upon every good thing, and condemn it not, ye certainly will be a child of Christ."

Also in the record of Moroni, Chapter ten and verses thirty and thirty-two and verse thirty-three is given the following: "And again I would exhort you that ye would come unto Christ, and lay hold upon EVERY GOOD GIFT!"

"Yea, come unto Christ, and be perfected in him, and deny yourselves of all ungodliness; and if ye shall deny yourselves of all ungodliness, and love God with all your might, mind and strength, then is his grace sufficient for you, that by his grace ye may be perfect in Christ; and if by the grace of God, ye are perfect in Christ, ye can in nowise deny the power of God.

"And again, if ye, by the grace of God, are perfect in Christ and deny not his power, then are ye sanctified in Christ by the grace of God through the shedding of the blood of Christ, which is in the covenant of the Father unto the remission of your sins, that ye become holy, without spot."

If you do not deny the power of God then you must BELIEVE in His power. You must believe in His power to fulfill all His PROMISES, for His words cannot return unto Him unfulfilled or void.

(Ibid. 4-5): "And when ye shall receive these things I would exhort you that ye would ask God the Eternal Father, in the name of Christ, if these things are not true; and if ye shall ask with a sincere heart, with real intent, having faith in Christ, he will manifest the Truth of it unto you, by the POWER OF THE HOLY GHOST.

"AND BY THE POWER OF THE HOLY GHOST YE MAY KNOW THE TRUTH OF ALL THINGS!" For "The Truth of all things is given to abide in you!" As you open up your sealed minds to accept and to seek to comprehend fully the greater Truths of God you will be led into the supreme "KNOWLEDGE OF ALL TRUTH!"

So has God Commanded me to write. And His words shall stand! They cannot be broken nor can they return unto Him unfulfilled and void!"

So be it! In the Name of the Father and His Son Jesus Christ and The Holy Ghost — Amen!

CHAPTER X

THE STRAIGHT AND NARROW WAY

In the book of Saint Matthew, chapter seven and verse fourteen, is given the following: "Enter ye in at the Straight Gate: for wide is the gate and broad is the way that leadeth to destruction, and many there be which go in thereat.

"Because straight is the gate and narrow is the way which leadeth unto life and few there be that find it!" This road which leads to LIFE is the road of OVERCOMING, in which a man need never die.

Such is a portion of Christ's precious teachings. And every waring organization in Christendom is positive that it alone is traveling that sacred Narrow Path that leads to life eternal. Yet they all follow the beaten path of earth into the grave as Isaiah proclaimed in his fifty-third chapter and sixth verse, as follows: "All we like sheep have gone astray; we have turned every one to his own way." Or as Paul declared in Romans 3:23. "For all have sinned, and come short of the glory of God."

Or as given in Psalms, chapter forty-nine, verses nine to fourteen: "That he (man believed that he) should still live forever and not see corruption.

"For he seeth that wise men die, likewise the fool and the brutish person perish, and leave their wealth to others.

"Their inward thought is that their houses shall continue forever, and their dwelling place to all generations, that they call their lands after their own names.

"Nevertheless, man being in honor abideth not; he is like the beasts that perish.

"THIS, THEIR WAY IS THEIR FOLLY: yet their posterity approve their sayings.

"LIKE SHEEP THEY ARE LAID IN THE GRAVE; death shall feed on them: and the upright shall have dominion over them in the morning; and their beauty shall consume in the grave - - -"

That men have followed like sheep to the grave is indeed their folly, especially since Christ came that men "might have LIFE and have it MORE ABUNDANTLY, EVEN LIFE ETERNAL, that they need never die!"

Christ's whole message is of life — *not death*. And then, that none might be mistaken, he proclaimed, "I am the Way, the TRUTH and the LIFE!"

"For the *law* made nothing perfect, BUT THE BRINGING OF A BETTER HOPE DID: by which we draw near to God." (Heb. 9:19)

Then comes the marvelous revelation given in II Peter chapter one, verses three and four: *"According as his* (Christ's) *divine power hath given unto us all things that pertain unto LIFE and* Godliness, through the knowledge of him that hath called us to glory and virtue.

"WHEREBY ARE GIVEN UNTO US EXCEEDING GREAT AND PRECIOUS PROMISES; *that by these ye might be partakers of the divine nature,* HAVING ESCAPED CORRUPTION that is in the world through lust." Here indeed is the definite promise that man could partake of the divine nature and escape corruption, which comes through lust.

Remember always is given this information: "The wages of sin is death!" But because we have gone on down the centuries satisfied with our mortal inclination, we truly have "All fallen short of the glory of God," though His *promises* of Life eternal have been there all the time for us to only open our eyes to see.

The above promise that we might be partakers of the divine nature and escape from corruption is verified in the ancient information that "Man can evolve from the man kingdom into the God Kingdom." If he partakes of the divine nature and escapes corruption then he would have to evolve beyond mortality. Man has, through love and devotion, the power to become a partaker of the divine nature and to escape the grave and death — that he need not follow the beaten path of mankind into the grave like sheep.

At first doubting man may hesitate to enter this Straight and Narrow Path, which so few find, because he has never beheld with his physical eyes, anyone who has attained unto these PROMISED POWERS. Yes, who has beheld anyone in this day and age who has *been born of the Spirit,* as Christ explained to Nicodemus — one who could come and go as the wind and no one would know from where he came, or where he went. These who are born of the Spirit are truly wrapped in the power and glory of their Maker and are sent forth to do the GREATER WORKS. But because individual, mortal man has not yet beheld such glorious manifestation of God's Almighty POWER, in fulfillment, many hesitate to make the slightest effort to travel the Highway of the Gods. They cling to the ugly, mortal way of corruption and death, thinking that is all there is.

But now let us examine II Cor. 4:18, which is as follows: "While we look not at the things which are seen, but at the things which are not seen; for the things which are seen are temporal (earthly, grubby, mortal); but the things which are not seen are eternal." These, as yet, unseen things are spiritual, indestructible and are the most real of all to those who follow that Straight Path into the Higher Way of perfection — where FAITH IS FINALLY MADE PERFECT and the existence of the spiritual is brought into tangible reality or manifestation.

This Straight and Narrow Way, which so few find, because it is not seen, and because it is entered into by the joy of FAITH. It is traveled in love and divine hope, which lights the Way of glory. This sacred Path is an unfolding of exquisite beauty as one's understanding opens to encompass the dynamic truths which it involves. It is a Pathway which is intangible to the mortal, physical senses and experiences, at first, but as one enters it his faith expands into knowledge as his spiritual attributes are quickened and developed.

This glorious Path is not an outside Path at all. It is an inner path in which one learns to PROVE the glorious PROMISES of Jesus Christ, by LIVING THEM. It is an inner exploring in which one takes hold of the PROMISES and begins to put them to the tests of PROVING. It is not a Path of narrowed, bigoted "dos" and "don'ts" or of restrictions and self-righteousness. It is not a road of darkness or bleak ugliness or skimped conformities. It is a road of Lighted glory and of increasing joyous ecstasy.

It is a road of PROMISES! The great and mighty *Promises* of God, the Eternal Father. It is traveled by FAITH, as one lays hold of the best gifts, casting out his own doubts. As one begins to look at the PROMISES and desires to PROVE them, which is actually to prove God and His power to fulfill, he must exercise Faith. No doubting man can travel this sacred road of fulfillment. Only by FAITH can it be traversed, this glorified "Road to Zion, in which a fool need not err, but over which the wicked cannot pass." To travel this sacred road of glory one must cast out his fears and his failures and his great wickedness of unbelief.

These books, which God has commanded me to write, contain the complete map to this exalting Pathway — and to the great glory to which the Pathway leads.

It is a road of Praise and of Love and of Singing Gratitude! There is no darkness nor sorrow nor evil for Christ IS THE WAY. He is the Light of it. He is the unfolding Revealer of It. He is the joy of it! And as one accepts the invitation to travel this sacred Road he soon learns that these great PROMISES have become a very part of his life without his striving or straining by any agonizing, self-denying misery or anguish.

As one begins to love God with all his heart, soul, mind and strength he enters the true Pathway of OVERCOMING. And he passes beyond the laws of mortal bondage. As he continues his love increases until he actually becomes the divine love of God. And he who is perfected in love is born of God. "Whosoever is born of God doth not sin, for his seed remaineth in him: and he cannot sin, because he is born of God." (I John 3:9) "He reaches the point where he overcomes the evils of his life and loses every desire for sin."

Or, as follows: "Beloved, let us love one another: for love is of God; and everyone that loveth is born of God, and KNOWETH GOD!" ("And this is Life Eternal!") (I John 4:7).

"For whatsoever is born of God, OVERCOMETH THE WORLD: and this is the victory that OVERCOMETH THE WORLD, even our FAITH." (I John 5:4). Or as Christ

Himself declared at his trial, "I have OVERCOME THE
WORLD!" (John 16:33).

Thus it is fully revealed that FAITH is the power of
OVERCOMING. And FAITH contains the knowledge and
the power by which one learns to cast out or OVERCOME
the doubts and fears and travels in a full HOPE of all the
holy PROMISES which God has given unto the children
of men.

"We know that whosoever is born of God sinneth not;
but he that is begotten of God *keepeth himself,* and that
wicked one touch him not." (I John 5:18). In other words
he enters upon this Straight and Narrow Way of PROMISE
and glory in which the darkness of evil and doubting and
of self is OVERCOME and left behind.

This divine Pathway is the Pathway of love being perfected until it casts out all fear and all doubting! It is the
Path of FAITH made perfect! This glorious Path is not a
long, difficult road, but one of prayer and hope and rejoicing as FAITH reveals each day its increasing glory and
unfolds its TRUTHS in the power of the divine PROMISES
of Almighty God.

As one continues along this road or Pathway of increasing Light and rejoicing he comprehends that his eyes have
truly become "Single to the glory of God!"

And the PROMISE is: "And if your eyes become single
to my glory you shall be filled with Light and comprehend
all things. And there shall be no darkness in you. And I
will unveil my Face unto you" etc. As one holds his eyes
single to the glory of God he begins to absorb that Light or
to bring it forth. How else could he "be filled with Light?"

And it is most assuredly true that as one travels this glorious, Straight and Narrow Path it becomes increasingly

more beautiful and joyous and desirable, for "The nearer man approaches perfection the clearer are his views and the greater are his enjoyments, until he *overcomes* the evils of his life and loses every desire for sin, and like the ancients, *arrives at the point of FAITH* where he is wrapped in the power and glory of his Maker and is caught up to dwell with Him!" This glorious condition is accomplished not through dying, but through LIVING and OVERCOMING. (Later on in this record the full wonder of this promise will be revealed).

This is a Pathway of almost unspeakable joy and glory as the weaknesses of the flesh are automatically OVERCOME and left behind like ugly, discarded, moth-eaten rags. Yet this is not a road of dark, dismal, ugly taboos and narrow-minded restrictions. It is not a Road of commands and obligations at all. It is a Pathway of choosing and willing and of glorifying God in a joy of exquisite gladness.

This Straight and Narrow Way is the Path of PROMISE as one travels it in an expectancy of joy and ecstasy as he perfects the love of God within himself until it becomes a fountain of "Living Water, springing up into everlasting LIFE!" This love becomes a fountain so life-giving, so real and so desirable one who partakes of it need never die. And Christ invited all to "Come and partake of the Waters of Life freely!" He invites all mankind to drink of these living waters, for they are offered without price.

These glorious, almost incomprehensible PROMISES have been waiting down the centuries for men to begin to open up their minds that they might BELIEVE. And in BELIEVING begin to travel this road of glory, by FAITH.

This Straight and Narrow Way is the Path of God! It is the Straight and Narrow Way which leads to Life Eternal!

It is the Road of unutterable glory—"Which so few find" because they are seeking with their mortal senses and their personal unenlightened understandings. They are not seeking with Souls alerted and with a humility that is enfolded in praise and love and gratitude and increasingly exalted through joy.

This is the Road which the wicked can never cross over, though a fool need not err therein. It can never be traveled by the self-righteous. Each church believes it alone has the keys of this sacred way of life. Yet each in turn has helped to fill the cemeteries with their dead. "Thus saith the Lord God; WOE unto the foolish prophets that FOLLOW THEIR OWN SPIRITS and have seen nothing!" (Ezek. 13:3) for they are only false prophets bearing witness of themselves, with eyes single to their own glory and not to the glory of God. These cannot travel this sacred Pathway of God.

As one travels this Straight and Narrow Way it becomes increasingly glorious. It is a Path of such praise and joy and ecstatic glory the darkness is overcome and forever left behind. But this great ecstatic joy is held and maintained in a majesty of divine power, not in outward manifestation.

Those who travel this Pathway in loving humility and increasing joy reach the point of Faith where all PROMISES ARE FULFILLED. It is the point of FAITH in which all doubts and fears have been OVERCOME and eliminated. It is the point of supreme, everlasting POWER. It is where FAITH itself is transformed into KNOWING. It is the point where one truly comprehends all things. And KNOWLEDGE IS POWER! It is the point of unutterable glory. It is the unveiling of man's soul as he stands face to face with God, purified even as He is pure, glorified as He is glorious for he will be a co-heir with Jesus Christ—a joint-heir with the Son of God.

"As one reaches this point of Faith where he is wrapped in the power and glory of his Maker and is caught up to dwell with Him, he can either choose to remain in that Celestial realm, or return to earth to "DO THE GREATER WORKS," which Christ promised. Christ explained that those who truly believed would not only be able to do all the works which He did but go on to do the greater works, because he was going to His Father. But it was not explained at that time that those who fulfilled the works of OVERCOMING, even as He OVERCAME, would be privileged to return to earth if they so chose, and only by this method could they possibly do the GREATER WORKS. And His word cannot return to him unfulfilled and void! Therefore, you who choose to lend your strength to the complete fulfilling of His Word and to fulfill all the *promises,* the very heavens are awaiting you—and the earth and all that in them is.

So marvelous is this promise to do even greater works than Christ did, it has been veiled down the centuries in a mist of unbelief. In two thousand years none have opened up their eyes to either see or comprehend how literal these words are, or exercised the FAITH TO EVEN TRY TO PROVE THEM. No one, in two thousands years of preaching and listening has ever done any of the works which Christ did, let alone go on to do the GREATER WORKS which He PROMISED!

Try to imagine what the greater works would be! Then know this, They are still incomprehensible to mortal minds. Yet how could anyone hope to become a joint-heir with Jesus Christ, or a co-heir with him, which means coequal, unless he did do the very works which Christ did—and then went on to do EVEN GREATER WORKS? How blind the world has been, and how steeped in the dark lethargy of mortality and unbelief. Rend the veil of unbelief and you will KNOW and be able TO DO the greater works, as PROMISED.

Man, when he has traveled that Straight and Narrow Path, of which Christ is the pattern, the Light and the glory, truly reaches the point of FAITH, where he is wrapped in the Power and glory of his Maker and is caught up to dwell with Him.

And only those who walk that Straight and Narrow Path of praise and love and glorious gratitude, as their joy and ecstasy increases, can possibly reach the point of FAITH where they can be made perfect as they are ordained of God and sent forth to do the GREATER WORKS. These PROM-ISES of Jesus Christ have been waiting down the centuries for those with enough humility to travel so glorious a Path of loving and praising and joyous Thanksgiving and believing in order that they might complete the journey of glory and OVERCOME the world! even as He overcame!

Only in the OVERCOMING OF THE WORLD, OR THE LITTLE MORTAL SELF with its demanding claim for superiority and attention, can this Straight and Narrow Path possibly be traveled. That is why so few have found it. But "Wide is the gate and broad is the Path that leadeth to destruction (or the grave) and many there be who go in thereat."

Yes, the whole wide world and all the creed-bound, self-righteous demonstrators of Christendom and of the heathen world and of the barbarians are traveling the broad Way of self, which leads to destruction and to death. No professing

can fulfill the greatness of the PROMISES. Only the LIV-
ING OF HIS WORDS can give one the POWER OF
FULFILLING.

Glorious, Wonderful God! How great Thou art!

Those who have eyes single to the glory of God instead
of to their own importance will eventually be filled with
Light and complete KNOWLEDGE as the darkness of mor-
tality is OVERCOME IN THEM. Then it is that "God
will unveil His face unto them. This is the great and last
PROMISE! "It is the very fulfilling of ALL PROMISES!
This is the point of perfect Faith in which one actually
KNOWS GOD! And "This is Life Eternal, to KNOW
THEE, the only True and Living God and Jesus Christ, whom
Thou hast sent!"

Then only, as this supreme point of FAITH IS reached
can one hope to DO THE GREATER WORKS, WHICH
are so needed and so necessary at the present time!

This Straight and Narrow Way — this Pathway of the
Lord—is the glorified Highway to Zion, THE PURE IN
HEART, of which Issaiah spoke as follows: "And an highway shall be there and a way, and it shall be called the Way
of Holiness; the unclean shall not pass over it; but it shall
be for those: *the wayfaring men* (Those who are traveling
the Straight and Narrow Path of complete purification of
the heart), though fools, shall not err therein." (Isa. 35:8)

This Straight and Narrow Road is the PROMISED road
to Zion, which means literally THE PURE IN HEART. It
is the road of holiness over which the wicked cannot pass. It
is the road of complete purification as one leaves his weakness automatically behind and travels with his eyes single to
the glory of God, and not single or centered upon himself
or his own self-importance. "And he, whose eyes are single

to the glory of God shall be filled with Light and shall comprehend all things!"

And it is only as one's heart is purified that he can behold the Face of God—which enfolds the gift of LIFE ETERNAL!

This glorified road of perfection and power cannot be traveled by the proud or the haughty; the greedy or the selfish or the lustful or by those who loveth and maketh a lie. Neither can it be traveled by the unbelievers nor the fearful nor the whoremongers nor by any whose devotion and love have not become purified as they developed and took on the virtues of perfection. There can remain no self-righteousness or self-acclaim to mar the lives of those seeking to behold the face of God.

Neither can this sacred road be traveled by those who cling to the old, backward methods of mortal concepts and injunctions. These methods were used down the ages to restrain mankind from searching to KNOW for himself and to prevent him from fulfilling any of the dynamic PROMISES OF ALMIGHTY GOD! Man has been held, and to a certain degree bound, as he has been restrained in the small crib that is too short! It is so short he cannot stretch himself in it to think, to observe or to either grow or progress in. And he has been furnished a covering so narrow it has brought neither comfort nor proved sufficient to cover his nakedness. And for centuries mankind has been satisfied with the outward show of things, the vain demonstrations of clattering cymbals and rattling, childish toys which has been the unprogressiveness of immaturity and make-believe.

This childish entertainment of the past is now outgrown and must be left behind. This is the day in which there are many who have been drawn from the breasts and weaned from the milk and who refuse to remain in their stupid, outgrown cribs, lulled into a semi-stupor of empty demonstrations or chanted lullabies and soothing syrups. And their restrainers have been blind men and wicked leaders who have followed the leading of the darkness.

Anyone who awakens enough to climb out of his outgrown crib as he refuses to longer partake of milk, will be answered by his Father and will begin to be fed upon the meat that will develop him and make a man of him. Only the meat, or food of the Father will longer satisfy one's hungering and thirsting after righteousness. And only as one's soul awakens and as he demands stronger food, even the food of the Father, can he possibly mature into the perfect stature of a man. It is of this meat that Paul spoke in Hebrews, chapter five. It is of this food of the Father, that leads one on to perfection as he leaves the creed-bound doctrines of the "law" behind. Study very carefully the 28th and 29th chapters of Isaiah and the record of Hebrews, chapter six, verses one and two.

"Blessed is he who hungers and thirsts after righteousness for he shall be filled WITH THE FULLNESS OF GOD," according to the original and complete record.

And so I have been called to bear witness of this Straight and Narrow Way, which can only be traveled by those who leave their infant cribs and their rattles and childish toys of immaturity behind and begin to hunger and thirst after righteousness, that they might not only be filled, but that they might mature into the very fulness of divinity.

Oh, Glorious, Wonderful God! How great Thou art! Oh, Glorious Path! Oh, fulness of Joy!

Chapter XI

DEMON-STRATORS!

It is most certainly true that "THE LAW MADE NOTHING PERFECT, but the bringing of a better hope did; by which we draw near to God." (Heb. 7:19).

When Moses returned from Mt. Sinai, with the sacred revelations of God, he found the people had thrown restrictions to the wind defiling themselves in a wild, unrestrained hysteria. Such was the pattern of the heathens and of all the Christians who have not learned to walk with God in a majesty of control and divine power.

Miriam, who was eight years older than Moses and his brother Aaron, who was three years older, assumed the leadership of the people after Moses had been absent longer than they thought proper. Both Miriam and Aaron assumed the responsibility of holding the people together. Then to prove their right to such claims of leadership they began to demonstrate their right of authority. They did it with the most righteous intentions. And those who gave them their support offered it as willingly as they had given their allegiance to Moses.

In the sincerity of their misguided self-ego they began to prove their powers in wild and unseemly demonstrations as they were carried along on a wave of abandon and uncontrolled hysteria. And they became subject to the spirit and not the spirit to them. Whatever power they could have been entrusted with was dissipated and squandered. It was wasted and a spirit of self-acclaim and self-righteousness gained possession of them as they abandoned themselves to be used by the forces of darkness, as their ego-selves responded to the momentary power they thought they were being edified by.

This is still a weakness of mankind today. And there are churches which still encourage such heathen, unseemly displays, not realizing that the Power of God is only manifested in divine majesty. Many think they are being led by the spirit as they hit the high pinnacle of an uncontrolled hilarity of spirit. But the road they travel is the road that is dictated by the little personal-ego self as it gloats in the supposed greatness of itself. And these misguided ones are on that broad, open Path that leads to destruction, because they will die as their leaders before them have died and gone into the grave. This is but one of the roads of that broad, open way that leads to destruction.

And as those who are carried aloft on the tide of the wave of a false exhilaration soon find themselves down at the very bottom and wallowing in the depths of despondency. Their emotions are like the rising and falling of a "yo-yo". This condition is not of God, this false exhilaration, this shouting and uncontrolled manifestation. It is only the little ego-self demonstrating its own imagined importance.

And so were the Israelites of long ago led astray by the outward show of shouted acclamations. When Moses returned to find all of Israel swept along on this false tide of heathen worship he dropped the sacred plates which God had engraved with His finger and they were shattered.

They had constructed a golden calf as they had offered their treasures to the Lord. The calf was to symbolize their devotion and their love. It was supposed to represent the symbol of their adoration. But almost immediately the symbol became the reality and they were worshipping the golden calf. In their wild abandon they were led completely astray, even as many professing Christians have been today.

God threatened to destroy the whole nation but Moses pleaded mightily for them. Finally, he said, "If they be destroyed, Lord, destroy me with them." And it was through Moses' pleading that Israel was given another chance and Moses was given the responsibility of getting them back into disciplined order and control.

The power of Moses, which was neither squandered nor dissipated, must have been terrific. He got the people back into line, then pounding their golden calf into dust he made them drink it in their water. Under the power of God their shouting acclamations and contorting were revealed to be but the noise of profanity.

After the people were brought to repentance and given an understanding of the power of God, Moses returned to Mt. Sinai.

Again Moses fasted forty days and forty nights as he waited on the Mountain top for God to reveal again the pattern for the people to accept and to live by. And according to the perfect translation of the record, it states: "And God wrote with His finger as He had done before, yet NOT as He had done before." The first time God had given the people an unfolding of the great and mighty PROMISES under which the Patriarchs had lived, through FAITH! The second time He did not write as He had done before. He wrote upon those two stone tablets the Ten Commandments —or the law. "And the Law came because of transgression!" (Gal. 3:19).

The glorious PROMISES of perfection and the Way of their fulfillment were withheld. And because of the wickedness of the people they were restrained under the law. And they have been under this restraint until this present day. "But the law made no man perfect." And the law is for the wicked. Yet in this day of gross wickedness, this evil generation cannot even abide by the law.

In Galatians we are informed that the law is not of FAITH and that no man is justified by the law, but the law was given because of wickedness. We are also told that Abraham and the Patriarchs of old lived not by the law but by the PROMISES, through FAITH. Then we are informed in Galatians5:14, that all the law is fulfilled in one word, "LOVE". And the information is plainly revealed that anyone who perfects love is no longer under the law. Or, as Christ so perfectly revealed the power and meaning of the First and Second Great Commandments, that any who *lived* these two wonderful laws had fulfilled ALL the laws and the prophets. So in perfecting love one passes from under the iron rod of the law and goes on unto perfection, as Paul admonished in Heb. 6:1-2.

Then is given this holy information in Galatians, chapter five, verse eighteen: "If ye be led of the Spirit, ye are not under the law." This "led of the Spirit" does not mean to be tossed about in any unseemly manner or in physical contortions or wordy displays as the spirit is permitted to rule until it goes completely out of bounds as it did with the children of Israel. The Spirit leads one gently and lovingly into the pattern of pure perfection as one learns to hold the spirit in subjection. Then only can one be giveen POWER! If one has not learned to hold the Spirit in control, by divine discipline and holy majesty, the power is squandered. It is dissipated and utterly wasted except for the feeding of the pride-filled little ego. The POWER can never be truly held by those who are always demonstrating the supposed greatness of their own little, mortal ego-selves.

Then Paul says, (Gal. 5:19): "Now the works of the flesh are these:" And Paul explains what the works of the flesh are and to his list is to be understood that any unseemly demonstrations that shame the majesty and the divinity of God's power are included. In verse twenty-two Paul explains that the fruits of the Spirit, are love, joy, peace, long-suffering, gentleness, goodness, FAITH, meekness, temperance, AGAINST SUCH THERE IS NO LAW." And we are told definitely that man will be known by his *fruits* not by his gifts.

This word "MEEKNESS" is such a powerful word and so little understood. It does not mean one who is a groveling, unassertive person, cringing and fearful. It means one of those dynamic persons who will inherit the earth! Meekness is POWER! It is the Power to hold one's eyes single to the glory of God, one who can glorify God under any and all conditions and circumstances as thanks is rendered in all things. It is a person clothed in the majestic, beautiful robe of humility as the individual seeks to glorify God instead of his own little, ugly, mortal-self.

This Straight and Narrow Way is no place for those seeking to exalt themselves or who are possessed with the unholy spirit of demon-stration. This sacred Pathway of Light and glory can only be traveled by those of perfected love and deep humility. "By their *works* ye shall know them," not by their *words*. When their prophecies fail and their words remain empty and unfilled all men will become aware that they are only demon-strators of the ego-self and not of God.

"Thus saith the Lord God; Woe unto the foolish prophets, that follow their own spirit, and have seen nothing!" (Ezek. 13:3).

And so I have been instructed to include this warning that none be deluded by the false acclamations of the demon-strators. Seek rather to KNOW GOD for yourselves. Let God alone be your Teacher. Let none block your way by their self-importance no matter how awesome or righteous they may declare themselves to be.

When John, the Beloved, was going to get down upon his knees to worship and adore the Angel of Revelation, he was commanded: "See thou do it not. I am thy fellow servant —" etc. Yet there are mere mortals who stand brazenly forth demanding acclaim from all they meet. They not only expect homage, they demand it, even while their hands are empty.

As one fulfills the First and Second Great Commandments he fulfills ALL the laws and the prophets. He is no longer under the bondage of the laws, which were formed for and apply to the wicked. He had moved up into the realm of the Patriarchs, and begins to live by and to fulfill the powerful wonder of the principle of FAITH.

Returning again to the gifts of the Spirit: "TEMPERATE" means to refrain from any fanaticism in anything, but rather let wisdom choose and rule in a mildness of gentle Love and Peace. "Against such there is no law!"

None can boast or brag along this glorious Pathway of Light! Those who do only block their own way with their little, mortal selves.

Anyone who declares boastingly that he is foremost on the divine, holy pathway is standing still as others pass him by. He may think he is traveling, but like one standing near a railroad track watches a train going by and begins to feel that the train is standing still and he is advancing though he has remained motionless. Such is the condition of the one who boasts and prophesies in his own mortal weaknesses, believing he has more gifts and powers than any other and therefore assumes he is nearest to the throne of God.

Anyone who thinks he is above and beyond all others is not on the sacred, holy Pathway at all. He is only off in a little whirlpool of his own.

These boasting, self-acclaiming ones are known as "demonstrators" as they perform in uncontrolled abandon, with the ego-self taking charge. Those who permit the spirit to take over in such abandon are working under the darkness of deception and are also deceiving those who yield themselves to stand before them in awe.

Do not follow such. Do not lend them your ear or your attention. Pray for them and pass on. Such are not on the sacred Pathway of holy Glory. They are but rushing along that broad, wide path that leads to destruction and death —and realize it not. But so have thousands before them followed like sheep into the grave.

No one so sacredly endowed with the power to perform miracles ever went forth proclaiming it. Imagine Peter and John, after healing the man at the temple gate, going forth boasting about it. Or imagine Christ ever boasting of either His powers or accomplishments. And so often He warned those who were healed not to boast of it. Rather he said, "Go thy way and tell no man."

"Charity (or the pure love of Christ) suffereth long, and is kind; charity envieth not; charity vaunteth not itself, IS NOT PUFFED UP, doth not behave UNSEEMLY!" It does not go into UNSEEMLY contortions or loud shouting. It is always majestic and under strict, divine control. It never behaves itself in an UNSEEMLY, repulsive manner.

Anyone who fulfills the First and Great Commandment will also have fulfilled the Second One. No one who loves with ALL HIS MIND could possibly think an evil, unkind thought against a living soul. In fact, "his mind and lips would have lost the power to hurt and wound, and his voice will be heard among the Gods!" He will have fulfilled ALL THE LAWS and the prophets and will no longer be under the laws or the Prophets. He will have moved into the PROMISES OF ALMIGHTY GOD, even as the ancient Patriarchs.

Such a one will become clothed in Light instead of in his own mortal nakedness. He will need none to teach him. Neither will he need any to prophesy over him. And God Himself will be his Teacher as he enters that Straight and Narrow Way that leads to LIFE ETERNAL!

This Straight and Narrow Path is so sacred and so holy and so filled with the POWER and the LIGHT of God that anyone who would assume to take over leadership or to display any degree of self-importance will be left behind in his own darkness.

Some of those who seek to display their imagined importance are often dangerously deadly, in that they are only standing at that wide, broad path that leads to destruction, enticing all who listen to them to enter therein. Such will deceive the very elect if possible.

Shortly the keys of DISCERNMENT will be revealed so that none need to be deceived. And the main safeguard against such is to keep a constant prayer of praise and love and gratitude singing in the soul. This glorious devotion keeps one in tune with God. And the word is: "My sheep hear My voice and they know Me, and a stranger they will not follow!"

Some of these deceiving ones are deceiving themselves most of all. They may believe they are at the very journey's end and are waiting to be invited to sit with Christ upon His throne, and realize not that they have never set one foot upon the sacred Path.

Any UNSEEMLY act or repulsive demonstrating is but the little, ego-self bearing witness of itself. Only majesty is carried by those who are truly on this Holy Path that leads to Life Eternal!

If one loves his neighbor as himself that ugly, evil ego-self is automatically OVERCOME in the great, glorious, triumphant OVERCOMING.

Those who permit themselves to become afflicted with the deadly "I DISEASE" will soon become completely blind as they go rushing headlong along that wide, broad path that leads to destruction. They are the blind, leading the blind as they shout forth their imagined instructions. These can never be taught simply because they already think they KNOW IT ALL. They cannot even LISTEN to anything except their own words as they continue to reiterate their own experiences and proclaim their own importance. If they do not humble themselves then God will humble them, in time, and it will be a great, public humiliating experience as they are invited down.

Those who travel the divine Highway of Light live in the present, not in the past. They do not drag the past along with them in their tedious recitals of ancient memories. They leave the past behind, for "he who looks back is not fit for the Kingdom."

If a past experience is ever repeated it must be used only to illustrate some lesson or to prove some point, but never in self-acclaim or in boasting, or deadly repetition. The dividing line between bragging, self-exalting and humble sharing is so fine the wicked cannot possibly detect the difference as they rush along their broad, open way to destruction.

In I. Cor. 14, Paul gives this beautiful picture of the gifts, saying: "He that speaks in tongues edifies himself, but the church is unedified." He also states that he would rather speak five words with his understanding, that by his voice he might teach others, than speak ten thousand words in an unknown tongue. He states that tongues were to be for a sign to unbelievers and not to them that believe.

Then Paul stated, that though *he had spoken in tongues more than they all,* yet he recommend that they be held in restraint at meetings. And here it must be explained that Paul traveled in his missionary labors from Jerusalem through Greece, Rome and all the countries between there and ancient Briton, where many areas and languages were unknown to him. There are records in the British Museum proving such travels. And in order to converse with these many peoples he was given the gift of tongues that he might testify of Jesus Christ, Son of the Living God, of His crucifixion and of His resurrection from the dead. This is why Paul spoke in tongues more than they all, because it was necessary. And Paul never used the gift except when it was needed.

Beware of those who go into physical contortions or UN-SEEMLY displays or who raise their voices to a high-pitched, rasping tone in their testifying or praying. The power of God is FELT, not necessarily heard, except as one's tones become richer and deeper as the power of God bears witness in a divine majesty of holiness. The Spirit of God is only manifest in glory and beauty and peace and divine majestic Power as the individual who receives such an outpouring holds himself under complete control. Then only can he possibly be a bearer of POWER.

Now, concerning the outpouring of the Spirit of God upon all flesh: "And ye shall know that I am in the midst of Israel, and that I am the Lord your God, and none else: AND MY PEOPLE SHALL NEVER BE ASHAMED.

"And it shall come to pass afterward, that I will pour out my Spirit upon all flesh; and your sons and your daughters shall prophesy, your old men shall dream dreams, and your young men shall see visions:

"And also upon the servants and the handmaids in those days will I pour out my Spirit.

"And I will show wonders in the heavens and in the earth, blood and fire, and pillars of smoke.

"The sun shall be turned into darkness, and the moon into blood, *before the great and terrible day of the Lord comes.*

"And it shall come to pass, that whosoever call on the name of the Lord shall be delivered." (Joel 2:27-32). The sun to be darkened is also recorded in Joel 3:15; Isaiah 24:22; Matt. 24:29; Mark 13:24 and Luke 23:45).

The word or name "ISRAEL" means literally "Men (or children) of Light and love."

And the promise of the Spirit of the Lord being poured out upon ALL flesh is the full preparation for those who are to be "Born of the Spirit that they can come and go as the wind" to give protection and service to those who have not yet fulfilled all righteousness. And only the righteous will so respond to the glorifying rays of the Spirit of Almighty God. The wicked will be in no way prepared to respond to this purifying light and they will lift up their voices and curse God and die, as is revealed in Rev., chapter sixteen and Isaiah 30:26.

Now, this must be made clear: When the righteous respond to the powerful rays of that released Spirit of God, according to the foregoing prophesy of Joel, there will be no wild, hysterical abandon in their actions or reactions. They will prophesy and glorify God in a power of humble majesty and in perfect control.

God's Almighty Power can only be made manifest in those who have brought the Light and the Life and the Spirit and the Power into subjection as it is released through them to glorify God instead of themselves.

This prophecy of Joel's first informs us that those who are of *Israel,* or who are men of light and love, are taken into God's special care and will be enfolded in His Power —and *will never be ashamed.*

Then comes the intensified pouring out of His Spirit upon ALL flesh. Next comes the signs in the heavens and in the earth, followed by the sun being darkened and the moon being turned to blood, or appearing deep red in color.

And after these things comes "THE GREAT AND DREADFUL DAY OF THE LORD". "For then shall be great tribulation, such as was not since the beginning of the world to this time, no, nor ever shall be. And except those days shall be shortened there shall be no flesh saved; but for the elect's sake those days shall be shortened." (Matt. 24:21-22).

Only in deepest trust and love and divine control can one be prepared to be "Born of the Spirit, that he can come and go as the wind" to render service wheresoever he is directed. And such as these are no longer classified as being of "FLESH" for they are so filled with the Spirit of Almighty God their very flesh has become spiritualized, else they could not have been born of the Spirit. These will never be ashamed nor dismayed nor distressed nor injured by those great tribulations which will be poured out without measure during this "GREAT AND DREADFUL DAY OF THE LORD."

Those who are "Born of the Spirit" will be spared for they will be immune to the things that afflict the flesh. "And they shall be mine, saith the Lord of hosts, in that day when I make up my jewels; and I will spare them as a man spareth his own son that serveth him. Then shall ye return, and discern between the righteous and the wicked, between him that serveth God and him that serveth him not." (Matt. 3:17-18)

This glorious "Birth of the Spirit", this complete control is best described by the NEW SONG, which none but the righteous can learn. None but the righteous can learn this sacred, powerful, dynamic Song because it cannot be uttered in words or by music, or in boasting, noisy, uncontrolled acclaim. It is a SILENT SONG of inward rejoicing of released "Glory to God" that arises from the depths of one's soul, in vibrations so powerful and so high no music or words on earth could ever express it. They could only defile it and squander and dissipate the power of its everlasting, purifying glory of Spiritual perfection and complete fulfillment.

In *silence* only is Power generated and held. The New Song is a song of everlasting Power, released in SILENCE as the full VIBRATIONS OF THE SPIRIT OF ALMIGHTY GOD ARE RELEASED THROUGH ONE'S BEING. This New Song is the Song of TRIUMPHANT OVERCOMING as the flesh is overcome and all that pertains to it.

Even the "Life more abundant" is contained in the singing glory of that "NEW SONG" of Eternal triumph—the Song of OVERCOMING as one uses the great Christ vibrations of Praise and Love and Gratitude as he spiritualizes himself to receive the full glory of the "Birth of the Spirit, that he can come and go as the wind" in a selflessness of service beyond words or demonstrations or self-acclaim.

THE PROUD AND THE MIGHTY!

I watched those high ones, from the side,
As they came riding on the tide,
Placing themselves upon the crest
With their heads held high, above the rest,

Demanding others to bear them along
As they sang their own self-righteous song
Of self-importance and self-acclaim—
The highest seats their only aim!

They demanded their place at the top of the wave—
Proclaiming their calling was to save
As they stepped on the shoulder and ground 'neath their tread
The ones from whom they gouged their bread!

Proud and haughty! The high seats theirs,
As they mouthed their great, self-righteous prayers!
They exalted themselves on the pinnacle high
As the wave they rode reached toward the sky!

Momentum increasing as it neared the land
    The wave crashed over the rocks and sand!
And the topmost crest was hurled out wide—
    While the wave returned on its ebbing tide.

And the far-flung and those whose claim
    Was the highest seats and demand for fame
Were left to crawl on their hands and knees
    Slowly back to the depths of the seas!

By NANSELA MATHEWS

CHAPTER XII

THE GIFTS AND THE FRUITS OF THE SPIRIT

The GIFTS of the Spirit I Cor. 12:8-11	The FRUITS of the Spirit Gal. 5:23
I. Word of Wisdom	I. Love
II. Knowledge	II. Joy
III. Faith	III. Peace
IV. Gift of Healing	IV. Longsuffering (patience)
V. Miracles	V. Gentleness
VI. Discerning of Spirits	VI. Goodness
VII. Diverse Tongues	VII. Faith
VIII. Interpretation of tongues.	VIII. Meekness (Humility)
	IX. Temperance— "Against such there is no law!"

These gifts are also enumerated in I Cor. 13, including the ability to speak with the tongues of men and of ANGELS, the power to move mountains, raise the dead, give all that one has to feed the poor and even his body to be burned—yet without the divine love these gifts are worthless, and in vain.

Anyone who has the Fruits of the Spirit made manifest in his life needs no other witness. The approval of God is stamped upon him for such a one would have perfected the unspeakable power of the First and Great Commandment of Eternal LOVE.

Without the divine gift of love bearing witness of the GIFTS they are but sounding brass and clanging cymbals. It is to these, the outward demonstrators, that Christ will say when they demand that He acknowledge them and their works as they proclaim, "Lord, Lord, did we not prophesy in your name? And in your name cast out devils? And in your name do many wonderful works?" Then comes Christ's answer, direct and without apology: "Then will I profess unto them, I never knew you: depart from me, ye that work iniquity."

"Iniquity" is from an old Anglo-Saxon phrase, meaning "lack of inner quiet" or contact with God. It is a condition of emotional disturbance or abandonment or an hysterical display of UNSEEMLINESS. In this condition the contact with God and His power is impossible. "The Peace that Passeth Understanding" is unknown. "Be still and KNOW that I am God!" Only in that inner stillness is this accomplished. Only through that deep, inner quiet or Peace does God operate. Only through that majestic, divine holiness can anyone contact or use the POWERS of God, or rather, permit God to do the works of accomplishment. And since these uncontrolled, emotional, immature ones are working entirely through their own displayed abandonment, without any contact with God, they are working in "iniquity".

Only through love, developed into a sublime devotion of selfless, melted humility of almost incomprehensible PEACE can God or Christ assist in any works. These demonstrators are truly working in "iniquity" without any contact with God. And in our day "iniquity" is understood to mean "great wickedness," which it is.

These abandoning ones are abandoned to themselves—and they demand the same "iniquity" of all whom they contact.

They realize not, in their emotional uncontrol that they are but serving the disturbed, immature, emotional cravings of their own mortal selves. And Christ will rebuke them saying, "I never knew you: depart from me, ye that work iniquity." What he will actually be saying is: "I had no part in your professed "mighty miracles." I was shut out by your own "iniquity" and I do not know you."

Only in and through the great peace, or inner contact, that passeth understanding and in perfect, selfless love can the divine, majestic powers of God operate. And when they work there is never an UNSEEMLY display. Divine majesty is manifest in every act of God.

Many of these demonstrating ones may be performing "Mighty Works" according to their lack of understanding or enlightenment, as they make their unrighteous demands for recognition upon the Lord. Their works are but their own works, performed in pride and arrogant self-righteousness; and their works will be rejected along with their mighty claims and their unrighteous demands for glory and rewards. And so it is that the GIFTS can be misused and abused and defiled by self-righteous, inferior mortals who work in unrestrained, unrestricted abandon.

It is not by the use of God's dynamic gifts that the righteous will be known. It is by their FRUITS only that they will be acknowledged and accepted. "By their *fruits* shall you know them."

There are some of these misguided ones who believe that the gift of tongues is the whole purpose and meaning of life and that those who do not possess this gift are totally unacceptable to God. In this they err greatly! The gift of tongues is the most easy gift for the evil forces to mimic in a counterfeit display of supposed power.

In St. Matthew, chapter twenty-four, is given a remarkable account of those, under the hands of Satan, who will shake the earth with their miracles. And all those who seek after signs and such displays will flock to them. In many instances the gift of tongues is but a demonstration of a person weakly yielding himself to a foreign, sometimes evil spirit who uses the mouth of the living to spew out his own pent-up words, without knowledge. There are thousands of such instances in which some defiled, discarnate, disembodied spirit, wishing to gain attention, takes over the tongue of some self-righteous, unsuspecting mortal.

There are the spiritualist mediums who lend their bodies and minds to disembodied spirits, to take over and to use. In Bible times they were rejected and condemned. And from the time of Moses on down they were placed under the penalty of death. They were designated as those with "familiar spirits" or as diviners or magicians or sooth-sayers. Today, those who are manipulated by these, often very evil, departed spirits, are coming back into vogue. They are highly sought after, though in the Book of Revelations, chapter twenty-one and verses six to eight, is given this information of what will happen to them at the coming of the Son of God. "And he said unto me, It is done. I am Alpha and Omega, the beginning and the end, I will give unto him that is athirst of the fountain of the water of life FREELY.

"He that OVERCOMETH shall inherit all things; and I will be his God, and he shall be my son.

"But the fearful, and unbelieving, and the abominable, and murderers, and whoremongers, and SORCERERS, and idolaters, and all liars, shall have their part in the lake which burneth, which is the second death."

And often those who are speaking in tongues have only been taken over by unclean spirits who desire to be heard, as they use the mouths of their gullible demonstrators to babble forth their "Words, without knowledge." And these are most certainly not approved or called of God. And the foreign words of some, defiled, evil spirit have no worth or value. And it is of these that Christ will profess that He knows them not.

"Yes, THOUGH I SPEAK WITH THE TONGUES OF MEN AND OF ANGELS and have not charity, I am but sounding brass and clanging cymbals."

Only in, and through love does God work. All the gifts can be demonstrated and performed by unholy ones seeking to impress others with their own powers and personalities as they place themselves upon the "HIGHEST SEATS" to later be invited down. Thus it is that the righteous are not recognized by their gifts or acclamations. But "BY THEIR FRUITS SHALL YOU KNOW THEM!"

And with the FRUITS the manifestation of *Love* and *Humility* are always made manifest as they bear witness of God's acceptance and approval, not in words, but in POWER.

"God will not be mocked!" And those who VAUNT themselves, or behave themselves UNSEEMLY are but mocking the majesty and the glory of God's sacred gifts and of God Himself! And these will stand under great condemnation at the last day.

As the Fruits of the Spirit alone can bear witness of one's true status it must be known that only as love is developed within the soul of man can he begin to bear these precious Fruits of holiness. These Fruits are gentleness and love and humility, and the precious attributes which Christ acclaimed, as He designated Himself as the Vine, and God as *the* Husbandman, and Man as the humble branch. It is only from the branch that the Fruits can be brought forth. And that bringing forth of the real Fruits of the Kingdom is always accomplished in a joyous ecstasy of selfless service for the glory of God and for the benefit of man. And Joy itself is the second Fruit of the Spirit. Without it nothing can be made perfect. And joy is not an hysterical, uncontrolled display. Joy is the glory of God flowing out from the depths of the soul, in perfect control and glorious humility.

Glory be to god for a privilege so great as being permitted to live upon this wonderful earth! And to live in this most dynamic age of all ages is an honor indeed! It is beautiful! It is glorious! It is divine!

Those who live only in the past, carrying their moments of inspiration and divine direction along with them, with no contact with God in the present, are truly burdened with the weight of their own wornout stairways as they drag each step along with them.

Those who live in the future, expecting it to fulfill their dreams of perfection, their hopes of glory, their desires for acknowledgment are also misplacing the dynamic impact of their creative powers in a far removed realm of accomplishment—beyond their reach.

Thank God with all the strength of the soul for every divine whisper of comfort or instruction or information— then go on unto Perfection, as Paul directed.

He who loves God with all his heart, soul, mind and strength is walking with God. And he is living in the great, eternal NOW! In this marvelous NOW do all things exist. It is within man's ability to "lay hold of the best gifts." And always the power of the Almighty is bestowed in the *living present,* not in the dead past or in the vague, distant future. Live as though you already had the complete fulfillment of your most sacred desires; this is how one *believes in his heart, and doubts not.* "Walk with God" and you will have constant contact with Him NOW. As one perfects LOVE NOW, the gifts and the Promises are fulfilled.

Live in the vibrating essence of your own dispersed LOVE as it flows out continually to heal and to bless and you are abiding in a new realm, in the perfection of the Celestial glory—NOW! It is necessary that each individual realizes this great truth as he takes upon himself the fulfilling of the wonders of his own divine perfection.

The greatest miracle of all time is the dynamic, breath-taking miracle of each man's unfoldment as he "purifies himself and loses every desire for sin," or lets go of his own drab mortality. As an individual advances into his own perfection he brings forth the greatest miracle of all. There is no other work so great and so utterly beautiful and holy. This is why it is so much more important to work upon oneself than to work upon others. As one brings himself into perfection he will have performed a work of the greatest glory and it will automatically help to exalt the whole world. There is no other work so sacred and so powerfully important. As one works upon himself he unloads the ugly burden of his little, mortal, ego-self and fulfills the promises of all perfection and all the glory. This includes the fulness of all things, not the ugly, imagined condition of the self-righteous.

In this humble, love-filled unfolding the great transition is accomplished and one "Evolves from the man (or mortal) kingdom into the God Kingdom!" "He is born of the Spirit." Which condition is the great reality of accomplishment. Such a one could never lift his voice in bragging or demonstrating self-acclaim or in defining boasts or contorting displays of ugliness. He could not possibly VAUNT himself. Neither could he behave in any UNSEEMLY manner of repulsive contorting as he seeks to demonstrate his own little, supposed greatness of empty mockery.

And such a one will know fully, even as Christ knew, "That only God is great! Only God is good!" And in the unspeakable joy of his own humility he will open wide the gates of heaven.

This is the purpose for which this sacred information must be placed within this record, that all may know that it is not in the demonstrating of the self, or even of God's divine gifts, that one is recognized as a divinely appointed messenger, sent of God. It is only "By their FRUITS that the righteous are known." And the Fruits of the Spirit are love, joy, humility and all the silent powers which are laid up in the center of the soul, or the kingdom of heaven (within) that are of any permanent value to him. These *fruits* are spiritual and those who receive them are appointed by Almighty God to become the greatest. And only they are acceptable to Him.

Now, I must share again with the world some of the sacred, holy truths given by that divine Writer of the Odes of Solomon, as revealed in the forty-first Ode, verses nine to seventeen, as follows: "For the Father of Truth remembered me: He who possessed me from the beginning:

"For His bounty begat me, and the thought of His heart:

"And His Word is with us in all our way;

"The Savior Who makes alive and does not reject our souls;

"The man (Christ) who was HUMBLED, and EXALTED by His own RIGHTEOUSNESS.

"The Son of the Most High appeared in the perfection of His Father;

"The Light dawned from the WORD, that was beforetime in Him.

"The Messiah is truly one; and He was known before the foundation of the world,

"That He might save souls for ever by the truth of His Name: A NEW SONG ARISES FROM THOSE WHO LOVE HIM!

Hallelujah!"

The above quotation is glorious! This blessed brother, this Writer of these Sacred Odes, from the long ago, OVER-CAME all the miseries of mortality—and death! In his sacred writings he unfolds the truths and the possibilities of complete OVERCOMING and of reaching perfection in the ability to glorify God. And this above quoted Ode explains the power of the "NEW SONG" which would arise from those who love God. This is true. And only they can learn it.

This "New Song" of *praise* and *love* and *gratitude,* this SONG of infinite power, which none but the righteous can learn is a song without words because no words could possibly express it. It is also a song without any specified music because only the released, joyous devotion from an exultant human heart can possibly express it. No shouting, no jumping, no contorting or words can ever express this Song of Holiness or send it forth. Only the silent, inner devotion of one who loves God with his entire being, mind, body and soul, can possibly sing this Song of eternal holiness and unspeakable power. And it can only be released in the vibrations of such dynamic POWER they cannot be heard by human ears or expressed with mortal tongue. This New Song is beyond all words and all professed acclaim. It is the instantaneous contact with the throne of God. And it is constant and continual and everlastingly perfect. And the one who learns to sing this Song truly becomes completely *"humbled and exalted"* by his own righteousness, even as Christ was. In the very humbling of himself, which only perfect love can accomplish, one seeks for the lowest seat as he becomes, in his own opinion, "The least." Then is righteousness established. It is this very humility that exalts one into righteousness, for then only can love be made perfect. Humility and love work always together.

This glorious brother, this Holy One, this Writer of these sacred Odes, foretold the coming forth of this work and of these books. It was his foretelling that makes them even more precious.

And this Writer of these glorious Odes of Solomon, which are contained in the Lost Books of the Bible, is awaiting all those who accept the truths which he revealed and who OVERCOME. Each one who fulfills these higher teachings, as he travels this glorified Straight and Narrow Path, will be welcomed and acknowledged by this Writer, this exalted one, for he too was exalted by his own humility, perfected into righteousness.

And this most gracious, inspired, exalted friend has commissioned me to extend his personal greetings and love to each of you as he invites you to enter the realms of the exalted. His loving understanding is held out to welcome and assist you. His love and his personal concern for each of you is great indeed. He is the friend of all who accept the higher truths of perfection. And to have such a friend is a blessing indeed.

Thanks be to God for such a helper! I would give his name but that is not yet permissible.

And glory be to God for such PROMISES as belong to this generation! Glory be to those who OVERCOME the self with all its desires to excel and to display its meager, skimped little merits, its contorting, *unseemly,* undignified, unholy, ungodly acclamations of supposed approval.

For "My Kingdom is not in WORD, but in POWER, saith the Lord." And that POWER can only be revealed in the Fruits of love, joy, mercy, humility, Faith and in a devotion that can only be displayed in a melted tenderness of inner glory as one sings that New Song from the very depths of his soul, not from his lips. "Yes, with their lips they confess me, but their hearts are far from me!"

Only from the heart can that Song be sung—that song of infinite love and praise and gratitude and devotion and everlasting exultation. That Song, released from a human heart, contains the power of every individual's exaltation. It contains the three major vibrations of utter glory, blended into the grand symphony of Celestial, triumphant OVER-COMING!

Yes, the gifts are but the implements of immature individuals as they use the gifts for self-aggrandizement or satisfaction. In Paul's glorious chapter, describing all the gifts he intermingles with every enumerated one their worthless mockery if love is absent or unmanifest. Then he describes the true powers, which hold all the fulfilling glory of perfection. These are the FRUITS of the Spirit, and are as follows: "Charity (or the pure love of Christ) suffereth long, and is kind, charity envieth not (is not jealous); Charity VAUNTETH not itself, IS NOT PUFFED UP.

"Doth not behave itself UNSEEMLY (or demonstrates in any repulsive contorting), seeketh not her own (credits or rewards), is not easily provoked, THINKETH NO EVIL;

"Rejoiceth not in INIQUITY, but rejoiceth in truth:

"Beareth all things, believeth all things (every Promise of God), hopeth all things, endureth all things.

"CHARITY NEVER FAILETH: but whether there be prophecies, they shall fail; whether there be tongues, they shall cease; whether there be knowledge, it shall vanish away." Then how could anyone boast or feel self-important? These gifts are but temporary substitutes given for the childish benefit of those who are immature. As soon as one leaves these things behind he is prepared, as Paul taught, "to go on unto perfection."

To continue with the precious quotation, starting now with verse nine: "For now we know in part, and we prophesy in part.

"BUT WHEN THAT WHICH IS PERFECT IS COME (or when we reach perfection), THEN THAT WHICH IS IN PART SHALL BE DONE AWAY.

"When I was a child, I spake as a child, I understood as a child, I thought (and acted) as a child; but when I became a man (A SON OF GOD), I put away childish things.

"For now we see through a glass, darkly (dimly), but then face to face; now I know in part; but then shall I know even as also I am known." This scripture is beautiful indeed. This point of being able to see even as we are seen is the complete unveiling of that higher realm of glory. Those on that higher level are able to behold us clearly and distinctly. They can behold our thoughts and the inner desires of our souls. They know the very workings and strength of our desires. Nothing is hid from them.

But from our mortal angle, even when we are permitted to behold heavenly beings, we see them only with our spiritual eyes, while they are still hid from our physical vision. And so even in this great gift of vision we see only vaguely the fulness of the glory of those who contact us.

However, when we reach perfection of glorified, perfect, selfless love and humility that veil will be completely removed and we will see with the clarity and exactness with which we are seen, for we too will "Be purified, even as He is pure!"

This state, when man's vision is completely purified, will be the great experience of being "Born of the Spirit." And this is possible! This is a condition or an achievement designated for those of this earth, for Christ said, "If I have told you of earthly things (in his explanation of being born of the Spirit) and you did not believe, how could you believe if I told you of heavenly things?"

This condition of promised vision in which we also will be able to see, even as those on that higher realm are able to behold us, is the glorious point where one is "Filled with Light and COMPREHENDS ALL THINGS!" This is a heavenly condition. But it can be reached by those on this earth as they "purify themselves, even as He is pure." It was meant to be accomplished right here and, as it is done one automatically, evolves from the man kingdom into the God Kingdom.

And now, to return to the last verse of that glorious thirteenth chapter of First Corinthians: "And now abideth FAITH, HOPE, CHARITY, these three; BUT THE GREATEST OF THESE IS CHARITY!" Or the pure Christ-like LOVE!

Only the gifts or qualities of Faith and Hope and Charity are eternal! Only these three are of lasting value. And only these belong to him who can stand before God as a Man —a true Son—who possesses these divine treasures which neither moth nor rust can corrupt nor thieves break through and steal. These are the jewels which are possessed by the soul as he purifies himself. "These are the treasures in heaven!" And these cannot possibly be put on display.

Then why should anyone boast or brag or behave himself in an UNSEEMLY manner as he pounds his little drum and rattles his brass toys and clangs his noisy cymbals of demonstrations in an unholy manner as he defiles himself and the holy gifts of God?

He who would be perfect, as the scriptures indicate in these words: "When that which is perfect is come," will understand that these inferior, partial gifts will be done away. This is true! But the greatest truth is this: as one develops that most holy Commandment, that First and Greatetst One of All, he does perfect LOVE right within himself. This is the one unfailing, glorifying accomplishment. It is the assurance of maturity or Sonship, for such a one will have put aside grubby mortality and will have advanced into a divine son of God.

This is a possibility for anyone who will lift his vision to behold the glory of God and then hold his mind focused upon that glory. In this exalted vision the little, childish, immature self, with its desire for show and its pride and VAUNTED demonstrating will be OVERCOME. Then only can one step forth into divine maturity.

The most marvelous truth is that one does not need to die in order to make this giant stride. For it is only in this life that the opportunity is held forth in its fulness for

COMPLETE OVERCOMING. It is while in this body of flesh that the soul can be most gloriously perfected.

This great, beautiful, eternal NOW is man's golden opportunity to fulfill all things. In this life lies the eternal challenge and opportunity to prove Christ's words by LIVING THEM—and so receiving the power contained in them.

Live that First and Great Commandment and all the Fruits of the Spirit will be brought forth in you—these sacred, holy treasures, these jewels of divinity. And these jewels are the Fruits of the Spirit. They will go with you into the next world. They will never be done away. And you have the power to clothe yourself in the glory of them. And they will bear witness of you. For it is only by your FRUITS that you will be known as an approved Son of God.

The *gifts* are only manifest in mortality and can be abused and misused. The *fruits* are spiritual and will endure forever for they are eternal. Yes, "By their FRUITS shall you KNOW them." It is only by men's true spiritual qualities that they can possibly be recognized, not by the gifts they display in open desecration.

It is in the proving and in the fulfilling of that most holy, divine, powerful Commandment that each individual advances into his maturity. And that Commandment is an everlasting challenge to test the integrity of man as its unspeakable powers are revealed. That Commandment is powerful beyond thought or knowledge! It is glorious beyond Words! It contains all the powers of fulfilling, even every glorious, dynamic, holy PROMISE of God. And these PROMISES are already held within the branch (or man) waiting to bud forth and to blossom into Celestial beauty— as the matured, ripened fruits of perfection yield the wonderful fulfillment of all that man was ordained to accomplish in the full measure of his own perfection.

This is how one matures into the perfection of all the glorified FRUITS of God, as he obtains the jewels of the Kingdom and lays up for himself the divine treasures of heaven. And it is only by the FRUITS of the Spirit that God's chosen may be recognized.

Perfect LOVE, the eternal jewel of everlasting glory and the Fruits of It will be yours and you will have the joyous power to hold them forth for the benefit of a hungry, starving world. And in bringing forth those precious Fruits you will be recognized or KNOWN.

In II Tim. 2:6 is given this full information, as follows: "The husbandman that laboureth must be first partaker of the FRUITS." In other words, he that works to bring forth these most holy Fruits of the Spirit within himself will also be the first to partake of them. Such will then be able to share those Fruits with the world. He will be recognized by these divine Fruits of purity and love and graciousness and joy and humility. And he will be clothed in the radiance of these everlasting jewels of the Spirit.

For shame to those who make such an open, noisy display of the holy gifts of God, as they defile them in a show of rattling brass and noisy, clanging cymbals, without the pure LOVE of Christ being first manifest in their lives.

Love is the key of perfection. It is the joy and the meaning of existence! It is the glory of eternity! It is the fulness of God! And in it are contained all the other jewels of the Spirit.

Then is given this powerful PROMISE to those who will lay hold of it and prove it, for it can be proved by every living soul upon this earth. I know, for I have fulfilled it.

"To him who *prayeth continually without ceasing* unto such is given to reveal things which never have been revealed; yea, and it shall be given unto such to bring thousands of souls to repentance."

To train oneself to pray continually without ceasing is the most marvelous blessing imaginable. This constant prayer is not a begging, "God, give me" prayer. It is the glorious "New Song" of praise and love and gratitude, which can only be expressed from a living heart in its pure perfection. It vibrates out in a radiance of ecstasy of glorious devotion. It is a divine melody of unspeakable power. It is the love of God being expressed in singing splendor as an eternal symphony of glorious, exquisite joy. It is LOVE made perfect. "And to such it is given to KNOW the mysteries of God, insomuch that he will be filled with Light and comprehend all things!"

Glory be to God! Glory and power and dominion be His forever and ever! And "he who prays without ceasing" or without letting this exuberant song die down, is releasing that song of increasing joyous ecstasy throughout his own being and in doing so is transforming or spiritualizing the very cells and atoms of his body and preparing it to "Be born of the Spirit." He is advancing into pure perfection as his body becomes exalted to the stature of the Spirit. And he will receive the powers of that spiritual birth and will be able to "come and go as the wind," in the divine service of Almighty God. He advances into the performance of the GREATER WORKS, as he brings thousands of souls unto repentance and to God. This is not done in WORDS—but in POWER! These are the Works of Jesus Christ. These are the GREAT-ER WORKS. And they begin right within each individual as he works upon himself instead of upon others. "Let your

Light so shine—." It does not say, "Let your Words so bear witness—."

Glory and power be to God forever and ever! Joy and everlasting Life be to those who fulfill His holy, divine PROMISES as the great and unutterable blessings become their own. And in fulfilling these higher possibilities one beholds with his eyes the things which have never yet been seen by human eyes. And with his ears he will hear the perfection of that divine Symphony of complete fulfillment and know the mysteries thereof. And he will contemplate and understand the great and marvelous things which God has prepared for those who LOVE Him!

Nothing is impossible! So I declare unto you anew! And I speak from knowledge and not from the letter of the law—and so may you too speak as you fulfill and prove the great truths which He gave.

————

(One little notation must be added here. Those whom Christ rebukes saying, "I never knew you; depart from me ye that work iniquity," is speaking of those who continually work through their own stirred up emotions as they work upon the emotions of others. These are working in "iniquity" or with a complete lack of inner contact with God. They lack that divine inner quiet so necessary for God's fulfilling.)

CHAPTER XIII

THE FULLNESS OF THE PROMISES!

"FOR BY THE WORKS OF THE LAW SHALL NO FLESH BE JUSTIFIED." (Gal. 2:16). Or as given in verse twenty-one of the same chapter, "I do not frustrate the grace of God: for if righteousness come by the Law, then Christ is dead in vain."

The Bible, which man has worshipped, has contained a minute record of all the laws, and those that have thought that by reading it they will have access to heaven itself, are mistaken. "The letter killeth, but the Spirit giveth Life!" Or, as Christ proclaimed in our mis-translation—the thirty-ninth verse of the fifth chapter of Saint John, in the King James translation, it states: "Search the scripture; for in them ye think ye have eternal life: and they are they which testify of me."

This translation is entirely in error. The correct translation reads thus: "YOU search the scriptures; for in them *ye think ye have eternal life*: *and they are they which testify of me.*

"AND YE WILL NOT COME TO ME, THAT YE MIGHT HAVE LIFE!"

Only Christ can give Life. Not the scriptures unless one uses them to live by the PROMISES they contain, that they might indeed go to Christ.

"Therefore by the deeds of the law there shall no flesh be justified in his sight: for by the law is the knowledge of sin." (Romans 3:20).

Abraham lived by the PROMISES through FAITH. In the third chapter of Galatians, verses eighteen and nineteen is given this marvelous bit of knowledge concerning Abraham: For if the interitance be of the law, it is no more of PROMISE; but God gave it to Abraham by PROMISE.

"Wherefore then serveth the law? It was added because of transgression, till the seed should come to whom the PROMISE was made." And that SEED is now upon the earth!

Not only did Abraham live by the PROMISES, but all the ancient Patriarchs before him—and those who followed him up until the time of Moses.

The whole world has struggled along that broad, wide way that has led to destruction, or death, or that road which held only the *law* for generations upon generations. But now, as the time of the restitution of all things is to take place man has the privilege, at last, to return to the great and wonderful prerogative of living under the favor or liberty of the ancient Patriarchs, that they no longer need to be bowed down beneath the burden of the law. The laws are the *commandments,* the certified restrictions. The PROMISES are the PATHWAY OF ALL FULFILLING. They are lived by the joyous willingness to serve and to love and to glorify. They are lived by FAITH according to the righteous desiring of each living soul as he seeks to glorify God instead of himself.

When Moses returned from the mountain the second time and the people, because of their wickedness were placed under the LAW, the PROMISES were henceforth veiled.

These great, all-enfolding PROMISES of Almighty God were not gathered into one glorious unveiling of dynamic, breath-taking unfoldment. Instead they were scattered and hidden in the scriptures as they were very cleverly wedged in, or sandwiched between various passages of scripture, which had a tendency to veil the great TRUTHS from the eyes of men.

This work, which God has commanded me to write, contains "The great and mighty TRUTHS which have been hidden from the foundations of the world, because of the blindness of men's minds, and the hardness of their hearts and because of the gross wickedness of unbelief."

And even the great Patriarchs of old were not given the fulness of all these glorious, mighty PROMISES in their completeness. Each Patriarch received but the PROMISES pertaining to his own era and time, except Enoch, who, through his faithfulness comprehended all things. And now, at last, all the great and holy PROMISES have been made apparent, these PROMISES which God has permitted to remain uncomprehended until this present day. And the PROMISE has always been that when the great veil of Unbelief should be rent the great and mighty PROMISES would be made apparent. The great veil has been rent and men need no longer walk in darkness, ESPECIALLY AT NOONDAY.

All that is required of man is that he open his eyes to behold these great and marvelous truths and everlasting PROMISES, and to begin to live by them as each individual rends his own little personal veil of unbelief. The great veil has been rent. But each person has his own little veil which he alone can rend. And each individual has the right and the power, if he will so exert himself, to lay hold of the PROMISES as he lives by them, through FAITH.

This is the ancient path of the Patriarchs, who lived before the laws. And as man fulfills the First Two Great Commandments, he passes beyond the law and all the prophets and prophecies into the Patriarchal order of the PROMISES. And the PROMISES MUST BE FULFILLED BY ALL WHO ACCEPT THEM, THROUGH FAITH, as doubts are OVERCOME. These are the "OVERCOMERS!" These are the ones who will do the works which Christ did, which work was to OVERCOME.

In Christ's teachings He was continually holding forth PROMISES and possibilities which mortal men have refused to believe or to see. Christ proclaimed the higher possibilities in so many ways. He declared that men were meant to be perfect, even as the Father in Heaven is perfect, and then gave the exact pattern of how such an almost unspeakable promise might be fulfilled. He also declared that He gave no commandment save He prepared the way for its ful-fillment. Christ also proclaimed that the Higher Way, which He represented, was the Way of Life, in which one did not need to die. And no one accepted of his PROMISES be-cause of the darkness of their own unbelief. Yet He unfolded the Pathway of OVERCOMING so plainly "even a fool need not err therein."

In the first few chapters of Revelations Christ revealed the seven glorified passages, written in flame, concerning those who would OVERCOME. Yet down the centuries no one has believed enough to even put His promises to the test—or attempt to prove them. Millions on the earth have proclaimed and still do proclaim that they believe in Jesus Christ, the Son of the Living God. Yet none have proved their words nor verified their claims, for none have ever done the works which He did. Nor have they fulfilled these words: "He that believeth on me need NEVER DIE!" And the professing of Christendom has been but a noisy, powerless declaration of words. No man has done the works which Christ did! And surely none have gone on to DO "THE GREATER WORKS!"

Many think they are doing the WORKS of Christ by their loud haranguements and shouting. Yet Christ never lifted His voice in unseemly shouting or loud acclaims. And we are told that His Kingdom is not in *words* but in POWER! Where is the power to do the works which He did? And surely none have done the "GREATER WORKS!" And at the present time no mortal man can even imagine what those greater works would consist of. But be it here remembered and noted, "His words cannot return unto Him unfulfilled or void."

Yes, Christ revealed the TRUTH by which man could rise forever above the bondage of sin and the law, under which the wicked were required to serve in bondage. But when one passes beyond the law he becomes FREE. "And he who is free is free indeed!" Such is the PROMISE!

By the fulfilling of the law of perfect love, those two divine, glorious Commandments, it is possible for anyone to pass beyond the laws of mortality and to go on unto perfection as Paul proclaimed in the sixth chapter of Hebrews, verses one and two. There is no possible way to make these divine truths plainer than Paul expressed them as he invited the saints to "Leave the principles of the doctrine of Christ, and go on to perfection; not laying again the foundation of repentance from dead works, and of faith toward God; nor of the doctrine of baptism and of the laying on of hands, or even of the resurrection of the dead and of the judgment."

As one moves into the higher promises of perfection, the law of repentance no longer has any place in an individual's life. Even his faith toward God will have developed into the point of FAITH where he will have the perfect KNOWLEDGE and will *"comprehend all things!"* This means he will actually KNOW GOD, not just know about Him. And "This is life eternal to know Thee, the only true and living God and Jesus Christ, whom thou hast sent!" This is the point where God will truly unveil His Face and that individual will be caught up to dwell with Him. Anyone who reaches this degree of perfected love will himself be made perfect for he will have overcome all the evils of his life.

From this higher point of PROMISE the ordinance of the laying on of hands is no longer necessary, for man, having "purified himself," will be "ordained of God and sent forth to become the greatest, notwithstanding he will become the least (in his own selfless, humble devotion, of exquisite love) and the servant of all."

And all things will become subject unto him, both in heaven and on earth: the Life and the Light, the Spirit and the POWER!"

As the gift of LIFE becomes subject unto one he does not need to die and the laws of death and of the resurrection and of the judgment will have no part in his existence. He will have no need or inclination to return to these doctrines. They will have been fulfilled and outgrown. In this enlightened road of perfection one does not go back to the dead works or teachings. Such an individual realizes fully that all the outside demonstrations were never of God. Those who are working under the divine direction and hand of God portray only majesty and divinity in their every act and word.

As one moves into the PROMISES, leaving the laws behind, he fulfills the Promises, by faith, even as Abraham did. These *laws* which Paul mentions and all laws for that matter, are left behind. Only as one travels this higher way of Faith in the PROMISES can he possibly enter and travel the Lighted Way, that Straight and Narrow Path of brilliant glory which leads to life eternal.

As one takes hold of these almost unspeakable PROMISES of Almighty God, casting out his doubts and fears, through his own increasing FAITH, as Abraham did, he moves into the order of the ancient Patriarchs, "and is no longer under the law."

As one continues along this glorified Path of FAITH in the PROMISES he realizes that those promises are the "Words of God, which cannot possibly return unto Him unfulfilled or void!" Then that advancing individual realizes that God's words can only return unto Him as some individual lays hold of His PROMISES (through faith) and holds them forth for God's fulfilling. This is how HIS Words (which are His PROMISES) are returned unto Him for fulfillment.

As one begins to study these great truths which I have been requested to write, they become breath-takingly beautiful and — every mortal man has the right and the privilege to lay hold of them and fulfill them. They are more exquisitely beautiful than anything that God has as yet released upon the earth. They are true and faithful. And God will fulfill them unto anyone who will lay hold of them, through Faith, and begin to live by them in a joy of eternal rejoicing.

These records contain all the great and mighty PROMISES which are possible to release at the present time. The others are only released as one fulfills these and travels that divine Highway of Light to the very throne of God. And these can never be shared in words, nor in teachings, but only by experience. "These great PROMISES that have herein been unfolded are the ones that have been hidden up from the foundation of the world because of the blindness of man's mind and the hardness of his heart and because of the great wickedness of unbelief!" When man will rend that veil of unbelief those who are seeking for truth and righteousness will begin to see out of the obscurity and the darkness (of the ages) and will begin to fulfill the PROMISES held in waiting since time itself began.

As any individual takes hold of these dynamic PROMISES OF ALMIGHTY GOD, with his mind and his heart he automatically holds them forth for God's fulfilling. Remember, it is as man holds them forth, so that they are returned to God, that they must be fulfilled.

As one takes hold of the great and unbreakable PROMISES of God he soon discovers that they have become a very part of his own life without great stress or striving. Very soon they become his very own. They become as much a part of him as the beating of his heart and the intaking of his breath.

Next, this dynamically progressing individual discovers that he has reached the point where these divine PROMISES of the ages have not only become a part of himself, HE HAS ACTUALLY BECOME THEM! And at this point he becomes literally clothed in Light and comprehends all things and God will unveil His Face unto him.

In the twelth Ode of Solomon, verses eleven and twelve, that inspired writer wrote: "For the dwelling place of the Word is man, and its truth is LOVE. Blessed are they who by means thereof have understood everything, and have known the Lord in His Truth!

"And as many as received Him, to them gave He the power to become sons of God". They were designated as "CO-HEIRS with Christ, even JOINT HEIRS with Him."

A "joint heir"or a "co-heir" is one who inherits equally and fully. These are they who fulfill the law of OVERCOM-ING, even as they begin to do the works which Christ did. It is then that they can go on to do the greater works, which none on the earth has as yet ever considered.

It is devil doctrine to believe that all one needs to do is to profess Christ's Name, then sit idly by and expect the Be-loved Redeemer to come and exalt him into everlasting glory. Those who believe thus are deceived and cheated by a lie. Christ said, "If you BELIEVE ON ME THE WORKS WHICH I DO WILL YOU DO ALSO!"

As one passes beyond the laws into the glorious PROM-ISES, accepting them fully, by FAITH, he becomes the literal fulfillment of all the holy PROMISES ever given to man since the foundations of the world. Then it is that God's divine Word, His holy, perfect plan will be accomplished, and His Word will again become flesh — the very inner-most part of everyone's being who lays hold of the PROM-ISES. God's WORDS are His PROMISES! And as man makes these PROMISES a very part of his own life, through FAITH, he becomes the WORD — the Living WORD of Almighty God, the Eternal Father, Who is a God of Truth and cannot lie!

Anyone who will lay hold of these PROMISES of perfection will evolve into the Patriarchal Order of the divine PROMISES of everlasting Truth and POWER!

"For all things are possible to him who believes!"

Leave the laws of mortality and evolve into the realm of immortality. It is the Straight and Narrow Way that leads to Life Eternal! Yes, "Glorify God in the body of you!" As you become perfect in love His Word is made flesh — your own flesh! And His Promises will be fulfilled in you!

Never before, since time began, have all the holy PROMISES of Almighty God been gathered together and held forth for man to behold them, to accept them if he chooses and to receive the boundless glory of their fulfillment.

Even the ancient Patriarchs of old did not have access to the fulness of the knowledge and the PROMISES contained in this work, except Enoch only.

However in this last day there is to be a people who are to "purify themselves even as Christ is pure!" "For when He appears we are to be like Him. We are to be purified even as He is pure." And "We are commanded to *sanctify ourselves!*" We are to do it for the glory and honor of Christ instead of expecting him to come and glorify us. His words and His teachings are for us to fulfill. We are commanded to do the works which He did! And His words cannot return unto Him unfulfilled and void!

It is in the perfection of the great holy gift of love that we complete the glorious, divine fulfilling, "For he who would interpret the wonders of the Lord will be dissolved and will become that which he interprets."

Interpret the LOVE OF GOD and be dissolved into that LOVE! And as John declared: "He who loveth is born of God and cannot sin."

Yes! Begin to interpret the PROMISES of Almighty God! And you will become these PROMISES, a being glorified and filled with Light, with all things subjected unto you, both in heaven and on earth!

This is the divine Highway of Jesus Christ, this Path of PROMISES, this ancient road of the Patriarchs who lived not under the laws, but lived by FAITH in the dynamic PROMISES of The Eternal! And the PROMISES TOO ARE ETERNAL!

"Through FAITH we understood that the worlds were framed by the Word of God, so that things which are seen were not made of things which do appear." Everything was first made of the divine substance of Spirit, held forth by a thought plan or pattern until the hope or idea was planted upon the element of spirit — and then it was brought forth into physical, tangible form. Hopes and ideas are the patterns conceived by intelligence; spirit substance is the material of forming as it is held in the mold of desire until it becomes apparent.

Chapter XIV

BEYOND THE PROMISES

The "Straight and Narrow Way" is the beginning and the fulfillment of perfection and power — and the only one that leads to LIFE ETERNAL.

Within that First and Great Commandment is contained not only the power to do the works which Christ did, but the power to do even the greater works, which no mortal mind has, as yet, begun to even fathom.

As one travels that glorious Path of joyous advancement, until he reaches the point where his Faith is made perfect and becomes absolute KNOWING, then he will be literally "wrapped in the power and glory of his Maker and *will be caught up to dwell with Him!*"

This information is profound indeed! And from here on it is difficult to unfold the things that remain to be made manifest. In order to receive this information it will be necessary to purify oneself. It is first just an overwhelming desire to receive the degree of righteousness that has been promised to those who OVERCOME. And one of the admonitions of Christ, to be able to receive this degree of righteousness is to "pray with all the energy of heart that you might be possessed of this great love of Jesus Christ."

All anyone has to do, in order to come out from under the dark burden of the make-believe, or counterfeit power, is to truly begin to live and to fulfill that First and Great Commandment. As it is fulfilled the Second One will be fulfilled also, for it is impossible to love God with all one's mind and still use the mind to think unkind thoughts or to cling to ugly resentments or nasty little hurts. "One's mind and lips will automatically lose the power to either hurt or wound. And his voice WILL be heard among the Gods," for he will have joined in their perfection.

As one steps into this perfection no church or orthodoxed, creed-bound ritualism can henceforth hold him in ignorance or human bondage. "He will become Free! And he who is free is free indeed!"

He learns the great difference between the GIFTS of the Spirit and the FRUITS of the Spirit. The gifts are that which one is permitted to receive — often just to test him — even as Christ was tested in the wilderness. Christ was given the power. The testing came to prove how He was going to use that POWER. In the *gifts* is contained the testing. In the *fruits* is contained the POWER! The Fruits reveal the degree of a man's worthiness as to whether he could possibly handle the POWER in righteousness. No man is exalted or glorified by the gifts. He may be utterly condemned by the misuse of them. One is only glorified by the Fruits of the Spirit. The gifts are distributed often just to prove who is worthy to be entrusted with the true power of heaven.

One can truly possess all the gifts possible and still be but sounding brass and clanging cymbals. And those gifts will profit him nothing. Again, the gifts are often just for testing. THE FRUITS ARE FOR GLORIFICATION AND FOR DIVINE SERVICE.

"By their FRUITS only can the chosen ones be known — by their self-effacement, their gentleness, their great love and their humble devotion. These fruits are manifested in a humility of divine love that none can deny. It is manifest by a vibration that draws people to it, like a light that cannot be hid under a bushel. It is felt! It is not demonstrated in words or proclamations. It is a reality of fact that needs no shouted acclamations to make it known or to establish its beauty. "For my Kingdom is not in WORD but in POWER saith the Lord. It is contained in the manifesting of love and understanding and gentleness.

"Every tree that bringeth not forth good fruit is hewn down, and cast into the fire.

"WHEREFORE BY THEIR FRUITS YE SHALL KNOW THEM.

"Not everyone that saith unto me, Lord, Lord, shall enter into the kingdom of heaven; but *he that doeth the will of my Father which is in heaven.*

"MANY WILL SAY TO ME IN THAT DAY, LORD, LORD HAVE WE NOT PROPHESIED IN THY NAME? AND IN THY NAME CAST OUT DEVILS? AND IN THY NAME DONE MANY WONDERFUL WORKS?

"AND THEN I WILL PROFESS UNTO THEM, I NEVER KNEW YOU: DEPART FROM ME, YE THAT WORK INIQUITY!"

All the mighty demonstrations in the world, all the professing and working of miracles are but as sounding brass or clanging cymbals if one has not brought forth the gift of perfect love from within his own heart. It is not by displaying the gifts that one proves his worth or his goodness, but by his fruits of patience, love, gentleness, meekness, "against such there is no law." Learn to look deep into the lives of men and judge them, not by their demonstrating or professing or spectacular works, but by the FRUITS OF THE SPIRIT only and you will never be deceived nor made ashamed.

All the laws of advancement and perfection and divine glory are fulfilled as one learns to travel that Straight and Narrow Way of unutterable beauty, to the very throne of God, in an adoration of divine, selfless love. Then it is that God will unveil His Face unto that individual, as has been *promised* to all who would learn to travel that Road of glory. This Holy Way is the Way which Christ marked. It is traveled through Faith, through living the laws He gave and by holding one's attention single to the glory of God.

As these greater things are accomplished and fulfilled, then only can one be prepared to do "THE GREATER WORKS" which, as yet, none have ever imagined.

And now, one thing more I am instructed to add to this chapter. It is contained in Matthew, chapter seven and verses thirteen to twenty-three and deals with the great and mighty truths of God, as follows: "Enter ye in at the straight gate; for wide is the gate, and broad is the way, that leadeth to destruction, and many there be which go in thereat:

"Because straight is the gate, and narrow is the way, which leadeth to life, and few there be that find it.

"Beware of false prophets, which come to you in sheep's clothing, but inwardly they are ravening wolves.

"YE SHALL KNOW THEM BY THEIR FRUITS" (not by their gifts). "Do men gather grapes of thorns, or figs of thistles?

"Even so every good tree bringeth forth good fruit; but a corrupt tree bringeth forth evil fruit.

"A good tree cannot bring forth evil fruit, neither can a corrupt tree bring forth good fruit."

And the following information is most important. As one fulfills the laws, through the perfecting of the great Commandment of divine LOVE he steps beyond the laws into the Patriarchal Order or realm and henceforth *lives by the* PROMISES, *through Faith.* He automatically begins to "evolve from the man kingdom into the God Kingdom" without tasting death.

"And the nearer man approaches perfection (along this Straight and Narrow Way of OVERCOMING) the clearer are his views and the greater are his enjoyments until he OVERCOMES the evils of his life and loses every desire for sin, and like the ancients (or Patriarchs), arrives at the point of FAITH where he is wrapped in the power and glory of his Maker and is caught up to dwell with him." And in that exalted glory he is given the choice of remaining in that Celestial Realm, or returning with his glorified, spiritualized body (which has been now born of the Spirit) to this earth, to render the GREATER SERVICE, of which Christ spoke.

It is only as these greater PROMISES are accomplished and fulfilled that one can possibly do the GREATER WORKS, which have been promised to those who would "BELIEVE."

It is only as an individual accepts God's PROMISES and lays hold of them, through FAITH, that he can possibly OVERCOME the evils of his life. This glorified Path of OVERCOMING is the Straight and Narrow Way that leads to Life Eternal. And it is upon this Path, as one holds his eyes single to the glory of God, that he becomes filled with Light and comprehends all things. This is how one learns to actually KNOW THE TRUTH, the very fulness of it, and is from henceforth forever abundantly free! All the great and marvelous PROMISES which God has given since time began are contained in the fulfilling of this Great Commandment of perfected love.

As one practices and so perfects that First and Great Commandment "the inside of the cup will also be cleansed."

It is the cleansing of the inside of the cup which Christ so stressed. It is in the cleansing of the inside of man that reveals or fulfills the glory and the truth of all the mighty PROMISES ever given since time began.

"The great and marvelous truths, which God has kept hid up from the foundation of the world because of the blindness of men's minds, and the hardness of their hearts and because of the great wickedness of unbelief," are now to be fully opened, for the great veil of darkness has been rent — and the time is at hand. It is true that each individual still has his own little individual veil of darkness and unbelief and doubting, which he must personally overcome. But the *great veil* HAS BEEN RENT. Yet, "There are still those who are walking in darkness at noonday."

The great and mighty PROMISES that have been veiled from man's profane, unbelieving eyes are at last made apparent to those who are only willing to look — and to *ask* — and to BELIEVE. Yes, "Ask and you shall receive, seek and you shall find!"

————

And now, the next step — that step into the world of glory must be made manifest. This step is beyond that great veil of darkness! It is a step into light and understanding. And as it is opened for man to step through into that higher realm, new glories and powers are revealed. And one may then enter that Glorious, spiritual realm "And come no more out!"

Daniel, in his twelfth chapter, reveals the wonder and the marvel of this precious time of glorious enlightenment. "Go thy way, Daniel: for the words are closed up and sealed until the time of the end.

"Many shall be purified, and made white, and tried; but the wicked shall do wickedly: and none of the wicked shall understand; but the wise shall understand." (verses 9-10).

"And they that be wise shall shine as the brightness of the firmament; and they that turn many to righteousness as the stars forever and ever.

"But thou, O Daniel, shut up the words, and seal the book, even to the time of the end: many shall run to and fro, and knowledge shall be increased." (verses 3-4). Knowledge is increasing so fast that no human mind can begin to comprehend a hundredth part of the information that has been gathered upon any one scientific subject. And yet, "Man has never been able to come to *a knowledge of the truth.*" There are more illness, more despair, more deformities in babies, more insanity and more desperate problems that need solving than there have ever been on the earth before. Yet man has been promised that if he will hold his eyes single to the glory of God he will be filled with Light and be able to comprehend all things. And there shall be no more darkness in him. In other words, "he will have overcome all the evils of his life."

Paul, in his first epistle to the Corinthians, proclaims the knowledge of great hidden truths that can only be received by the Spirit of God. Paul is quoting from the sixty-fourth chapter of Isaiah, in which it is revealed that eyes have not seen, nor ears heard, neither has it entered into the heart of man the great things which God has laid up for those who LOVE Him.

Then Paul bears witness that he had received this knowledge of these unspeakable truths and reveals the method

of receiving such divine enlightenment, as follows: "Howbeit we speak wisdom among them that are perfect: yet not
the wisdom of this world, nor of the princes of this world,
that come to nought.

"But we speak the wisdom of God in a mystery, even
THE HIDDEN WISDOM, WHICH GOD ORDAINED
BEFORE THE WORLD unto our glory:

"Which none of the Princes of this world knew: for had
they known it, they would not have crucified the Lord of
Glory!

"But as it is written Eye hath not seen, nor ear heard,
neither have entered into the heart of man, the things which
God hath prepared for them that love him.

"But God hath revealed them unto us by His Spirit: for
the Spirit searcheth all things, yea, the deep things of God.

"For what man knoweth the things of man, save the spirit
of man which is in him? Even so the things of God knoweth
no man, but the Spirit of God." (I. Cor. 25-11).

These great things which God has reserved for those who
love Him and which mortal eyes have never yet beheld nor
read about, and which no physical ears have ever been taught
or heard and which no human heart has as yet dreamed of,
are now to be opened to the understandings of men until
they are worthy and prepared. These dynamic, glorious
truths, which only the chosen ones of old were permitted
to glimpse, through the revelations of the Spirit of Almighty
God, are now ours to receive as we humble ourselves before
God and glorify Him.

Jesus Christ, the Lord, the divine Son of God, said: "The
Kingdom of God cometh not with observation.

"Neither shall they say, Lo here! or Lo, there! for behold,
the Kingdom of God is within you." (St. Luke 17:20-21).

Christ also said, "Seek ye first the Kingdom of God — and its righteousness and all else shall be added unto you." (Matt. 6:33 & Luke 12:31).

The "righteousness" of the Kingdom means literally the "Right Use" of its privileges and its powers as one uses them in divine majesty.

Then we are informed definitely by the Lord Jesus Christ, that "The Kingdom of heaven *is within* you!" Many of those who have taken hold of this with their unpurified minds have used it only to utter blasphemous statements as they have gone about proclaiming their own greatness as they defile the very altar of God with their own unglorified, mortal selves. These have not stepped one foot upon the divine Pathway of OVERCOMING. They are clothed in hypocrisy and self-righteousness without even being aware of the darkness they are carrying.

Along with the powers of this divine Kingdom, which is within, must be mentioned again the following: "It is given to ABIDE IN YOU the record of heaven, the Comforter, the PEACEABLE things of immortal glory; the truth of all things; that which quickeneth all things, which maketh alive all things; that which KNOWETH ALL THINGS, AND HATH ALL POWER, according to wisdom, mercy, truth, justice and judgment."

As one ceases from all outward striving and searching and begins to fulfill that First and Great Commandment he learns, as the inspired writer of the Odes of Solomon revealed in his seventeenth Ode, verses seven to ten: "And he who knew and brought me up is the Most High in all His perfection. And He glorified me by His kindness, and raised my thoughts to the height of His truth.

"And from thence He gave me the way of His precepts and I opened the doors that were closed.

"And brake in pieces the bars of iron; but my iron melted and dissolved before me;

"Nothing appeared closed to me; BECAUSE I WAS THE DOOR TO EVERYTHING!"

Through the fulfilling or living of the First and Great Commandment that inner door to the realm of Heaven is opened wide! The effulgent light is beautiful beyond the power of words to unfold. There are really no words to describe its unutterable beauty, therefore no ears have ever heard of it. And no mortal eyes have ever beheld it because as one has attained unto this inner realm he is no longer just a mere mortal and would not desecrate the glory of this divine Kingdom by boasting of having entered it. As one enters this holy Kingdom of God (within) all else is truly added unto him. As he breaks those hardened seals upon his own heart they melt away and he realizes that he, truly, is the door to everything.

One having fulfilled all the laws of mortality by perfecting that First and Great Commandment he is no longer under the laws OF MORTALITY. He passes beyond the earthly, physical laws and evolves into the realm of immortality — and that realm becomes his own.

Such a one realizes that he is standing in the "Holy of Holies," not as it was in Solomon's Temple, but as it is in the realms of heaven. It is beautiful beyond all the words of the earth to describe. It is truly so far beyond anything that physical eyes have ever beheld no ears can truly hear about it fully because there is no language on this earth capable of describing it. It is a condition of fulfillment.

At first one becomes aware of shimmering, glorious

jewels! These jewels are spiritual and beyond anything mortal man has ever seen. They are priceless and exquisite beyond compare. These are the real jewels of eternal glory. There is no counterfeit, no sham, no shoddy display of hysterical acclaim. They contain the eternal, glorious wonder of all perfection. These jewels or fruits are Spiritual. They are the treasures in heaven, which no contamination could ever touch. They are the divine virtues which, by OVER-COMING the human weaknesses and desires the divine jewels will be forever established in the soul of man as his everlasting, crowning virtues. They are never placed on noisy display by hysterical shouting. They cannot be thus defiled. They are eternal and apparent and glorious beyond mere mortal man's finite comprehension.

When one first is privileged to behold the exquisite splendor of these spiritual treasures, which he has established right within himself, he stands silent and awed realizing he is standing in that divine "Holy of Holies" and that it is most real. He knows with a positive knowing that he has entered "The Secret Place of the Most High," the glorified center of his own divine, purified soul. Then a new wonder opens to that individual's understanding as he realizes fully that he is indeed "THE TEMPLE OF THE LIVING GOD!"

Those glorified jewels are the treasures of one's own virtues which he has laid up in his own OVERCOMING of the little, mortal ego-filled self of mortality. And he knows those jewels are alive and effervescent with the glory of immortality and eternal life. And those jewels are his! And he is them!

Within man's own self is contained all the wonder and the beauty and perfection of all that could or does exist, in the glory of his own OVERCOMING.

Then one realizes there is still another step to be taken. He must clothe the outside of himself in the glorious radiance of those magnificent, inner jewels. Mankind has forever sought to cleanse the outside of himself by his accepted rituals and formulas and often hypocrisy. But the outside can never be perfected until the inside is completely purified.

As one, by diligent seeking, enters or finds that divine Kingdom of God, the inside of the soul is purified and glorified. It is then one has the power to fulfill the perfection of the writer of those sacred Odes of Solomon in which he stated: "I cast off darkness and clothed myself in light; and acquired a body free from sorrow or affliction or pain!" In this glorious achievement one receives the eternal virtues and blessings of a physical translation. He truly becomes clothed in light or in the radiance of all the sacred virtues he has developed in his own divine OVERCOMING as he placed them into the living center of his own soul.

And, as one steps into that "Kingdom within," "he need go no more out!" There is an ancient record of Christ, which states: "He never once dwelt in the external after his illumination."

One may return to the mortal sphere of action to render service in this physical world, even as Christ did, but he is no longer of the world, nor can any outside happening disturb him.

Each individual, in that moment of unfoldment, realizes he is the fulfillment and the eternal reality of all the wonders of which he could possibly desire. He is that very thing! Glory itself!

Then it is he becomes a living, vibrating part of the Celestial Symphony. He is a living part of the divine harmonies and the heavenly music of the eternal ages as they are released to enfold a universe in the healing rhythm of eternal grandeur.

As one clothes himself with the pure radiance of those spiritual jewels of his own perfected OVERCOMING he comprehends why mortal eyes have never beheld the glory of those things which God has reserved for those who love Him.

In reaching this Kingdom within, and laying claim to it through the perfecting of that divine gift of love, one fulfills all the laws. Then, automatically, he steps beyond the order or realm of even the Patriarchs. He steps through and beyond the PROMISES — into the complete fulfillment, which is perfection itself.

Then in one moment of realization the progressing individual becomes aware that the divine key to the Door to Everything, that First and Great Commandment, has been with man from the beginning of time. Yes, it has been with man from the foundation of the world. Moses gave those two great Commandments of *overcoming* all physical laws and boundaries and conditions ten times in his writings. Christ reaffirmed it two thousand years ago. And until this day few have ever put it into practice — or PROVED ITS POWER. And the very few who did live it previous to this day were not permitted to share or to reveal its dynamic power and glory.

Now, at last, it is man's privilege to comprehend the literal power and meaning of those divine words — AND TO PROVE THEM!

As this glorious, inner Kingdom is earned and entered into one literally clothes himself in Light. He clothes himself in the radiance of those Celestial jewels, his own sacred treasures of divine integrity and perfected love. Then he knows why "Solomon in all his glory was not arrayed as beautifully as even the lilies of the field."

The materials in Solomon's robes were made of earthly elements, spun by mortal hands and fashioned with only human skill. As one clothes himself in the Light or Radiance of the pure perfection of his own priceless virtues and divine qualities of selfless purity he realizes the wonder of Christ's invitation for man to seek for the Kingdom of God, that he might be rich indeed, or that everything else will be added unto him. Then one realizes that the gold that has been tried in the fire of his own soul is himself purified with the testings and the OVERCOMING of life. He himself becomes the radiance of each fabulous jewel or divine virtue. These are his own earned treasures which none can steal or no moth or rust mar or corrupt. They are eternal.

As one clothes himself in the pure radiance of his own priceless treasures his light begins to shine forth so that others seeing it, or realizing that that individual carries something beyond mortal manifesting, will seek to bring forth that Light within themselves, for the glory of God.

And God has said: "This is my work and my glory to bring to pass the immortality and eternal life of man!" Glorify God with your Light and you will become glorious! "Hold your eyes single to the glory of God and you will be filled with Light."

CHAPTER XV

"THE UNSPEAKABLE TRUTHS HIDDEN UP FROM THE FOUNDATIONS OF THE WORLD."

The witnessing radiance of Light is not revealed in WORDS, but in POWER and in majesty and in the perfecting and the bringing forth of divinity right within oneself.

"Seek not for the things for which the Gentiles seek," as Christ warned. "But rather seek ye the Kingdom of God; and all else will be added unto you." (Matt. 6:33 and Luke 12:27).

It is only as the heart of man is opened, by the great love, that he can possibly enter that divine Kingdom of God and receive the unspeakable glory which God has held locked within each individual's soul. And as one exerts himself to "think only the most beautiful things possible," he will automatically develop that love and will become as beautiful as possible. And as one sends that love forth with all the energy of heart, soul, mind and strength he generates a power beyond the natural mind of man to fathom. And forever will he be clothed in the spiritual radiance, "that the shame of his mortal nakedness will never appear." "And though his sins were as scarlet, they will become white as snow, to him that OVERCOMETH. And they will never come in remembrance before the Lord."

Such a one will "walk in glory and be clothed in Light," as Christine Mercie declared.

These greater blessings can never be claimed by those who are satisfied with all the failings and weaknesses of mortality. It is most assuredly true that "The wages of sin IS death!" And it is also true that those who OVERCOME sin also have the power to OVERCOME that last enemy — DEATH!

The possibility of OVERCOMING and of becoming "perfect, even as the Father in heaven is perfect," has been there down the endless centuries, awaiting those who were willing to look beyond the common, orthodoxed vision of grubby mortality. This promise of perfection is possible else the command would not have been given. Man has failed to even look or to contemplate it because of the hardness of his heart and because of the great wickedness of unbelief. Yet this invitation to become perfect, "even as the Father in Heaven is perfect" is but the unveiling of the gifts and power of manhood to a small, grubby child. He is invited to grow into such possibilities. And growing, itself, is a natural process.

In the exercising of love and forgiveness is the growing accomplished. And in accepting such a possibility one begins to mature or to "evolve from the man kingdom." He leaves the realms of childhood and develops into the full stature of sonship. God has at last made apparent the method of passing beyond all mortal laws into the Order or Realm of the ancient Patriarchs.

As one lays hold of the PROMISES, through FAITH, and lives that First and Great Commandment, he is no longer under the laws of mortality. It is as one takes hold of the Promises, through Faith, that he discovers he is traveling that Straight and Narrow Way, and IT IS BEAUTIFUL. It is the path of PROMISES and one need travel it but a very short distance before the door to that Kingdom of God is

opened wide. Its reality and its powers and its glories become the divine possession of that individual as he has
opened his heart to be-live.

No one can possibly travel that STRAIGHT AND NAR-
ROW WAY of OVERCOMING without reaching the great
ultimate goal of all existence. As he travels that divine
Highway of Light his vision closes to the darkness and the
Light becomes ever more real and perfect and glorious. This
is a point of development where one reaches the point of
Faith or progress where Light and perfection and joy and
ecstasy are all that is left — and "he is wrapped in the power and glory of his Maker and is caught up to dwell with
Him!" This has been waiting for man to only begin to contemplate and to believe.

As one travels "This Straight and Narrow Way, that
leads to Life Eternal" he naturally, and quite easily progresses beyond the Order of the Patriarchs and the PROM-
ISES. He receives the fulfillment of the PROMISES. He
becomes the radiance of their glory.

But no Promise on the earth, or in heaven for that matter, is of any worth unless it is possible to fulfill it and to
receive its limitless power. And God said, "Behold, I never
give a command or a Promise except I prepare the way for
its accomplishment." And He is a God of truth and cannot
lie! Neither can His Words return unto Him unfulfilled
or void!

To comprehend and to receive the fulness of the marvelous
wonders of those great Promises, that were hidden up from
the foundation of the world, because of the blindness of
men's minds and because of the hardness of their hearts and
because of the gross wickedness of unbelief, comes the unveiling of the unspeakable glories of that which has been

awaiting man from the beginning of time — even before the dawn of history. And these great blessings are for this life — and for all eternity. *They are for the great, living* NOW — and the forever.!

As one opens his sealed mind, his hardened heart and his entire being or soul to BELIEVE, the unfolding will come. And the blessings become his own. Thus he begins to travel that Straight and Narrow Path of desiring for things beyond the grubby, mortal level of drab existence. His exerted power to *believe* will open his mind to begin to desire. And his *desiring* is the "asking" which is required for fulfillment. Yes. "Ask (or desire) and you shall receive — FOR EVERYONE WHO ASKS RECEIVES." One cannot possibly ask or desire without first opening up his mind to behold, his eyes to see — and his heart to believe. It is all one and the same thing.

As one goes beyond all orthodoxed, dull, accepted, dead beliefs into the spiritual promises and possibilities he begins to rend that dismal, gross, deadly veil of unbelief. And only then can one's eyes be conditioned to behold the Light and the glory and the possibility of all that the awakened heart of man can possibly hope for or desire. This is how one steps through the door of grubby mortality into the divine Pathway of OVERCOMING as mortality and all its curses and evils are left behind. And this is a Path anyone on this earth can travel if so be he DESIRES.

This Straight and Narrow Path, of which Christ held forth the keys, is the Highway to Life Eternal — in which a man need never die. And even with the unfolding of this tremendous Truth, of which Christ constantly bore witness, there are those who are dull, unprogressive and so self-centered in their orthodoxed conformity they will proclaim that they are not *afraid* to die. They are mediocre individuals and completely without understanding. One does not travel this road because he is AFRAID to die, but because he loves God.

The love of such a one will continue to increase, if his heart is sincere, until he truly loves God with all his heart, all his soul, and all his mind, then with the strength of his entire being that love will be rayed out in a dynamic glory of OVERCOMING. And that individual understands fully that he is not traveling that divine Highway of the Gods because of any groveling fear. The very first miracle accomplished by LOVE is to CAST OUT ALL FEAR! One travels this Road of Holiness because his own soul is reaching forth to glorify God with everything he has to offer. He also realizes that, because he has the courage and the fortitude to become a pioneer along this wondrous spiritual Path, he is building a Highway, paved with the transparent gold, for those who follow. Such a one is a privileged being indeed, for it is a far greater privilege to travel by FAITH than by knowledge. One becomes the trail-blazing guide to those who come later, traveling in comfort and ease.

As one loves with ALL his soul his entire being is renovated and purified and spiritualized and beautified and made perfect.

And only such are prepared to "Be born of the Spirit." It is then one is prepared to behold the things which mortal eyes have never seen, nor mortal ears ever heard and which have never before entered into the heart of man. Such a one, having fulfilled all the laws, through the perfecting of LOVE, will be prepared to enter into that divine Kingdom of God, which pertains only to those WHO LOVE HIM!

Such a purified one enters the jeweled Holy of Holies and

discovers that he has become all the glories and the wonders it contains. Anything that is on the outside of man is never really his own. He can only claim definitely and permanently that which is within him—or which he himself IS! He becomes the love and the purity and the perfection of all that he could possibly desire, in righteousness. He is those very things. He is filled with the radiance of those inner jewels and knows fully that all the virtues of perfection have become his own. It is then he is able to send forth the divine radiance of those precious jewels or virtues, for he himself has become divine.

The Straight and Narrow Way that leads to Life Eternal is the Pathway of LOVE made perfect, joy fulfilled, perfection established and glory accomplished.

But, as Christ said to Nicodemus, "If I have told you earthly things and you have not believed how can you believe if I tell you heavenly things?" All the things that have been written in this record have been earthly things, or conditions that must be taken hold of and fulfilled while in this mortal life. If it is seemingly almost impossible to comprehend being "born of the Spirit" and taking on immortality, then how is it possible to even give a hint concerning the fulness of the things which are spiritual?

"All that the Father has is yours!" The power of perfection! Divine LOVE glorified! Divinity accomplished and Godhood not only a possibility but a reality!

In the eighth chapter of Romans is given the information that "There are Lords many, and Gods many!" "And the scriptures cannot be broken!" Then stand forth Christ's dynamic words partially quoted from Pslams, eighty-two: "If he called them Gods unto whom the word of God comes * * * then why should you seek to stone me because I said,

I am the Son of God?" Here Christ was pointing out that he had only claimed to be a son of God, though God had proclaimed that they were called Gods unto whom His words came!"

Christ also testified many times of "The Father within who doeth the works!" This Father within, of Whom Christ so continually bore witness is truly the Great God, "in whom we live and move and have our being!" This is the contact with God within, the divine power of the Almighty that "doeth the works." So Christ testified and bore witness of the Father within. Yet when He came forth from the tomb, after his three days and nights of teaching the Spirits in Prison (according to St. Peter), and Mary dropped at His feet to embrace and worship Him, He forbade her, saying, "Touch me not, for I have not yet ascended to My Father which is in heaven!" So the Father in Heaven was not the Father within with Whom he was in constant contact. There is truly "the Father within," and "the Father Which Art in Heaven!" And both are real and in complete agreement.

Warring, wrangling Christendom and all the heathen nations alike have contradicted each other and battled verbally over What or Who God is, as they have continued to tell *about God* without ever having KNOWN Him. Yet each and every soul is invited to seek God that he might KNOW HIM—not just about Him.

"Seek me early and ye shall find me!" Yes! "Seek me diligently and you shall KNOW me!" And the Promise is: "That they might KNOW ME, THE ONLY TRUE AND LIVING GOD AND JESUS CHRIST WHOM YOU HAVE SENT!" This invitation has been waiting down the centuries for man to fulfill the conditions of its fulfilment.

One does not need to get involved in profane arguments about God. It is most assuredly true that there is the great God Who does fill all space, "in whom we live and move and have our being, and out of which all things were made —and do exist," This is the God "who is nearer than hands and feet"—THE FATHER WITHIN!

And there are also "Lords many, and Gods Many!" Which indicates that there are personal, individual Gods also, set to rule the heavens above and the earth beneath. And we are informed that this world itself is "THE SCHOOL FOR GODS!"

And what about this revelation: "As man is God once was! And as God is man may become!"

Over individual worlds and planetary systems, and over solar systems and galaxies and over universes there are Gods, set and appointed to rule in majesty and power and understanding as they have progressed along the Eternal Pathway of the Gods! There is no end to progress and to advancement to those who work upon themselves to fulfill all righteousness—not self-righteousness. And only LOVE can fulfill all righteousness—for of all the gifts it is the most divinely powerful. And it is eternal!

Those who accept the holy Promises of God, and fulfill them while in this life, will have the power to "evolve from the man kingdom into the God Kingdom." Such will have the comprehension to be informed of heavenly things, of which Christ could only vaguely hint when speaking with Nicodemus.

The very Road of Godhood is that Straight and Narrow Path and it must be traveled while in this life in order for one to receive the fulness of its Promises and powers along with the keys of Eternal Life, continuing forever along that upward Path of everlasting advancement.

The Path is so simple a fool need not err therein. It is the Road of "Love for God made manifest," and the love for one's fellowmen so filled with forgiveness and mercy and compassion the self and all its negative, mortal traits are completely OVERCOME. This Straight and Narrow Path IS the Road of Triumphant OVERCOMING! And Praise and Love and Gratitude are the rhythm and the vibration and the music of its accomplishment.

These are the divine realities beyond Mortal Boundaries.

These are the heavenly things which man has never lifted his vision to behold because of the gross wickedness of his unbelief, which has held him down the centuries in his earthbound condition of grubby mortality.

It is true that very few indeed have been able to comprehend or behold the "Great and marvelous things God has hid up from the foundation of the world!" Even the things pertaining to this earth have been ignored and smothered in that great, dark, dismal veil of unbelief.

"All that the Father has is yours!" — The LOVE — the understanding — the power of creation and the unspeakable glory of Godhood.

The Straight and Narrow Way — the Pathway to these dynamic PROMISES and the door to the Path is LOVE fulfilled and made perfect! Love for God and love for one's fellowman.

Truth itself is the great reward for those who are willing to ACCEPT IT, WHEN IT IS REVEALED TO THEM. But most people would rather perish than change one preconceived belief, regardless of its erroneous deception. It is easier for many individuals to relinquish their lives than one cherished false belief. However, he who desires to KNOW TRUTH must be willing to pay the price for it. He must be willing to open up his sealed mind and his hardened heart and to "ask God for knowledge to comprehend TRUTH!" Then only can he rend the black, dismal veil of unbelief which does cause him to remain in his awful state of wickedness, through which the great Truths can never penetrate. Few on this earth, at the present time have the stamina or the COURAGE to seek to Know TRUTH! But the Promise is and has always been: "KNOW THE TRUTH AND THE TRUTH WILL SET YOU FREE from error, false beliefs, doubting, darkness, negation and evils! "AND·HE WHO IS FREE SHALL BE FREE INDEED!" He will have the freedom and the power to "Come and go ·as the wind and no one will know from whence he came or whither he goeth!" Yes. *He will be born of the Spirit.* And, unless you have been born of the Spirit and have its great powers YOU DO NOT HAVE THE TRUTH, no matter what your claims may be.

Then God gave this information: "No man is ever damned for believing too much, but only for believing too little!" It is in the narrow, conformity of all skimped little orthodoxed ideas and petty doctrines that man is DAMNED or his progress is stopped, which the word "damnation" means.

The great miracles of the future will not be to awe the minds of men or to impress them with one's gifts and professed powers. The great miracles will be the miracle enacted within each individual as he rends that veil of unbelief, knowing that nothing is impossible with God. As one rends that veil of darkness he will have overcome the evils of his life and he will henceforth be clothed in Light as he acquires a body free from sorrow or affliction or pain. He will receive a body filled with Spirit insomuch that the flesh will be transformed into the glory of its own true, spiritual substance.

And as God is loved with the whole soul or entire being of man that individual will be transformed or translated into a "new being." He will truly be "born of the Spirit" as he becomes a divine instrument in the hands of Almighty God to help redeem and save individuals—and the world. He will be a co-worker or a co-heir with the Lord Jesus Christ Himself—a joint-heir with Him, having OVERCOME he will be co-equal. The physical, mortal cells of his body will be transformed and will take on immortality or the fulness of their divine counterpart.

All atoms were composed from the rays of Living Light, or the substance of things hoped for, in the beginning. Their very essence and foundation is Spirit—and in the great transformation they are glorified by the spirit which is given to abide in them. And so is man himself glorified and redeemed and translated.

"These are the great and marvelous things which have been hid up from the foundation of the world." These are the things which eyes have never seen, nor ears heard, nor which have never yet fully entered into the heart of man. And even now, that they are made plain, so plain a fool need not err in fulfilling them, only the righteous will have the spirit of understanding which is required to behold the greatness of God's unspeakable blessings which He has in store for those who love him!"

These TRUTHS have never before been unfolded because man has refused to believe anything which his five mortal senses could not verify or which his orthodoxed mind has not been conditioned to accept. They have been hid because man has refused to believe them as his scanning of the Word has opened to his eyes only the things he desired to behold in order to verify only that which he has already accepted. And so the great truths have remained hid up from the foundation of the world.

"And the LETTER" has killed as men have accepted only of the *letter* and so have filled the cemeteries with their relinquished bodies as they "GAVE UP THE GHOST." Yes! They gave it up! Though it was not required of them, if they had accepted the divine PATH OF OVERCOMING —that Straight and Narrow Way that leads to Life Eternal!

These great and eternal PROMISES have at last been unveiled so that those who are humble and searching may discover them and apply them—for they are LIFE! And every person on the face of the earth may live and prove them if so be he is desirous to KNOW TRUTH. TRUTH goes beyond any small, orthodoxed group! Truth belongs to God! It is eternal! And no man in existence has a monopoly upon TRUTH! One may know Truth if he is only willing to seek for it—and as it unfolds apply its glorious unfolding in his own life—and then? He becomes the great eternal TRUTH! For "He was that TRUTH in the beginning!"

THESE TRUTHS AND THESE PROMISES of Almighty God belong to you!

And if you "ask," God will be with you in your desire to accept and fulfill.

So be it, in the Name of Jesus Christ! Amen!

CHAPTER XVI

THE FULFILLMENT

The door to the Straight and Narrow Way is the FIRST
AND GREAT COMMANDMENT when it is LIVED.

This First and Great Commandment is also the very Path,
which Christ trod and left the map for. One travels this
Way of Holiness, this Highway to Zion, or to the complete
purification of the heart, through perfecting love right within himself. To love God with all one's heart purifies the
heart and removes its hard, iron bars of unbelief. It also
holds the keys to the very gates of heaven.

All mortal laws are fulfilled in the living of this dynamic
Command. All Spiritual laws are fulfilled in this most powerful invitation as the method of seeking God is fully revealed. And this great offering of love is not for God at
all. God does not need it or demand it for Himself. This
love is required for the benefit of man. In learning to
develop and to release this love one is glorified completely
as his heart, soul and mind are opened to the vision of a
new realm of unutterable beauty and fulfillment.

As one loves God with his whole being it is a most natural
thing to become thankful—even in ALL things. Love is a
part of gratitude. Gratitude mingled with love embraces that
refined attitude of appreciation, which releases that ecstatic
vibration of singing, joyous praise. It is in the pure gift of
appreciation that joy and ecstasy are fully released. And these
gifts contain the deepest happiness of life.

The gift of divine *appreciation* is the very perfecting of love and obedient acceptance of all that comes or goes in one's life, with all the powers of the soul alerted and singing in sublime, joyous ecstasy. This condition is not a dead, dull, stupid acceptance of misfortunes and evils. It is a condition of dynamic power as love is released. This attitude holds no possibility of self-pity. It is a power which exalts every calamity and dismay and evil as they are totally disarmed of their destructive forces. And "ALL THINGS WORK TOGETHER FOR GOOD, TO THOSE WHO LOVE GOD!" This "being thankful in all things," holds no resentments, no groveling, cringing attitude of abuse. It contains the dynamic powers of godhood released through a mortal being as he lifts himself above the grubbiness of mortal adversities and sends his song of glory singing out across the universe. This is power in action. And this is man's privilege to use at all times to dispel the darkness until it is completely overcome in his life.

As any individual advances into this knowledge, or begins to live it so that he actually PROVES Christ's words, he lays hold of the powers of eternity and begins to "evolve from the man kingdom into the God Kingdom." And he learns that every adverse condition is but a privilege or a stepping stone into the higher realms of existence.

"HE WHO IS THANKFUL IN ALL THINGS SHALL BE MADE GLORIOUS!" It is as one perfects this law of *appreciation* that everything becomes more beautiful. One's food tastes better. His dwelling becomes a temple, sacred and divine. His very clothing begins to take on the radiance of inner light and singing ecstasy. And it is as one perfects this law of *appreciation* that he becomes attuned to the enfolding glory of God and begins his advancement into the everlasting realms of Light. He truly becomes GLORIOUS! And within himself is released the singing love and gratitude and praising ecstasy of heaven.

These are the PROMISES of Almighty God and they cannot fail. As one practices that Great Command, to love God with his entire being he will receive the fulfilment of *every* PROMISE. Nothing will be impossible to him. He will not only learn to BELIEVE, he will reach the point where Faith is made perfect and becomes knowledge as his mind opens to comprehend all things. "Then he will be assuredly wrapped in the power and glory of his Maker and will be caught up to dwell with Him!"

Another of God's dynamic PROMISES, which can be easily PROVED by the LIVING of this glorious Command is: "If your eyes be single to my glory your whole bodies shall be filled with Light; and there shall be no darkness in you. And that individual will not only be filled with Light, he will behold the Face of God and be given a comprehension of all things." And in this work man is instructed to "SANCTIFY HIMSELF!" No one can have "eyes single to the glory of God" without loving God. It is only through the great love that any of His dynamic, breath-taking PROMISES can be fulfilled. And it is up to man to PROVE THEM.

The great unveiling of the Face of God to any individual is the final end of that Straight and Narrow Path! It is Life Eternal! It is glory unutterable! It is everlasting beauty and joy and perfection! And the command is and has always been: "Seek me diligently and you shall find me!" "Seek me early and you shall find me!" Then one truly KNOWS GOD and will need none to teach him. He does not merely know ABOUT GOD! He actually KNOWS HIM! "And this is Life eternal, to know Thee, the only True and Living God and Jesus Christ Whom Thou has sent!"

As one loves God with all his heart, soul, mind and strength, that one, of necessity, becomes Spiritualized, and will be "Born of the Spirit" with all of its powerful, exalting perfection. And "He will be able to come and go as the wind," even as Christ bore witness to Nicodemus. The cells of the flesh and the atoms thereof will be transmuted into the Spiritual radiance of divine loveliness. *This is being born of the Spirit,* and unless one has received this power to be able to "come and go as the wind" in a supreme service of divine love, he is boasting in vain and is but a grubby mortal.

This being "Born of the Spirit" is the completion of all righteousness. And to complete the explanation, Nicodemus was asked, "If I have told you earthly things and you believe not, how can you believe if I told you heavenly things?"

This being "born of the Spirit" is an achievement which must be accomplished while in the flesh, for as Christ testified, it is an earthly accomplishment. Or, in other words, it is only in and through the flesh that one can OVERCOME to this extent. It is a privilege and a possibility open to anyone who will take upon himself the responsibility of PROVING the words and PROMISES of the Lord Jesus Christ. And His words were: "Live the laws and you will KNOW of their power."

Those who receive this purifying glory and are given the power to "come and go as the wind" are performing the GREATER WORKS for they will be opened unto him. Such a one will be able to travel in the invisible, to appear as required or requested, to administer love and blessings and healings according to the needs and faith of those he is sent to assist. And such service will more often be rendered without WORDS. "For MY KINGDOM IS NOT IN WORD, BUT IN POWER, saith the Lord!" There will be no personal demonstrating or wordly acclaim. It will be a work and a benediction of outflowing, selfless love and Light.

These silent, glorified ministrations are the GREATER WORKS upon this earth. And as yet few have advanced to the point where they can have any part in this wonder because few have accepted that First and Great Commandment, to prove its power and its dynamic glory. Those who advance into this perfect love and POWER of being able to perform the GREATER WORKS, will be unannounced, and unacclaimed — and POWERFUL! Without waiting to receive credit or to be acknowledged or praised or thanked such a one will leave his blessing of everlasting power and will be upon his way, and no one will know from what service he came or to what service of divine love he has gone. The childish, immature desire to receive praise and acknowledgement will have been OVERCOME. It is overcome in the journey along that Straight and Narrow Way of perfected love.

As one perfects this divine, holy love, "The clearer are his views and the greater are his enjoyments, until he OVERCOMES the evils of his life and loses every desire for sin, and reaches the point of Faith where he is wrapped in the power and glory of his Maker and is caught up to dwell with Him!" This is true and faithful! The PROMISE cannot fail! Only man can fail as he refuses to believe the Words of Almighty God and His divine and Holy PROMISES.

As one perfects the great love for God he naturally leaves the evils of his life behind. All the evils of mortal life are contained in the flesh, with its physical cravings and wanton, corrupted desires, which are often self-developed. As one perfects the love for God the claims of the flesh are overcome and the very flesh becomes spiritualized. And one is automatically "Born of the Spirit!" He is made perfect in his entire physical being as he overcomes the evils of his life.

Anyone who lives and fulfills that First and Great Commandment will have his belief in God not only strengthened but confirmed as his faith is developed into absolute KNOWLEDGE. And he will naturally be able to fulfill Christ's breathing PROMISE of being able to do the GREATER WORKS.

And in this exerted, exercised love one learns of the perfection of Christ's everlasting, standing invitation to all, regardless of background or degree of righteousness or accepted church affiliation, for the PROMISE is: "Come unto me, *all you who labor* (either with physical work or mortal weaknesses) and are heavy laden and I will give you rest, WHICH REST IS THE FULNESS OF MY GLORY!" This glorious PROMISE was left out deliberately by wicked and designing men who wished to hold men's attention upon themselves instead of upon God. Then to continue with Christ's glorious words of mercy: "Take my yoke upon you, for my yoke is easy (for it is LOVE) and my burden is LIGHT—even the great Light of eternal glory!" Could any PROMISE be greater than this? And it belongs to every man regardless of race, color or creed. It is an eternal, everlasting invitation and can be PROVED by anyone who will take hold of it.

As one lives the lesser laws, whether physical, temporal or spiritual, with a sincere heart, he will be automatically drawn into the glory and power of this greatest of all Commands if he only seek to KNOW the TRUTH, not thinking he already possesses it all. This sacred First and Glorious Commandment fulfills ALL the others. As one practices this dynamic, perfect, powerful admonition he becomes all the living glory it contains. His doubts and fears are forever banished, for "perfect love casts out all fear." He becomes more and more powerful as his vision is opened to behold the increasing wonders of Almighty God.

Man is then instructed to "Pray with all the energy of heart that he might be POSSESSED of this great love, that it might be well with him at the last day." As one becomes POSSESSED of this great love, that love not only fills his being, it owns him. He becomes so filled with love, so enfolded with love that no evil could possibly come near him. He becomes clothed in Light and the divine love of God so that he can literally walk through the exploding terror of an H Bomb and be unharmed. And no experience of destruction could be so devastating or disastrous as to be able to harm or touch him. And these dynamic destructions will be poured out to the extent that "The wicked will become ashes under the soles of your feet." But—"If one is possessed of this great love IT WILL BE WELL WITH HIM AT THE LAST DAY!" The day of destruction. This is the PROMISE.

"To pray with all the energy of heart," simply means to center the desires of the heart upon achieving or upon the receiving of the gift of perfect love. And ALL WILL BE WELL WITH THAT INDIVIDUAL. The First and Great Commandment automatically fulfills this desire. No one can exert himself in prayer to develop this love until he is possessed of it, or by it, who would not be exalted and glorified by its fulfilling.

"And the Fruit of the Tree of Life *is* the love of God, which is shed forth through the hearts of the children of men." It is the very power of LIFE and as one opens his heart to receive its fulness no power on earth can take his life from him. As one exerts his own little trickle of love he releases the seals upon his heart and as these are removed God begins to send His great, boundless, powerful, limitless love through that heart as "THE FOUNTAINS OF LIVING WATER." To "Come and partake of the fountains of living water—FREELY"—is an invitation which has been offered to mankind from the beginning. "Yes, Come and partake of them, WITHOUT PRICE!" This love contains all healing for the physical, aging body, all the blessings of abundance and the boundless, ecstatic joys of the soul along with the great gift of ETERNAL LIFE!

Now, to "Pray with all the energy of heart" means simply to focus the desires of the inner being upon so great a gift as Pure, Divine, Christ-like LOVE. Desire it! Exercise love! Use it constantly and pray for it with all the energy of heart and the PROMISE of God is that you shall be possessed of it and it will be well with you. Such a one will indeed receive the very fulness of the divine gift of love, insomuch that he will be literally *possessed* or owned and controlled by this divine and holy love at all times and all occasions. "And It never faileth!" It increases with use. In such a condition only beauty and happiness and understanding could possibly come into the life of such an individual. The song or vibration of joyous, glorious love would forever fill his entire being and then flow forth from him to bless and heal and glorify all that he contacted either in thought or casual passing. And especially those whom he concentrated that love upon, in prayer, would receive the blessing it held.

As one takes hold of this First and Great Commandment and PROVES its unspeakable POWERS, he will clothe himself in its glory. In it is contained the key to the doors of heaven as he completes his journey along "That Straight and Narrow Way, which leads to Life Eternal!" Or to the unveiling of the Face of God!

This First and Great Commandment is the door that opens up and reveals the Straight and Narrow Way so that one may begin to travel that glorified Highway of Holiness, to the complete purification of his heart."

As one enters that sacred doorway to the Straight and Narrow Way he also learns that that First and Great Commandment is not only the door but is also the very Way itself. As one brings forth and perfects that LOVE within himself he is literally walking with God. This greatest of all privileges, this opportunity to live and fulfill that greatest of all glories, the perfecting of love within oneself, he will find the power of his own divine completion and perfection. Within that holy, divine bit of instruction is contained all that heaven holds as it is perfected in the heart and soul and mind of man. And man becomes that LOVE, pure, glorified, powerful and dynamically eternal. He is no longer a mere mortal. "He has evolved from the man kingdom into the God Kingdom" as he has traveled that Straight and Narrow Way that leads to Life Eternal.

"God is love!" As one becomes POSSESSED of this great love he is literally "Born of God" as is PROMISED in the epistles of Saint John. "And he can henceforth commit no sin!"

The GREATER WORKS which Christ talked about were not the ones performed in words, but in POWER, unheralded and unspoken in most instances — and unacclaimed as love is released and poured out to heal and to bless and to glorify.

In Matthew, chapter four, is given the account of the great exploits and seeming miracles which will be performed by those who are evil and wicked and who are the workers of Satan's kingdom, as "They go forth to deceive even the very elect, if possible!" Many will be deceived by their words and their demonstrations and miracles. These deceived ones will rush to and from one acclaimed prophet or false Christ to the next. Or it may be that they will be so blinded by the show of false power they will yield their beings, minds, bodies and souls to "The worshipping of the beast."

"At the time of the end," the angel informed Daniel; "Many shall be purified, and made white and tried" (to see if they, like Christ, can resist the temptation to manifest their powers and so prove that they are actually of God, as they suppose). "And the wicked shall do wickedly; and none of the wicked shall understand; but the wise shall understand." (Dan. 12:10).

"And they that be wise shall shine as the brightness of the firmament; and they that turn many to righteousness as the stars forever and ever.

"But thou, O Daniel, shut up the words, and seal the book, even to the time of the end: many shall run to and fro, and knowledge shall be increased." (Dan. 12:3-4). And though "Knowledge is increased they will never be able to come to a knowledge OF THE TRUTH!"

Only as one "LIVES THE LAWS CAN HE POSSIBLY KNOW OF THEIR TRUTH AND THEIR POWER!" As one lives that First and Great Commandment he will have fulfilled ALL the laws and the PROPHETS. He will no longer be under the laws and will have advanced beyond them. Having fulfilled all things he will have OVERCOME the world, even as Christ did. He will also be doing the works which Christ did, in POWER, rather than in WORDS. And he who OVERCOMES to this extent will naturally OVERCOME DEATH — THE LAST ENEMY.

And those who OVERCOME to the extent that death is required to back down before them will find that they have fulfilled all things. They will be joint-heirs or co-heirs with the Lord Jesus Christ, for such is the PROMISE. In other words they will be co-equal with Him. "And they will sit down with Him on His throne!" (Rev. 3:21). They will have fulfilled that dynamic admonition of Saint Paul, "Let the same mind be in you which was also in Christ Jesus, who being in the form of God, thought it not robbery to be equal with God!"

As the great love is perfected the little, ego, mortal-self is put aside. And with eyes solely "single to the glory of God," and with nothing but love flowing forth from one's entire being that individual will go forth, "Born of the Spirit" and in the power and majesty of Almighty God, to render the greater service and to do the GREATER WORKS. He will literally be a member of the Kingdom of God, not a self-acclaimed, bragging, preaching individual, but one clothed in Power and Light. "For My Kingdom is not in WORD, but in POWER, SAITH THE LORD!"

These GREATER WORKS, which Christ promised, will be performed in POWER—not in words. One "Born of the Spirit will have the POWER to come and go as the wind," to render service according to the need as he blesses, performing some act of love and comfort and healing. Then, without fanfare or waiting to bask in praise or thanks or self-acclaim or acknowledgement, he will go on to some other assignment and the one whom he has just assisted will not know from what assignment he just came, or where he has gone. These will be the GREATER WORKS—works without fanfare or demonstrating and often without WORDS.

Those who have.not perfected love, who are still following the little, ego, mortal-self will want it to be made known and proclaimed aloud that it was through them that the healing was accomplished, the miracle performed, the need supplied—and they will be but the workers of darkness.

Those who cannot relinquish such desires for credits and acknowledgements will never have part in the GREATER WORKS. These, like Christ, will be tempted to make a great demonstration of the power vested in them as being something personal, and may, unlike Christ, fail to resist such a temptation. They who cannot relinquish their cravings for outward show will seek to exalt themselves in a flame of self-righteous demonstrations and so will join the miracle workers who will have power to even "call down fire from heaven."

These pitifully misguided ones will be the individuals who will flock to the false prophets and the false Christs and to those who shout and contort and do UNSEEMLY things insomuch that they will not only be deceived themselves but will assist in "deceiving the very elect, IF POSSIBLE."

The elect will be those who love God with their entire beings, their hearts, souls, minds and strength. They ARE HIS SHEEP! And they will know His voice, and the voice of a stranger they will not follow. Their very love will exalt them to the status of the "ELECT"—The "Sons of God!" "And they are called Sons of God who are led by the Spirit of God." And the keys of the Kingdom, which is POWER, will be placed in their hands. And they will be co-heirs with Christ—to reign forever and ever in the Light of Eternal Truth!"

Thus, the GREATER WORKS can only be performed by those who have OVERCOME. They will be performed in silence, not in WORDS. Their Fruits will continually manifest and bear witness of their status and worth. And no matter how the wicked may manifest the gifts of the Spirit and their proclamations testify of their being chosen of God the evil within them will be made apparent to those who truly love God. The very Spirit they carry will be repulsive and abhorrent to those who love the Lord and who are His elect. And it is the righteous, or the "elect" only who will be endowed with that most gracious, wonderful gift called the "Spirit of Discernment!" This gift of discernment holds the keys of being able to discern between the righteous and the wicked.

As those who are truly servants of the Living God perform some great work of mercy and blessing and then go upon their way, not waiting to receive either praise or acknowledgement or credit, the power of God will be continually increased upon them. They have, within themselves, become the very least, or servant of all, which is required in order to become the GREATEST.

This greater glory and these GREATER WORKS of everlasting value pertain only to those who have "eyes single to the glory of God" and not to their own aggrandizement. And those who wish to demonstrate will find this holy Path is not for them. These Greater Works can only be performed by those who have OVERCOME all things, "even as He *overcame*!" And the OVERCOMING is of the little, mortal, ego-self with its evil cravings for glory and recognition and importance.

Not having sought for glory or acclaim, those OVERCOMING, love-filled individuals will be glorified. Having developed "eyes single to the glory of God, they will take on that glory and be filled with Light and comprehend all things!" They will "Shine forth as the firmament and be as the brilliance of the stars forever and ever."

The power of God will not be made manifest in either WORDS or in UNSEEMLY demonstrations, or even in the gifts, as Paul proclaimed in the thirteenth chapter of First Corinthians, "for these former things will be done away—these childish things—when that which is perfect is come." And it is true that those who truly love God, and who perfect that Love, will have grown into manhood. They will have left the milk and the breasts and the out-grown crib and the childish, rattling brass toys with the clanging cymbals for they will have progressed into the status of son-ship and perfection. They will no longer behave like children or be beguiled by childish enticements and noisy demonstrations. They will be free! Powerfully, dynamically free—free from all inferior ways and mortal, childish demonstrations. They will walk with God, their Father, in power and majesty.

This First and Great Commandment is indeed the road of glory as one travels it, along that Straight and Narrow Path of unspeakable joy to Life Eternal. And this Way is not a hard, arduous Way as the unrighteous may suppose. It is a Way of singing, joyous ecstasy. One becomes the singing, triumphant glory.

But "He who puts his hand to the plow, or sets his mind upon the fulfilling of an invitation as great as that First, divine Commandment, then looks back, is not fit for the

Kingdom." He who looks back to repeat or to retell some individual experiences, in which he had been touched for a moment with the finger of inspiration, is *not* fit for the Kingdom. This Path is the way in which the individual learns to glorify God, by developing "eyes single to His glory!" It is only in this manner or in this developing of the great attitude of gratitude, which is LOVE made manifest, that one can possibly become glorious. As one glorifies God for each supreme moment of enlightenment he must then pass on and leave it behind in order to hold that living contact in the eternal NOW! God's kingdom is not in Words—or in repeated retellings or in hammered exhortations, but in POWER. And the POWER is in the PRESENT. Learn to carry or hold that contact with God Now and you will become powerful!

The miracles, or the divine gifts of God, will automatically "FOLLOW those who believe!" They will be as natural and perfect as breathing and living. They will follow in the wake of those who let the perfected love flow forth through their beings, and that LOVE always leaves a divine blessing upon these that are contacted. And in this silent, perfect blessing there is no demonstrating or self-acclaim. There is just the outflowing power of God. And from one's very robes the power to heal will be made manifest.

It is through the living of that First and Great Commandment that the Promises are unveiled and the powers of Almighty God are released into one's life. Every dynamic PROMISE ever given, when fulfilled, leads one to that great DOOR beyond all mortal concepts. The very boundaries of mortality are dissolved and one becomes a translated being, truly "Born of the Spirit," "Ordained literally of God" and filled with Light insomuch that he comprehends all things! *Every* PROMISE blends into this promised fulfilling of everlasting OVERCOMING AND ETERNAL POWER, beyond the boundaries of mortality.

———————

This record is sealed with the power of God, and no man can loose its seals. He who will attempt to do so shall himself be destroyed.

And the power and the grace of God will be upon you chosen ones who understand, for you shall be clothed in Light and in the power of fulfilling. "But the wicked shall do wickedly and none of the wicked shall understand."

And he who offers to God the great burden of his own anguished weaknesses will be given the power to let go of them, if so be he loves God more than he loves his weaknesses. The greatest offering one can give to God is his own intense misery as he refuses to be held in bondage by the cravings of the flesh. And in that supreme anguish he shall be given the power to overcome. "I gave men weaknesses that they might become strong!" They become strong and mighty and glorified in the anguish of their own *overcoming*. And the anguish is transmuted into eternal strength and glory! Such anguish as is held on one's mortal relinquishing is very short, when that suffering is offered freely to God. It may be but momentary. At the most it will be but for a few days, for as one relinquishes it to God then God will lend His strength to the accomplishment, or to the OVERCOMING. And it is true that the length of one's endurance will be measured by his own intensity of desire as he reaches for perfection. In the flesh this testing is but the relinquishing of the cravings one has established in the cells of his mortal flesh. If permitted to remain they are carried on by the spirit into the realms beyond the grave.

It is in the OVERCOMING of those evil, little, personal cravings, or developed dynamic ones, of one's inferior habits that one becomes strong and mighty and the anguish, which could have endured for ages in the next world, have right here, on this earth, been transmuted into eternal power.

As one offers the anguish of his physical cravings and desires to God his very flesh will become spiritualized. Such a privilege and opportunity is boundless. As one lets go of his intense cravings of the flesh, God will accept his offering and the very angels will rejoice over him. "Come unto Me, all you who labor with your mortal weaknesses and physical lusts, AND I WILL GIVE YOU REST—WHICH REST IS THE FULNESS OF MY GLORY!" As one, through his own intense desiring to serve God and to perfect himself is thus offered to Christ, his grubby, mortal, physical cravings will be transformed into spiritual strength —the divine, eternal strength and power of OVERCOMING. This is the very wonder and marvel and the breath-taking privilege and power of OVERCOMING. It transforms weaknesses into STRENGTH. It transforms a mere mortal into a radiant, divine being with the power to fulfill all things.

Every person on the earth has the power to transform his body into beauty and youth and perfection, or as the Writer of the Odes of Solomon expressed it: "I clothed myself in Light and acquired a body free from sorrow, affliction or pain" or from all ugly, physical, degenerate lusts and cravings and habits.

One can partake of the waters of the "Fountain of
YOUTH!" He can bathe himself in those waters. Yes.
"Come and partake of the waters of LIFE—*freely!*"

As one trains his mind to think only thoughts of love
and mercy and compassion and to mentally bless all whom
his thoughts enfold and those he contacts, he will soon
establish those vibrations in his living emotions and they
will become a very part of his entire being. They will become the habitual feelings which are but himself in expression. In this process of retraining oneself to think and
feel only the most beautiful things possible one becomes
one of the most beautiful beings possible. And it is in this
process of transforming himself into a love-filled being
that one passes beyond mortality into immortality.

As one is transformed by his own thinking and feeling
habits into a radiant, beautiful person he truly "becomes
a new being," filled with love and light and joyous youth.
Every cell of one's body can thus be transformed from a
physical cell into a spiritual one. And when one has, by
the very power and privilege of his own thinking and feeling, completed this conversion, he will be matured spiritually and will "BE BORN OF THE SPIRIT!"

This holy transition belongs to every human being who
will only BE-LIVE and who will but exert himself to
prove that First and Great Commandment—the key of
eternal glory. In the LIVING of that law are held all the
keys and the powers of Eternal, unspeakable, everlasting
beauty and perfection and glory.

"Come! Partake of the waters of *life*—FREELY!" For
they are yours.

Chapter XVII

BEYOND MORTAL BOUNDARIES

Yes, it is quite possible to transform and translate the physical cells of the body into their divine, spiritual essence, cell by cell, as the body takes on the radiance of the spirit in a gradual process of OVERCOMING.

But there is an even speedier way to bring about this divine transition right within oneself.

The keys of glory are each man's to use. It is the privilege and within the power of every human soul to "Clothe himself in Light and to acquire a body free from sorrow or affliction or pain." In other words, each individual on this earth has the power and the equipment to transmute his physical body into a glorified spiritual one, "Born of the Spirit, or into a completely spiritualized, transformed, exalted being, beyond the powers of all negation, suffering—and DEATH!

"As a man thinketh in his heart, so is he." As a man transplants his thoughts into the depths of his being they become EMOTIONS. E—MOTIONS are but *energy in motion*. Direct the motion of your own released energy of thought and feeling and you will realize the dynamic powers which are yours to harness and to control.

With the comprehension of this creative force, right within himself, man can easily become the Master instead of the slave of his emotions.

Thoughts, directed into the emotions, establish VIBRATIONS. And vibrations are the living energy of which all

things are composed. Vibrations are the reality of all creative power.

"Think the most beautiful things possible," *at all times*
and you will become beautiful! Think the most glorious,
powerful things possible and you will become powerful,
in personality and in thought, word and deed. And you will
be exalted into the fulfilling of your own thought desires.

"He who is thankful in all things will be made glorious!"
The singing gratitude, released from the depths of a man's
heart will exalt and glorify him. As "Gratitude, the Greatest Attitude," is released, triumphant, life-giving, spiritual
energy is generated. It is first released right through the
entire being of man himself as he uses it.

"Whoso offereth praises, glorifieth ME!" And in glorifying God one is himself glorified. The very vibrations he
releases, in such inner praise, become the living essence of
his own existence.

This "gratitude" that glorifies; this "praise" that exalts,
along with the dynamic love for God as it is sent out from
one's whole being, heart, soul, mind and strength, is the
power and the very process of OVERCOMING, simplified.
As one develops and releases only the exquisite vibrations
of the Highest pulsating energy possible to generate, his
entire being will be transformed thereby. He will become a
spiritual being clothed in Light or the radiant wonder of
Celestial beauty. He automatically becomes a glorified being and is "born of the Spirit." He becomes a person who
has evolved from the man kingdom into the God Kingdom.
He is no longer a mere earthly mortal. He becomes a translated being, FREE—Eternally, beautifully FREE—Free to
come and go as the wind—in a service beyond all mortal
thought.

Now, for a moment it is necessary to digress from this highest place of accomplishment, into the mortal reality of everything that clings to earthlings—until they put forth the effort and exert the desire to OVERCOME. Any negative, hateful thought, every resentful desolating feeling become a part of man also as he permits them to take over his being. He can and will become all the ugly negation of diseases and evil possible to crawl into by his own thinking and feeling and encouraged habits of self-pity, resentments, jealousies, fears or greeds and lusts, which he may nourish within himself. Man is what he *thinks* and FEELS. And man is the creator of his own personality and whatever attributes he may acquire in his journey of life.

This fact is given so very plainly in Ezekiel, chapter twenty-eight and verses thirteen and fourteen. Ezekiel, a choice prophet of the Lord is commanded by God to give a divine rebuke upon the head of the King of Tyre. And with that rebuke comes an explanation of the reason for his rejection.

It is as follows: (Thou, King of Tyre), "hast been in Eden the Garden of God; every precious stone was thy covering, the sardius, topaz, and the diamond, the beryl, the onyx, and the jasper, the sapphire, the emerald, and the carbuncle, and gold . . . Thou hast walked up and down in the midst of the stones of fire.

"Thou wast perfect in thy ways from the day that thou wast created, till iniquity was found in thee."

Like Lucifer, the King of Tyre was a divine and beautiful **being, clothed in the exquisite radiance of these inner jewels** of perfection—as all were in the beginning. Then, like Lucifer, his own thinking began to bring forth the evil and the wickedness, which greed and jealousies and pride develop. And in such released vibrations he changed himself into an evil person, rejected by God — and eventually by man.

Such is man's power to mold himself. He can also re-mold himself into a radiant son of light, a glorified being as he clothes himself in Light, or gathers the exquisite radiance of those jewels, or living attributes of the heavenly treasures unto himself.

The following is from James Allen's little book, "AS A MAN THINKETH." "Man is made or unmade by himself, in the armoury of thought he forges the weapons by which he destroys himself; he also fashions the tools with which he builds for himself heavenly mansions of joy and strength and peace. By the right choice and true application of thought, man ascends to Divine Perfection; by the abuse and wrong application of thought, he descends below the level of the beast. Between these two extremes are all the grades of character, and man is their Maker and Master."

"As a being of Power, Intelligence and LOVE, and the lord of his own thought, man holds the key to every situation, and contains within himself that transforming and regenerative agency by which he may make himself into what he wills." (Ibid).

As one develops and perfects that Celestial Song of Praise and Gratitude and Love he naturally becomes clothed in Light. These are the vibrations of Light. There is no darkness in them. There could not possibly be. And as one sends out these singing vibrations from the center of his soul he clothes himself in Light. He acquires a body free from sorrow or affliction or pain. He will, by continually holding himself in the radiance of those three master color vibrations of pure spirit, become a living part of the

Celestial symphony. Those glorious jewels of radiant perfection, those divine treasures held within or laid up in his own divine kingdom of heaven, become his own and all the interest and power possible to generate and increase.

Clothed in the inner radiance of these heavenly attributes the physical body becomes transmuted and exalted and one is automatically "Born of the Spirit. He becomes a translated being of beautiful perfection. This is the OVER-COMING that is required in order to fulfill the dynamic PROMISES OF Almighty God. This is the OVERCOMING REQUIRED TO DO THE WORKS WHICH Christ did and then go on TO THE GREATER WORKS!" This is the glorified Path that exalts one into complete equality and heirship with Jesus Christ, Son of the Living God. And the Path is easy and most desirable and the road is sure.

It is a Highway of exalting splendor, a Path of Purification of the heart, without bigotry or stress or striving or condemning. It is a Highway of exquisite, increasing joy and dynamic glory! It is the Path to Godhood.

And it is no longer a secret, hidden path, though few find it, simply because they look for it outside themselves. This Path is the Inner, transparent, gold-paved Highway of inner, jeweled perfection. And it is now opened wide that all who so desire may enter, and "THE WAY IS SO SIMPLE A FOOL NEED NOT ERR THEREIN—though the wicked can never cross over!" even as Isaiah testified.

But anyone who travels this Path overcomes all his self-developed, or inherent wickedness and becomes a radiant being clothed in Light and exalted in the radiance of his own heavenly treasures of perfection—a divine son of God!

Thus, this transition from mortality into immortality can be speedy or slow, according to one's power to believe and according to the intensity of his desiring. It is possible to transmute the physical body slowly, cell by cell. Or it is possible to so hold oneself in the vibrations of singing effulgence, refusing to let the darkness of evil take over, that one can transform himself into a divine being very rapidly. Take on the vibrations of praise and love and gratitude and it is possible to pass very speedily into the realms beyond mortality.

Mortal boundaries begin right where each individual stands. Each human being is bounded on every side by his own mortal thinking and feeling habits. He is not only bound by them, he is often enslaved by these boundaries for they can be narrowed down until there is no space nor outlook, nothing but a dim, murky glimpse of gray skies visible through the iron bars of his self-constructed prison cell. Mortal boundaries can be as confining and as heartbreakingly dismal as any ancient, underground dungeon. Or one can be as free as mortal thinking can make him in an expanded joy of abundant living.

But it is entirely possible for man to go beyond all mortal boundaries. These boundaries are man-made and man himself can crumble them into dust and nothingness. They are of man's own making and by man are they upheld and maintained.

The narrowest cell can be expanded and enlarged by one first expanding his mental vision as he trains his mind to think beyond his normal daily habits.

As one trains himself to think beyond mere mortal thinking his spiritual vision is opened and enlarged. His powers of visualization are invigorated and developed and become usable. "For without vision the people perish!" Or, "Without hope one must needs be in despair; and despair cometh because of iniquity!"

Now, at last it is possible to give the final keys to those doors that open up the fulfillment of glory and go beyond all mortal boundaries.

When your troubles have increased until your desperation has reached the very climax of your endurance and your world crumbles into dust and disintegrates into murky fog, then lift up your heads and rejoice. For out of the slivers and the dust of your old, crumbled world a new and better one can be formed. Out of your despairs can strength be born. "Yes! I gave men weaknesses (and troubles) that they might become strong!" This is how one becomes strong—in the OVERCOMING of the weaknesses and the utter desolation that can be increased and multiplied until the little, fighting-self is completely exhausted and is licked. And in this greatest of all calamities one will be given the vision and the power to "STAND FORTH, NEW BORN!" if so be he accepts the divine opportunity opened to him through such drastic testings.

This is so simple and so beautiful and so powerful it has been unbelievable up until the present time. And even now, only those who use this power will be able to prove its unutterable expanse of miraculous releasing as they become KNOWERS OF THE TRUTH!

When the heaped-up vicissitudes and calamities come, and they usually come in twos and threes and fours, don't panic and start frantically grabbing at the pieces in a desperation of hopeless frenzy. "Be STILL and KNOW that I AM GOD!" Yes! Stop! BE STILL! For one brief moment stand perfectly quiet. Don't start working on the fallen

roof, the caved-in wall, the collapsed garage, the mangled
car and the leveled fences.

WORK ON YOURSELF!

And you will become the greatest miracle of all! You
hold the keys of miracles in your hands. You are a living
dynamo of unbelievable power! But you can only contact
this power and use it as you control yourself and your own
vibrations.

In the great, heartbreaking emergencies learn to be
STILL, for only a moment, as you quietly whisper to the
great and All-Powerful God, the Almighty Creator of heav-
en and of earth, your own Loving Father, "Dear God, I
love you! I love you! I love you! I love you!"

Perhaps, at that moment, you can think of nothing for
which you can possibly love Him! Do not let that disturb you. Just continue to repeat those words of love and
in doing so you are releasing your disasters into His loving, capable, all-knowing, willing Hands. You are, in that
instant of relinquishment, lifting yourself into a higher
vibration in which a full contact can be made with His
Powers.

And though your expression of love may seem to be but
an empty declaration of hopeless despair and even mockery,
you are lifting yourself above the storm and the tempest
and the wreckage and disasters surrounding you and you
become the Master of that impossible situation.

You release, in that declaration of love, a higher vibration of power. It is a vibration that reaches out beyond all
mortal boundaries. And within a few minutes peace will
come. And in and through the inner vibrations of this divine contact God can begin to take charge of the situation
and "Do the works!"

You will, almost in the instant of your released panic, begin to receive comfort and assistance and wisdom and knowledge. And divine help will be sent to assist you in straightening out the disasters. And "all things will begin to work together for your good!" And you will reach a place where nothing in all existence can disturb you or distress you for you will walk in the released power of Almighty God. As you declare your love for God, in your great emergencies, you are beginning to transmute the evils and vicissitudes of your mortal life into blessings. Thus you "OVERCOME THE EVILS OF YOUR LIFE!"

Use this power upon every occasion and you will KNOW the power of God and your own divine contact with Him. Use it always and as you walk the earth you will become a worker of miracles, for they will fall into step with you — "For these miracles are to follow all those who believe!"

And soon you will realize that you are the greatest miracle of all! You will live with miracles following at your heels. You may not always comprehend the full extent of such power as you pass along your way giving out praise and love and blessing in a silence of unspoken words. But miracles will be there, unannounced and unacclaimed and so naturally brought about there will be no need of rattling brass or of clanging cymbals to bear witness of God's great powers. These are the GREATER WORKS, unheralded and unacclaimed.

As that faint little, doubtful whisper of "Dear God, I love You! I love You! I love You!" expands and increases, you will KNOW that you yourself are a divine, glorified miracle of all fulfillment. As that silent little whisper of love is increased the increasing glory of divine gratitude includes each new wonder as the miracle of yourself and your own

OVERCOMING becomes daily more apparent. Thus you OVERCOME the darkness of your life and become clothed in Light and acquire a body free from sorrow or affliction or pain — and reach the point of Faith that turns into absolute KNOWING, as you become wrapped in the power and glory of your Maker and are caught up to dwell with HIM!"

This is not fantasy! This is fact! And it is yours to prove! And it is yours to live by as you leave the desolating boundaries of mortality behind.

Begin that whispered releasing of miracles, "Dear God, I love You! I love You! I love You!" And shortly, instead of you putting forth the effort required to sing so simple a phrase, it will be singing forth in infinite power from the depths of your own being in the dynamic glory of that New Song. It will not be in words. It will be in the silence of everlasting, increasing, expanding, eternal glory. And in the releasing and perfecting of that Celestial Song of the Universe you will realize fully that you are a mighty, living miracle. And that song will be perfected by the united vibrations of praise and gratitude being added in their full perfecting of limitless power! This is the all-powerful Christ vibration being perfected and released through you. "And he who is thankful in all things shall be made glorious!" "And whoso offereth praise glorifieth me!" And with your own whispered acclamation of "Dear God, I love You!" you will have opened the doors into the realms beyond all mortal boundaries.

You will become fully aware that you are a glorified child of God, just as you were intended to be from the very beginning, for you will become glorious! And in that glory you will have the power and the Light and understanding to step beyond all mortal boundaries — FREE! Forever Free! And you will know that you are the very glory of God!

This too must be made clear, this key to take hold of and maintain that higher vibration, in which there is no darkness, is so simple anyone on the face of this earth can use it who has a mind to do so. And as one lifts his own vibrations with the glorious acknowledgement that there is a God and signifies his respect and love for Him that acknowledgment is accepted.

And no one in existence, no matter what their mental, emotional or vibrational level can remain on their present level who begins to whisper, within himself, "Dear God, I love You! I love You! I love You!" And in the development and release of that supreme key of devotion one's eyes become "Single to the glory of God!" He does become filled with Light, for this releases that vibration of Light and one becomes enfolded in it. He begins to comprehend all things! And his comprehension expands until God, in response to that glorious vibration, now perfected in the heart of man, unveils His Face. "AND THIS IS LIFE ETERNAL!"

"One evolves from the man kingdom into the God Kingdom" as he learns to control his own vibrations. Mortal, earthly emotions or vibrations can be mastered completely by anyone who so desires to evolve beyond grubby, physical mortality.

As one generates only the highest vibrations, he evolves into a condition or place of higher, joyous frequency of everlasting power, in which the darkness is overcome. Man is the selector of the realm of his existence, whether it be dismal, ugly, Hellish or perfect and sublime, according to his own understanding and desires—and according to the effort he is willing to put into the divine privilege of living his life instead of letting it live him.

The road between the two extreme realms, the lowest and the highest, is the great Highway of which Isaiah spoke, "over which the wicked can never cross." And yet he explains that it is so perfect and so simple a fool need not err therein. This road between these realms *is* the Pathway of OVERCOMING. It is the STRAIGHT AND NARROW WAY, of which Christ spoke, and which so few find. It is the Path that leads to Eternal Life, in which one need never die. It is the Path of exalted faith in which all doubts are overcome. It is a Path of high vibrations as one casts out the darkness of fears and ugliness and "OVERCOMES the evils of his life!"

This sacred, holy Path is a condition rather than a location. It is an attitude of Faith and exuberant, glorious gratitude and praising love. It is a Highway of continual, increasing rejoicing. It is the Pathway of love made perfect. And this Pathway is man himself. It is each individual, for only with man can this Pathway be selected and followed. Man is the one who must choose it. He is also the guardian of it and the traveler who fulfills its glory and receives of its effulgent rewards.

Christ truly said, "I am the Way." So is each man the Way—his own way—as he OVERCOMES the darkness and the bondage of mortality and evolves into the higher realm as his own vibrations are perfected and held in a divine symphony of singing, triumphant OVERCOMING. Then truly can mortality and all its darkness and negations be left behind.

This is the Path that leads to Life Eternal! It is more! It IS Life Eternal! And no human soul can possibly travel this

Path of learning to control his own thoughts and emotions, which are vibrations, without "arriving at the point of Faith where he will be wrapped in the power and glory of his Maker and be caught up to dwell with Him." Or he will have the privilege of choosing to return to the earth plane, having been "Born of the Spirit" in which he will have the power to do the GREATER WORKS!"

The Path is wide open! And it is yours! Come!

Chapter XVIII

THE PATHWAY OF THE GODS

"The Tree of Knowledge of Good and Evil."

And the command of God goes out: "Let there be Light!"
As He directs His thought the Light goes out in a living
flame of everlasting power as the thunders of creation roll
forth to follow that pattern and to fulfill the Almighty de-
cree of His command.

And a new world takes form from the essence of His
thoughts as that vision is manifest, first as a tangible reality
within the mind of God. This is spiritual creation. This
thought, this inner vision is the pattern to which the elements are drawn into the power of its forming and its be-
getting. For all things were first a thought, a vision, a breath
of life divine breathed into the birthing of each holy need,
to give it body and to make it live. This is creation as it
follows the pattern that the light of thought designs or
draws for is fulfillment.

"AND ALL THAT THE FATHER HAS IS YOURS!"
To man God gave the priceless gift divine, *the mind!* To
each man was given a mind with which to think, to dream,
to fashion and to form the vision his heart holds forth, for
man too is a creator — a God in the making. And for man's
use God set the universe and all that it contains! The creative force of Light is ever man's to use, even as it is God's.
It is man's to command and to form into atoms as it is

215

drawn into the pattern of his dreamings. For out of these infinitesimal rays of living, cosmic light, which fill the universe, are atoms formed.

And atoms are the foundations and the substance and the essence of all tangible, solid, material things. And each atom holds a living spark of God held lovingly enfolded within its embrace. Within each atom is contained the love, the intelligence and the power of God. Atoms are the building blocks of all that is visible.

Atoms, created from the rays of living light are gathered into form by thought, until reality becomes apparent to the most ordinary and dense of men as their lowered vision beholds only the dust.

And so to each man God gave a mind with which to think, to dream, to form the patterns of his inner musings, by the living force and energy of his own brooding. And those thoughts will take form, to flourish or to die, according to the attention with which one's garden of desire is nourished and sustained.

Such is the power of that divine "Tree of Good or Evil" which each man holds within the center of his being, which is his own Eden — his soul. Each man, by the selection of his thoughts, can bring forth an abundance of all that his thoughts embrace.

This is the Tree of Creation — the "Tree of Knowledge of Good and Evil." This is the tree of which man is a branch, and each man produces and brings forth either the *good* or the *evil* of his own thinking. And some produce a contaminated mixture of both love and the hates of their own creating. And *each man will be judged by his idle thoughts*. This is truth indeed. "A man is WHAT HE THINKS, not what he thinks he is."

That man will be judged by his idle thoughts is most assuredly true. And he will be destroyed by his wicked, polluted, selfish thoughts. Or he can be eternally exalted by his noble thoughts. A man is noble, or craven or mediocre or completely defiled by the caliber of his thoughts. And from the moment the fruit of that Tree of Knowledge was tasted all men henceforward until the end of time have been and will be held accountable for the products of their minds.

This amazing mystery or "mist-tree" has been ignored as man has tried to blot from his mind the memory of its producing. He has sought always to close his eyes to his own responsibility in regards to the fruit of that tree. He is only childishly seeking to be held unaccountable for his thoughts, his moods, his tempers and his mortal leanings. But he will be held accountable even for his idle thoughts. And the fruit is good or evil according to the thoughts of each individual.

This is the TREE of which Christ is the Vine — and men are the branches — and God is the Husbandman. And man is the producer of those fruits. And whether they are "good" or whether they are "evil" is entirely of man's choosing.

The Tree of Knowledge of "Good or evil" is also the Tree of Death. For by its fruits came death into the world. And every living soul is fed and nourished upon the fruit of his own thinking. And he who thinks only filthy, angry, evil or selfish, greedy, defiled thoughts is required to subsist upon the evil of his own corrupted, degenerate, contaminated poisons of lusts, dishonesties or selfishness, his hates and evils is feeding upon deadly pollution—and HE WILL DIE! For this is the Tree that brought death into the world — and is still bringing death into the world for each individual who brings forth its evils.

However, the fruits of that Tree *can be* beautiful and glorious and eternally life-giving, instead of bitter and poisonous and deadly.

It is entirely according to each man's thinking as to which type of fruit he will bring forth through the power or the use he makes of his golden gift, the mind. "For as a man thinketh in his heart so is he!" And as he thinketh in his heart so will he produce or bring forth the fruit upon which he himself will be nourished. "For man does not live by earthly bread alone." He lives (or dies) upon the fruit of his own thinking.

This is the law of eternity! It cannot be changed! Neither can it fail! It is as definitely positive as the rotation of the earth, as its days and its nights and its times and its seasons. BUT, MAN CAN CHANGE HIS THINKING HABITS AND THUS NOT ONLY CHANGE HIS LIFE BUT GLORIFY IT. The *law* itself *is justice*. The power to be able to change one's thought habits *is mercy!*

"The land thou seest will I give unto thee!" Yes! The fruit you produce through your thinking habits, or inner vision, I will give unto you as the diet upon which you will be required to subsist, for the harvest is of your own planting and your own bringing forth.

"*If your eyes be single to My glory your whole bodies will be filled with Light and there shall be no darkness in you.*" (There will be no evils, no poisons, no deadliness or corruption). "And you will be filled with Light and comprehend all things!"

If one is filled with Light, so that he begins to comprehend all things, he will first of all comprehend and KNOW fully the law which brings about all conditions, either good or evil, according to the inner vision, or according to the thoughts he holds within his mind. He will comprehend the full meaning of that "Tree of Knowledge of Good and Evil." He will understand fully and with reverent awe, that he is a branch of that Tree and is therefore responsible for the type of fruit he produces.

If an individual wallows in the slime of self-pity, gorges himself on the lusts and corruption of his flesh, seethes in the wraths of his hates, robs or cheats, through the greeds of his blind selfishness, then the fruits he is subsisting upon are sour, evil, shriveled, contaminated and poison. And his body will be corrupted and defiled and will rot in the grave as his spirit, naked and unclothed with the precious gift of the flesh will wander forth to await its judgment: "For ALL THE DEAD, small and great *must* stand before the throne of God and be judged." And the shame of their nakedness will appear as they are held accountable for the loss of their bodies. And for those who "Overcome", which overcoming means also the overcoming of death, there is no judgment — but only glory!

It is only possible for one "To receive a fulness of joy when the body and the spirit are inseparably united!" And this condition was meant to be achieved while in this life. The body can be exalted, purified and so spiritualized through love and the worship of God and a reverence for one's fellowman the physical can take on the purity and eternal vibrations of the exalted status of the Spirit — and DEATH CAN BE OVERCOME!

As one understands the dynamic wonder of that Tree of Knowledge and produces only the "good" of that glorious Tree, he becomes powerful! He fulfills completely the laws of Christ in a splendor of divine love and gratitude and exulting praise. He becomes purified and is cleansed from all sin. He becomes exalted and naturally, and without effort or striving, he overcomes death — the last enemy, according to the promises of Jesus Christ. Christ not only taught by words, that a record might remain, he proved His words by fulfilling them. He proved everything He taught by His own life. He overcame death and left this challenge for us: "If ye believe on me, the works which I do shall ye do also, even GREATER WORKS THAN THESE SHALL YE DO!"

And so, that great mystery or "mist-tree" that has been veiled in the mist of the ages, becomes fully revealed in its breath-taking glory as the "TREE OF LIFE" also! It is the veil or mist that has enshrouded this Tree down the centuries that must now be rent.

One has but to guard his thoughts and so control his emotions, his actions and his reactions with a glory of released love and good-will, and joy and happiness will be the banquet of his feasting as "he begins to grow and wax strong" in the perfection of his diet.

As one fulfills those first two Great Commandments he truly fulfills all the laws and rises above the law in a triumphant *overcoming of mortality,* and in so doing he will be "Wrapped in the power and glory of his Maker and will be caught up to dwell with HIM!" Such is the promise!

As man learns of the power of his thoughts and the meaning and the effects of them, first upon himself and then of their effect upon the world, and uses that KNOWLEDGE, he becomes a master. And from mastery he progresses onward into a glorious, radiant being, completely freed from mortality and death. Then he is prepared to move onward toward divinity and Godhood.

The fruit of the Tree of Knowledge is to make one wise.

But wisdom only comes to those who benefit from experience, whether their own or that of others. One does not need to personally live in the eternal gloom of despondency, the agony of despair, the filthy evil of hopelessness in order to gain wisdom. Too many who permit themselves to be entrapped in these slimy bogs of darkness have willingly descended into those hideous depths through their own thinking habits. No one can be forced to wallow in such contaminated defilement unless he is WILLING or completely *unwise.*

"*And if your eyes be single to my glory your whole body shall be filled with Light and there shall be no darkness in you. And that body which is filled with Light comprehends all things!* And I will unveil my face to you!" Such is the promise of Almighty God and His promises fail not!

And if one's eyes are single to the glory of God it is utterly impossible for him to dwell mentally upon a negative, dark, dismal plane of doubt, fear, frustration, greed, lusts, hate, envy or self-pity. And as his thoughts are consciously held upon that highest level, he is gradually spiritualizing his body as he feeds upon the most perfect of all fruits, the "Good" of that precious Tree of Knowledge.

In this divine control of thoughts and feelings and perfect adoration, love will pour out through every living cell of the soul and the body. "And the fruit of the TREE OF LIFE *is the love of God* which is shed forth through the hearts of the children of men." And man's heart is prepared for this glorious experience as he trains his mind to "*Think only the most beautiful things possible!*"

This precious fruit of Life Eternal is man's to partake of always. And in it is contained the fulness of joy and a complete KNOWLEDGE OF GOD for "He will unveil His face to you! It will be in His own time, and in His own way, and according to His own will!" And *His time* will be when that individual is ready and prepared for so great a glory.

It will be after one has been "tested and tried in all things, and God finds that individual is determined to serve Him at all hazards. Then will he find his calling and election made sure!" This holy preparation is accomplished by the controlling of one's thoughts. It is achieved in the releasing of praise, in the joy of happiness, in the cultivation of singing ecstasy as one rejoices in every blessing. And as he thus gives thanks and rejoices his blessings will multiply and increase. Such is the law!

This complete glory of revealing will be open and unfolded and will become one's own as he arises in his faith to lay claim to his own divine heritage, accepts the responsibility of doing his own thinking. And as he knowingly and with full understanding selects the caliber of his thoughts, holding his mind single to the glory of God, in an inner joy of praise and love and gratitude, then will the wondrous everlasting GOOD of his own divine thinking bear the fulness of its perfection for his joy and glorification. In this divine KNOWLEDGE, as one uses this knowledge, he truly "Evolves from the man kingdom into the God Kingdom!" "And all things will become subject unto him, both in heaven and on earth; the Light and the Life; the Spirit and the Power, sent forth by the will of the Father, through Jesus Christ, His Son!"

PROMISES?! Yes! The promises are great and endless and impossible to comprehend in their fulness until one begins to use his mind and his will to explore, to live and to lay claim to them. "For God is a God of truth, and cannot lie!" "He is no respecter of persons!" These most holy, divine, almost unspeakable promises are yours to PROVE and to "take hold of, as the best gifts," as Paul revealed.

Oh, come with me, you blessed ones! Leave the dark, dreary road of mortality behind! Let your minds become single to the glory of God, to the splendor of His perfection, to the breath-taking beauty of His creations, to the love of His sharing, to the gratitude of His blessings, to the joy of His existence! And begin to think as He thinks! Hold your thoughts high! Keep your vision exalted! And rejoice evermore!

This Tree of Knowledge is most assuredly alive and precious. It has been alive and producing for each individual according to his own thoughts and actions and reactions since time itself began. Few indeed have comprehended the stupendous import of that Tree. Many have assumed that that Tree contains the instinctive knowledge of right and wrong. It most certainly does just that! But it does far more than that! It is the Tree upon which grow the fruits of every man's thinking and acting habits. Thus the responsibility of one's own thinking habits is his own. And the results are his. And he will be held responsible for them. He is accountable for every vibration he releases from within himself. For he is assuredly a branch of that Tree and from his own thought energies the fruits he brings forth into his own life are produced.

When one accepts of the "evil" of that Tree of Knowledge there come into his life all the desolating experiences, the nagging vicissitudes, the heaped-up mountains of seeming bad luck, the dismaying misfortunes of ill health and deterioration as one plods his weary way along life's difficult, burdensome road to that dreary back door of DEATH!

It is possible that one may be unaware that through his greedy and dishonest procedures he is carrying the curse of the broken law of gravity which is one of the physical, mortal laws. The law of gravity and the law of mortality and the law of death are one and the same law. This physical law is the law of "seeking for one's own." The higher law as revealed by Paul in I Corinthians, the thirteenth chapter, is the law of Charity, which "Seeketh not its own!" In breaking the lower law of gravity and of mortality one usually goes a step lower and seeks for more than is his own or for more than he is rightfully entitled to. He grasps that which he has no right to, through dishonest procedures or greed. When the earthly law of gravity is broken the burden of its curse follows beyond the grave and into eternity. Those who break this mortal law are doubly subject unto death, which is the fulfilled law of earth and mortality and gravity — or the grave.

But this road is one of individual choosing. No one need travel it. It is a loathsome road, paved with the slimy evils of pride and falsehood and broken lives. It is the road of DEATH!

But "death has no claim on him who overcomes all sin!" so declared the ancients. And many of them proved it. Christ reaffirmed this higher law. And it is yours, this wondrous law of glory and of life everlasting and of joy unspeakable and of power ineffable! It is yours to live — and to PROVE!

The stupendous, glorious wonder of living His words — and of PROVING THEM—belongs to every living soul who desires to put them to the test. And as each individual assumes this responsibility he will need none to teach him, for God Himself will become his teacher! And as one *lives* the teachings he not only KNOWS of their power, he is able to use that power — the power of creation in its fulness — the power of healing and of bringing forth from the universal substance that which will satisfy every good desire, and his daily needs, for all these things will be added unto him. Such will walk with God!

As one takes hold of the KNOWLEDGE of the power of the "good" and the "evil" of the *Tree of Life* — or *death* — and uses his precious gift of choosing his thoughts for "good" and for the glory of God, he begins to take upon himself that same glory. He truly becomes glorious! Or, as the precious writer of the Odes of Solomon declared: "He who would interpret the wonders of the Lord will be dissolved and will become that which he interprets!"

Interpret the love of God and become that love personified! Interpret the beauty of God's fabulous creations and in your own life become the personification of exquisite beauty! Interpret the breath-taking glory of that Celestial Song of Creation, of praise and love and gratitude, and become the creative power of all perfection.

Lift your thoughts to the Glory of God and hold them there and you will become glorious! Radiant! Filled with Light!

CHAPTER XIX

A GOD IN THE MAKING!

A desire to become a servant in the hands of God can only be understood by the righteous. The wicked and the rebellious can never comprehend a desire so great because they would not be willing to relinquish one single selfish wish for anything in all of "Kingdom Come!" Only their own level of mortal, degraded concepts and lusts are desirable to them.

They do not realize that behind this devotional service a great and mighty truth lies hidden. "He who becomes a follower will of necessity advance until he becomes a leader!" This is the law of progression and of responsibility and of service. It is the divine law of fulfillment, though one may not even give it a thought. For there are those who desire to serve for pure love — love for God — love for their fellowmen and the love that requires action and fulfillment in a devotion of self-sacrifice.

It is desire which plays the role of unfolding in this revealing chapter, even as it does in the preceding one.

Only those who have advanced to the point where they love God above all else are capable of holding within them the desire to serve Him completely.

And those who wish to serve Him must seek first to know His will. They truly wish to train their own minds to be able to hear, that they "might speak no word save He commands it — or perform no act except He reveals it." This is the

Christ type of service — and only through such service is it possible to begin to do the works which He did, for love and joy are the power of its perfecting.

There are many of those precious ones who are being prepared, or who are preparing themselves, to become servants in His hands in very deed. Yes — in very deed — and in all things.

And there are many who are desirous of attaining this point of service who do not yet know the way of its fulfilling. And many erroneously think it is done by shouting and preaching in a fanatical disquietude. Be it known, this higher type of service is accomplished in humility and not by flinging oneself from the temple pinnacle. This perfect type of service is reserved for the *elect*. And those are the *elect* who *elect* to serve God fully and completely and not themselves or their pride or their proud self-righteousness.

All things are fulfilled through growth and desire. Even Christ, so we are informed, "Grew from grace to grace!" So must each man grow and develop from one step to the next. No individual can possibly take that complete stairway of perfection and overcoming and power in one stride, no matter what his pre-existent training or calling may be. And there are many who think God should set aside His holy laws of fulfillment for them as soon as they catch the first glimpse of this higher way. This is as impossible as it is for an infant to become a man in an instant. This requires the progress of growth and of development.

Growth can only come through LIVING THE LAWS — not just through believing them. "Be ye therefore doers of the word, not hearers only, thus deceiving your own selves." To be a doer of any law one must not only accept it, but he must fulfill it by performing it. This entails the practice of actually experiencing all that is connected with the power of fulfillment of that law, whatever it may be. One must experience growth by fulfilling the laws pertaining to it. And this takes a great deal of living.

And only "after one has been *tested and tried* in all things will he find his calling and election made sure." Every lesson one learns, along this upward path, must needs be followed by a *test* to see if that individual is "determined to serve God at all hazards." And that word "hazards" is a big word. It can include many things.

This testing is that which will prove whether one will hold his thoughts exalted regardless of the circumstances which he may be called to face. It is the test to find out if one "will be *thankful in all things* that he might become glorious!" It is the test to see if he can abide on that high level of living, exulting, joyous praise and refuse to sink mentally into the "evils" of despair. This testing holds the power of his exaltation.

One may be tested like Job. Or one may be tested like the prophets of old or the Apostles of the Lord, but there is not one of them who would change places with any one else on earth — not for all the honors and wealth of this world. And theirs was the greatest choice. And their testing was easy because of their love for God. Love makes all things easy and beautiful!

One may be required to pass every test possible — and some that seem to be impossible. Yet, through love they become but golden opportunities. And it must be remembered that "God never gives a commandment save He prepares the way for its fulfillment." It is the love and the willingness alone that is being tested, after all. And to those who love greatly every test is but a divine and holy privilege.

Let the wonder of His comfort enter your hearts in these holy words: "Your peace was prepared for you, before ever your war (or testing) was." (Ode of Solomon 8:8). No difficulty or test can possibly come that does not have within it the great peace and reward which was held in reserve for you before ever the test was given.

Anyone can PROVE this point. All that is necessary is to accept of the irksome condition and bless it with an increasing song of praise and love. And no matter what that condition is it can be transmuted into beauty and perfection. This glorious law of transmutation is every man's to use, even as it was Christ's to use as He glorified His death upon the cross. All tests are blessings in disguise. All difficulties are but the stepping stones to glory.

And no law or commandment was ever released that does not contain the seed or the germ of its own fulfilling.

Those tests can only become glorified stepping stones as one keeps his vision and his thoughts high in a continual singleness to the glory of God. Then, as one treads upon those trials of dismay they become paved with gold— and he becomes flame-shod.

NOTHING IS IMPOSSIBLE either to endure, to overcome or to achieve! No testing is greater than one's strength and endurance if he meets those difficulties with pure adoration in his soul. There is no testing or law or condition that cannot be glorified and exalted. Within man is the power of transmutation and glorification!

This higher law is one of *giving* and of *forgiving,* of relinquishing and of blessing. It is the pathway of love and of praising and of *giving thanks in all things!* It is the law of rejoicing even at what might appear to be a violent setback. Yet within those seeming setbacks and trials may be the keys of one's graduation—the glory of his victory. This is the pathway of progress, this road of "overcoming" —this divine highway to the stars!

And this sacred path of advancing and of refining and of purifying is the path one must travel willingly. If one travels it in joy and gratitude the tests are not even felt as tests or trials or impossible burdens. They are the divine opportunities of continual advancement.

"And he who is thankful in all things shall be made glorious! And the things of this earth shall be added unto him an hundred-fold! Yes! More!" These are not just words! These are promises of Almighty God and they can be fulfilled and proved by anyone who is willing to LIVE them.

Never permit a mere straw to be your stumbling block or block your way.

Never stumble without picking yourself up and going on with renewed determination and energy.

Never allow the magnitude of this glorious pathway to overwhelm you. It is traveled by taking just one step at a time. In traveling it thus the Way is easy and the journey a joy. And it is only as one joyously travels each step that he ascends unto the heights.

Nothing is impossible. And this path of love and service and gratitude is the road divine in which one "evolves from the man kingdom into the God Kingdom" if so be he is willing to unload the burden of his own weaknesses and faults.

And no one can travel this divine "Straight and Narrow Way" without reaching divinity. This is the path of love and mercy and compassion and all are invited to step out of their ugly, physical rags of mortal thinking into the realms of inspired, holy thinking, into the realms of divinity.

No one can possibly live nobly without becoming noble! No one can worship and adore without becoming adorable, if he does it in joy. No one can give thanks or "become thankful in all things without becoming glorious!" No one can possibly hold compassion and mercy and a tender desire to assist, when needed, without becoming a literal co-worker with God.

And there is no law or rule or commandment given that is not possible to fulfill as each becomes an experience of utter glory—when LIVED! It is only in the LIVING of God's holy laws that their unspeakable power and beauty can be revealed.

Every command is but the loving invitation of God towards one's own exaltation. Every law contains the divine pattern of one's own fulfillment. Every tiny bit of instruction becomes the pure gold as one ascends along that divine and holy pathway into Godhood.

And in the living of the laws one becomes the master of them. Such a one becomes radiant and filled with Light as he comprehends all things and becomes endowed with power.

"A servant in His Hands?"

No! A feasted, divine Son of glory!

There is nothing impossible in existence! The very word "IMPOSSIBLE" is God's greatest word of POWER!

God will always be God! And each individual will always be himself. But there will be a difference between them according to their own preparing. Only those who learn to travel that glorious "Straight and Narrow Path" of triumphant OVERCOMING can possibly become Gods and Goddesses—or "Elohim!" Only these can become joint-heirs with Jesus Christ. Only these will be allowed to create, for the others have never brought the Light into subjection. And Light is the "Substance out of which all created things are formed." It is "The substance of things hoped for!" It is the material out of which atoms are fashioned and form into nebulous gatherings. And out of this ethereal substance moisture is condensed into seas. And out of the seas the dry land appears. Thus from one step of creation into a more dense, tangible substance "The worlds were formed by faith."

As these advancing ones travel the pioneering road of their divine OVERCOMING along that Straight and Narrow Way they are traveling the road of Godhood. And the key to that door is to "Love God with all your heart, soul, mind and strength" for out of your love a God is being formed—YOURSELF!

As these advancing Sons of God continue to move onward and upward, in their own struggle of "overcoming," the darkness is forever banished. They not only become filled with Light; they actually *become that LIGHT!* And "That Light becomes subject unto them" according to the dynamic, unbreakable promise of God. And as that Light becomes subjected unto one he henceforth has the power and the intelligence to command it—and to send it forth to form atoms and to create any substance or material or object needed. These creations will come forth according to the vision and need of that dynamic one. Such advanced ones have the power to command that Light to "STAND FORTH" and it will obey as they focus their attention upon it. This is the power of creation in action. This is the power of Godhood.

Or, as Paul revealed in I Cor. 8:5-6, as follows: "For though there be those that are called Gods, whhether in heaven or in earth (AS THERE BE GODS MANY, AND LORDS MANY,) But to us there is but one God, the Father, of whom are all things, and we in him; and one Lord Jesus Christ, by whom are all things and we by him."

Yes, there are Lords many and Gods many. But no matter how high we ascend, our own gracious Father and our beloved Savior, Jesus Christ, will always be ahead of us, leading us ever onward and upward as they, too, continue to ascend and progress along that glorified spiral of eternity.

Again, that testimony of gods many is verified in the following: (Psalms 82:1) "God standeth in the congregation of the mighty; HE JUDGETH AMONG THE GODS."

And in the sixth verse of the above quoted Psalm is added this pertinent information; "I said, Ye Are Gods; and all of you are the children of the Most High." This holy scripture is verified by Jesus Christ, Himself, the perfect, infallible authority, as recorded by St. John 10:34-35, as follows: "Is it not written in your law, I said ye are Gods?

"If He called them Gods unto whom the word of God came, and THE SCRIPTURE CANNOT BE BROKEN: say ye of him, whom the Father sanctified, and sent into the world, Thou blasphemest; because I said I am the Son of God?"

Yes, there are Lords many and Gods many. And they are the Sons of God who are taking upon themselves the responsibility of this divine journey toward Godhood.

And with these Gods there are Goddesses. The ancient Hebrew name of God was "Elohim" which is a masculine plural of a feminine noun, meaning God and His Mate.

When Christ called upon "Eloi" from the cross, he was speaking to His Father in the singular. But in the ancient Hebrew, the title for Deity was Elohim — "For man is not without the woman or woman without the man in the Lord"—or when they reach the state of Godhood.

And this holy Pathway Christ revealed, of power and Truth and Light, contains "the great and mighty things that mortal eyes have never looked upon, nor mortal ears ever heard"—For these things have never before been revealed in the fulness of their breath-taking glory. This brief glimpse is disclosed partially to the heart of man in order that this journey to the very stars might be comprehended.

This progressing group of anointed ones who are taking part, or who will take part in this great Spiritual journey of the present day, will go onward to the point of their own complete purification. And they are, perhaps without fully realizing it at first, preparing themselves for Godhood.

These mighty, progressing ones will continue to go onward, forever onward.

And after they have visited many realms and many spheres and many galaxies and continued in their gathering of wisdom and knowledge and perfection they will be sent out into the great realms of "Outer Darkness" where the Light of Gods has never penetrated. And there, in the far-out reaches of the universe, they will use that Light which they have developed and brought forth right within themselves, to light up that darkness. For that Light has become truly subjected unto them in all its vast fulness of power.

And they will have the authority and the power to issue that dynamic command, "LET THERE BE LIGHT!" And that Light will go forth as living rays, which will curl upon themselves to form atoms when the distinct plan of their fulfilling is presented. Thus will form atoms from the rays of living Light—and those atoms will congeal into tangible materials to form worlds.

This Light is the "Substance of things hoped for." It is the FAITH out of which the worlds were created—and will continue to be created to the end of eternity and beyond. Those living rays of Light are this very substance—and can be directed to form tangible materials according to the plan and the vision and the need. This is the substance of "Things waiting to become" understood anciently.

Heb. 11:3: "Through faith we understand that the worlds were formed by the Word (or command) of God so that things which are seen were not made of things which do appear."

And since "Faith is the substance, or material of things hoped for, and is the evidence of things not seen," as revealed in verse one of this chapter of John, it is plain that this great power or element of Creation was used even by Gods in the formation of worlds. And this same material or substance is man's to use—for "All that the Father has, is yours!"

And these great and mighty ones, graduates from the school of gods, with a Holy Trinity—and with their fulfilling quorum of Archangels, will watch to see that their commands are obeyed. Or they will hold forth the plan or pattern until it takes form and "IS GOOD!" or perfect, according to their visioning.

And for these great and mighty Elohim the road of their progressing has only then found the full purpose of its long training, the striving and the "overcoming" of all the past darkness and negation—and the fears.

From this point, as the eons of glory move onward, so will they continue to progress in the unending system of "Eternal glory!" They will go on to create solar systems— and galaxies and eventually universes—and to rule over them in love and mercy and wisdom and compassion—for by this time they will be directing or assisting their own spirit children who have also advanced into the status of Gods.

This is the eternal plan and the pattern of our Almighty God, our Heavenly Father, Creator of heaven and of earth and of His Beloved Son, Jesus Christ and of the Holy Ghost and of the divine Quorum of Archangels. For as God proclaimed, "This is my work and my glory, to bring to pass the immortality and the Eternal Life of man!"

This is the path awaiting the treading of man as he paves the road he travels with the transparent gold of his own advancing footsteps.

"Beloved, now are we the sons of God, and it doth not yet appear what we shall be." (I John 3:2-3). At the time when John, the Beloved, spoke these words it had not yet been revealed—the full glory of man's possibilities as he moves ever upward along that Holy Pathway of the Gods. But now, in this last day, in this glorious age of revealing, it is made manifest—yea—all that man shall or can be.

Those who think they have achieved all, when they shout aloud to be heard of men that they have been *"saved,"* thinking they have reached the end of all goals, are but small children indeed.

The great goal is not merely "salvation!" It is exaltation! It is even more! It is Godhood! It is eternal glory with all the power of knowledge and of doing and of creating, held forever in their hands! And be it here known, there is no FATHER in existence, whether mortal or heavenly, who does not desire and expect his children to be all that He IS!

This holy glimpse of the "Promised Land" am I permitted to unveil for a moment to your understandings.

Open your eyes to see and your hearts to comprehend. And listen to the inner teachings of your own souls—for within you is contained the very "Record of Heaven!"

Our own Mighty God, Creator of our heaven and our earth is calling us back into His presence to be assigned and prepared to build worlds—and solar systems and galaxies and eventually universes—"And the end of His doings none can find out!"

At the present time our work is to finish our schooling along this pioneering pilgrimage before us as we travel this divine Highway of our own complete purification as we PROVE ALL THINGS—in order that we may use them.

This divine Path is more accessible at the present time than it has ever been before since the creation of this world. And it is quite possible to travel this "Straight and Narrow Way" that leads to the very throne of God.

This is the day of that Journey's beginning! This is the day of its revealing and of its unfolding! This is YOUR day! You and the great and Mighty Sons and Daughters of Eternal, glorious God of Creation as you progress into Creatorship yourselves.

By the power of Almighty God have I been commanded to write! And I lie not!

Chapter XX

THE DIFFERENT DEGREES OF GLORY

The world has been deluded for centuries by the idea of a heaven and a hell, with nothing in between except a narrow line. The realms between those two extreme degrees are as varied and numerous as there are degrees of righteousness and evil.

With the information concerning godhood and the possibility of individuals from this earth finally being able to attain unto such ultimate glory it should be quite evident why it is so necessary to begin right here in mortality to develop divine self-control and majesty.

The only thing that really matters in eternity is not what one knows or has or professes to be but only what he IS! God-like virtues and qualities alone can make one God-like and prepare him for dominion and rulership among the high hierarchy of heaven as he travels this sacred Highway of the Gods—"This Road to Zion or to the complete purification of the heart!" This Straight and Narrow Way, which leads to Life Eternal, is the one in which one need never die. But to live forever without a goal or a purpose is meaningless nonsense.

Only those who OVERCOME and are truly "Born of the Spirit" can possibly become co-heirs or joint-heirs with the Lord Jesus Christ! And this must be partially achieved while one is still in the flesh, otherwise the flesh cannot be exalted and glorified and then one is required to relinquish the body for a period of time or until the appointed season of the resurrection when he will have to stand before God and be judged, according to everything he did or failed to do, while in mortality.

Rev. 21:7: "He that OVERCOMETH shall inherit all things!"

The resurrection does not change anyone too much except to return to them their bodies, no longer subject to death. Rev. 20:12-14: "And I saw the dead small and great stand before God; and the books were opened; and another book was opened, which is the book of life: and the dead were judged (AND WILL HAVE TO ANSWER) out of those things written in the books, ACCORDING TO THEIR WORKS!"

This is the resurrection and this is the judgment, which Paul admonished the Saints to leave behind, as he counseled them to "GO ON UNTO PERFECTION," in which these lesser things would have no part. (Heb. 6:1-2)

In I Cor. 15:40-42, is given the following information: "There are also celestial bodies, and bodies terrestrial; but the glory of the celestial is one, and the glory of the terrestrial is another.

"There is one glory of the sun, and another of the moon, another glory of the stars: for one star differeth from another in glory.

"So also is the resurrection of the dead!"

This glory of the stars, which is as varied as the stars in heaven in brilliance and in dimness and in the stages in between, is called "Telestial glory." Though in some realms or upon some lesser stars there is very little glory at all. The myriad degrees of glory in the Telestial realms are prepared for the numerous types of individuals of this earth who are resurrected with their sins and their weaknesses still upon them.

The pickpockets and petty thieves will probably be placed together where they can pick each other's pockets until they are satiated with the futility of such perverse, wasted, contrary behavior and with all their souls yearn for a way of escape.

The liars will automatically seek their own realms where lies can be told and retold until only the liar himself is listening to his tales and is eventually awakened to the point of sheer agonizing frustration as he begins to comprehend the desolation and the dreariness of his condition, and begins to yield himself to a new desiring.

The lust-filled, greedy, murderous individuals will be sent out to worlds as insignificant as those most obscure, dim, pinpoints of light—worlds completely without glory—stars without honor. These are the souls who will be clothed in "eternal shame" as Daniel describes.

In Revelations 21:8 is given this dynamic information: "The fearful, and unbelieving, and the abominable, the murderers and whoremongers; and sorcerers, and idolaters, and all liars, shall have their part in the lake which burneth with fire and brimstone; which is the second death."

It is at first most startling to hear that the FEARFUL and UNBELIEVERS are the ones who head that list of desecrated, defiled individuals who receive no glory whatsoever.

Why are the FEARFUL and the UNBELIEVERS the first on the list of great sinners, those listed for a degree of damnation, known as the second death?

Let us examine this information. We learn that it is not the "MEEK" who are the timid, groveling, cringing weaklings, but the FEARFUL! The fearful are the ones who lack courage! They lack initiative! They lack the qualities to probe into anything their orthodoxed minds have not already accepted, that they might KNOW TRUTH! They have a deadly fear of TRUTH lest it undermine their false sand castles of error and dethrone false ideas and their false gods. They are cringing cowards, living in their own dark prisons of unprogressiveness. They are damned and realize it not. Damnation is only the state where one's progress is stopped and he ceases to advance because of his own rejection of Light.

The fearful can never accept the divine challenge of Jesus, Christ, Son of the Living God, "TO PROVE ALL THINGS!" They can prove nothing, not even their own erroneous beliefs. By shouting louder than anyone else they seal their ears and their minds to any new information or divine enlightenment. They do not even have the courage to look at one single new truth or to seek to compare the light with their own darkness.

TRUTH itself is the greatest reward in all existence. And those who seek to prove any idea in prayerful humility, will be "taught of God" and will receive a KNOWLEDGE OF TRUTH. And those who KNOW THE TRUTH are forever free! Abundantly, Gloriously FREE! They step forth with courage and in joy as they travel the Straight and Narrow Way of eternal progress.

Those who are cringing cowards know nothing of "The Life More Abundant" which Christ came to give! They do not really know how to live in joy and happiness. They are bound by every conformity and by their lack of confidence in God or in His powers to protect them from evil. How can "they trust in Him with all their hearts" when they trust only in their own understandings? These FEAR-FUL ONES deny the Holy Ghost, refusing It the power to function in their lives as the Revealer of ALL TRUTH. Their very lives become skimped and warped and ugly and they know nothing at all about "THE LIFE MORE ABUN-DANT" which Christ came to give.

No wonder the FEARFUL are the first on the list to be cast out with the dogs and the unbelievers and the whore-mongers and the sorcerers and murderers.

The FEARFUL lack love completely. In fact, they have never known love, either for God, or for others. Nor do they have any love or desire for the TRUTH—the great emancipator! For the PROMISE is: "KNOW THE TRUTH, AND THE TRUTH WILL SET YOU FREE! AND HE WHO IS FREE SHALL BE FREE INDEED." Neither do they understand nor believe in this eternal Truth of Al-mighty God: "PERFECT LOVE CASTS OUT ALL FEAR!"

Man is commanded to *"search all things* and HOLD FAST TO THAT WHICH IS GOOD!" In order to know fully what is GOOD one would have to search into all things, discarding that which is evil as he trusts in God with all his heart. Then only can one KNOW TRUTH— and HOLD FAST TO IT!"

The DOUBTING or UNBELIEVERS are those who are always looking for an excuse to disbelieve in order that they might be exempt from all responsibility or FULFILL-ING the great TRUTHS and admonition of God. They never seek to PROVE anything but only to DISPROVE. They dig deep into the darkness in order to cling to every adverse doctrine that they might justify themselves in seek-ing to escape every divine responsibility. It is more difficult for these who flee from TRUTH to open up their own sealed minds than it is to relinquish their lives to the darkness.

And so it is that the FEARFUL and the UNBELIEVING are the leaders who stand at that broad, open Way which leads to destruction. And giving their full allegiance to that broad, open path of darkness they stand insisting that the entire world enter therein. To these who have refused to accept the Light of Christ or the powers of the divine Holy Spirit to lead them into ALL TRUTH can only follow the erring multitudes, the popular dogmas as they close their eyes to TRUTH. Only in mass conformity can they feel secure. These are the weaklings and the cowards, not the MEEK.

"Behold, I come quickly; and my reward is with me, TO GIVE TO EVERY MAN ACCORDING AS HIS WORKS SHALL BE:" (or rather, has been).

"I am Alpha and Omega, the beginning and the end, the first and the last.

"BLESSED ARE THEY THAT DO HIS COMMAND-MENTS, *that they may have right to the Tree of Life, and may enter in through the gates into the city.*

"For without are dogs, and sorcerers, and whoremongers, and idolaters, and whosoever loveth and maketh a lie." (Rev. 33:12-15).

This quotation and the previous one telling of the second death are both from the Book of Revelations and each verifies the other and substantiates the dynamic truth that there will be many who will come forth in the resurrection without any glory whatsoever.

Daniel verifies this fact in the twelfth chapter and the second verse of his sacred work, as follows: *"And many of them that sleep in the dust of the earth shall awake,* SOME TO EVERLASTING LIFE, AND SOME TO SHAME AND EVERLASTING CONTEMPT."

Then we have this beautiful record of Christ's prayer: "Now they have known that all things whatsoever thou hast given me are of thee.

"For I have given unto them the words which thou gavest me; and they have received them, and have known surely that I came out from thee, and they have believed that thou didst send me.

"FOR THEM I PRAY: I PRAY NOT FOR THE WORLD, but for them which thou hast given me; for they are thine." (John 17:7-9).

Always there have been the *rewards* and the *penalties* attached to every action. And yet there are still many who see not and who believe not the words of God, but accept rather the Devil's doctrine that all will be redeemed with equal glory through the atoning blood of Jesus Christ, regardless of what they did or did not do in this life. And such make God a liar and make His word null and void.

Each and every soul will be exalted or retarded in his eternal progress according to his own desiring and fulfilling as he lives according to the cravings of the flesh or according to the righteous desirings of his own inner soul.

Then this word stands forth in a PROMISE *of eternal meaning*: "THE MEEK SHALL INHERIT THE EARTH!" Not the unrighteous, not the proud and selfish, not the wicked, not the lustful or the dangerously greedy or the profane—BUT THE MEEK!

And now, the "MEEK" must be introduced in their full robes of glory. The "MEEK" are not the weaklings, the cringing, fearful, groveling, apologetic nobodies that the world has supposed.

The "MEEK" ARE the MIGHTY! They are the ones, like Jesus Christ, who have learned to control their every vibration in a majesty of power so dynamic they could rock the very earth with their continued silence as they were mocked or tortured or slain. And their reactions to mockery or persecution would have the power to silence their mockers, bring their accusers to repentance or to even paralyze their persecutors, if so be they were led to use their accumulated powers in such a manner. But regardless of how they used the overwhelming strength of their controlled, righteous vibrations, they would themselves be Masters, standing unharmed, uninjured and divinely powerful as they would hold their SILENCE, even as Christ did at His trial. They would have the power to radiate only the glory of released love. And this is MAJESTY! This is MEEKNESS! And such as these will be the inheritors of this earth when it is glorified.

Christ's atonement was given as a gift of choice. It is the glory of man's free agency to receive or to reject. He who desires that gift of redemption and who seeks for the eternal blessings connected with it also is proving his BELIEF in the PROMISES and in GOD and in JESUS CHRIST and in all the teachings which are involved in such a glorious privilege.

There is another prophet's words concerning the resurrection which definitely states: "And in the resurrection those who are filthy will be filthy still; and those who are unhappy shall be unhappy still!"

Death and the resurrection does not change a wicked person into a saint. Each individual will indeed be held accountable for the deeds done in the flesh—unless he OVERCOMES and sanctifies his body—and follows Paul's admonition to "GO ON UNTO PERFECTION!" Or as Christ commanded, "Pray for those who despitefully use you and persecute you *that you may be perfect, even as your Father in heaven is perfect!*" In this great command is given the law of perfect forgiveness, *the law of being forgiven*—the law of utter glory, and none have ever BELIEVED IN IT!

Paul gives this positive statement in I Cor. 15: "Behold, I show you a mystery; WE SHALL NOT ALL SLEEP, (or go through death) *but we shall all be changed.*

"In a moment, in the twinkling of an eye, at the last trump; for the trumpet shall sound, and THE DEAD SHALL BE RAISED incorruptible, and we shall be changed.

"For this corruptible must put on incorruption, and this mortal must put on immortality." etc.

This scripture has been used to help justify the false belief that ALL will be resurrected into a status of eternal glory. This is not so!

When one fails to use the privilege of his own purified desiring "and fails to OVERCOME the evils of his life," they overcome him. And those very evils bring on the full power of corruptibility as disease or old age or some dreaded calamity finally lays him in the grave. In this way one carries his mortal, corruptible body with him into its fulness of corruption right on into death. And the body is placed deep in the earth, "sown in corruption." "For the wages of sin is death". Thus the wages of his sin and failure to OVERCOME and fulfill all righteousness is truly complete corruption.

But when any body is brought forth from the grave, through the power of the resurrection, it cannot again be destroyed by illness or by death, though that individual, as Daniel declared in his Twelfth chapter, may only be resurrected to *"eternal shame"*—not into glory, though he does receive a body that can not again put on corruption or the diseases of the flesh.

The erroneous doctrine of complete purification and glory for every evil, wicked, abhorrent sinner is totally without scriptural foundation.

Often those who have looked only at the WORDS (WHICH KILLETH) without the Spirit of enlightenment, have assumed such a complete forgiveness from the parable of the laborers in the vineyard—those who went to work at sunrise and worked all through the heat of the long, arduous day—those who went to work the second hour—and the third—and the fourth, etc., until the last hour. And those who worked only that one short hour in the cool of the day yet received a full day's wages. But those who put such a meaning on this parable are without understanding.

This parable is telling of the "WORKERS" who were eager to work, those who waited patiently in the Market Place through those long, tiresome hours, hoping, perhaps praying that they might be called to serve in some way. This parable is speaking only of those who were prepared to work, eager to work and most desirous of finding a place of service. It is not speaking of the slothful, the unwilling or those desirous of escaping all responsibility. Neither is it speaking of the residents of the city in which the Market Place existed. Neither is it speaking of the realm where the LABORERS resided. And it certainly is not speaking of the inhabitants of the world. It mentions only those who were prepared to work and who were desirous of working, not of those who had no intention of ever doing an honest day's labor. The LABORERS, of which this parable deals, are the ones prepared, and hoping and eager to render service to some master. They were not slothful, nor were they seeking to gain rewards through any evil, cheating means or methods of violence.

This is indeed a glorious parable. It is a parable of mercy and love—and rewards for those who find their niche or place of service, mayhap, at the very last hour. But with God it is intentions that count. And in this parable the righteous desires and intentions of men will be the measuring rod of their reward. Such will be God's rewards for the honest in heart and those who are willing to serve Him, even though they only enter the ranks of the workers at the last possible hour.

Justice is for those who die because they did not OVERCOME while in the flesh. And each of these will be judged according to his works. And even the worst sinner will acknowledge that God's judgments are just—and that the rewards or punishments were according to their merits, even though they are cast out of the city with those who have no part in glory or in rewards.

Mercy is for those who OVERCOME, even as Christ OVERCAME! Mercy is for those who love God with all their hearts, souls, minds and strength. These will receive MERCY insomuch that their sins, though they may have been as scarlet, will never come in remembrance before the Lord. They will even be blotted forever from the memory of him who committed them, TO HIM WHO OVERCOMES!

Those who OVERCOME will inherit the highest degree of glory for they will have done the works which Christ did, the works of OVERCOMING. Thus they will be co-heirs, yes, joint-heirs with the Lord Jesus Christ, or be co-equal with Him. And only those who OVERCOME while in this life, have any such PROMISE.

This divine Pathway of OVERCOMING is the divine Highway of the Gods and as Isaiah proclaimed, "only the righteous can travel it." "The wicked can never cross over it, though a fool need not err therein." (Isa. 35:)

For the multitude who will have traveled that broad, open way of corruption and sin, that leads to death or to destruction, there is awaiting the resurrection—AND THE JUDGMENT. Paul, however, in Heb. 6:1-2, admonished the saints to leave this doctrine behind as they would go on unto perfection. In perfection, which is the fulness of OVERCOMING, neither the resurrection nor the judgment have any part.

Those who travel the Straight and Narrow Way of OVERCOMING, (which is the works which Christ did) will have OVERCOME ALL THINGS—even DEATH! For them there is no judgment. And their bodies having *overcome* sin, which brings on corruption and death will have no need of the resurrection. For them there is nothing but glory! Just everlasting glory! "For when He appears they will be like Him—*And everyone who has this hope purifieth himself* even as He is pure!"

Herein are stated the eternal truths of progress and of divinity and of Godliness and the absolute knowledge that our mission in life is to glorify Christ—in majesty and humility, in the perfection of love and in the purification of our hearts until we too OVERCOME, EVEN AS HE

OVERCAME! Then only can anyone go on to do the GREATER WORKS or to receive the highest degree of Celestial glory. This reward must be earned through a love and devotion that reaches beyond mortality and all the laws thereof into eternal fulfillment — even Godhood.

Mortality itself is a condition halfway between the highest heaven and the lowest hell. And it is right here in mortality where one must make his choice as he lays hold of the laws of the kingdom he will inherit.

Those who approve Christ's sayings only as they nod their heads in acquiescence to these glorious promises and laws, yet do not live by them or fulfill them, are truly only deceiving themselves and in doing so OVERCOME nothing at all. They are still just grubby mortals. "Even the devils believe, and tremble!"

He who breaks every mortal law has only qualified himself for an existence with the lawless. The lower the laws an individual lives by the lower will be the realm to which he automatically is consigned when the judgment or future assignments are made. Each man is going to be judged out of the books or out of the record of his own doings, undoings or misdoings, according to his works.

This is not the parable of the workers in the vineyard. This is the eternal truth and reality of the judgment. And no man can change it. "It is irrevocable!" It is JUSTICE and it will be the great JUDGMENT in action for it is God's! And He is just and so are His judgments.

However the laws of God are eternal progress! This is the power of Christ's glorious atonement. When the wicked, mayhap from the lowest depths of hell, which in itself is only a condition of burning regret, have paid the uttermost farthing of their debts to God and to humanity, they will eventually be released to receive new opportunities as they slowly evolve from their stations of remorse into new paths of progress.

But they can never, "Worlds without end," inherit the same degree of glory which the OVERCOMERS inherit because, without any delays or retardments to restrict them, the co-heirs with Christ go on without delays or restraints into the realm of Godhood. And worlds without end the others can never catch up. They may reach a high point of glory in the eternities but always the OVERCOMERS will be far, far ahead.

There are *Saints* and there are *sinners* and there are rewards and there are PROMISES and there are judgments and condemnations. And he who denies these conditions denies his own intelligence and the wisdom and the truth of God.

If one can prove that any child who refuses to abide by the laws of learning can receive a degree of higher qualifications, then that one only proves that all efforts are wasted and in vain—all love is non-existent or squandered—and all promises and rewards are a lie and worthless. Rewards must be EARNED else they cannot be used for they would be of no value.

Even as one puts new information into his mind, by the exerted effort of application, so one implants virtues and divine qualifications into his own being by the continual effort and desire of his soul.

All rewards must be EARNED. And in the *earning* one grows into a person of quality and honor and majesty and renown. Power can only be entrusted to those who master the use of it in a concentrated control of emotions and thoughts as they grow or evolve into perfection.

"Those divine treasures in heaven" which are to be laid up in the innermost part of one's being are the virtues developed through application. And man becomes those virtues, the wearer and possessor of those jewels. He becomes the divine recipient of all the glories of heaven! He becomes divine because he has *earned* divinity. And in no other way can it be given — or received.

If such jewels of divine perfection were given to the wicked they could not appreciate them or use them. They would trample them under their feet and again turn to rend the GIVER. And after they had been cleansed and glorified they would still be themselves and would fulfill fully the parable of Christ, "returning like dogs to their vomit or like swine to their wallow". The traits they have built into themselves through their thinking and acting habits are what they really are. And they will remain just what they are until and unless they eventually begin to change through their own efforts and desiring.

"Come unto me all who LABOR (or who are struggling to OVERCOME MORTALITY) and I will give you rest; *which is the fulness of my glory!* Take my yoke upon you for my yoke is easy, for it is love; and my burden is Light, even the great Light of Eternal glory!" But even in this only those who are desirous and who are laboring are invited to partake of the glorious blessings Christ is so freely offering to the world.

Only those who LABOR or who are working to achieve can possibly receive or appreciate such glorious rewards. THEY MUST BE EARNED! This is the everlasting law of eternity.

"There is a law irrevocable decreed in heaven, before the foundations of the world, upon which all blessings are predicated. And when one receives any blessing from God it must be upon obedience to that law upon which it is predicated!" So is the irrevocable, eternal law of God! And God changes not! Neither does He change His laws to conform to some mortal's sinful hope, or mere "say-so!" And God gave His word before the foundations of the world that that law would govern the rewards given upon this earth as long as this earth would stand. And He gave His word that that law was irrevocable and even He could not change it because He had given His Word! And certainly no man's erroneous beliefs can make the least difference in this eternal TRUTH—either of its fulfilling or of its rejection. It stands with the absolute Promise of God backing it up. And only by the living of the laws upon which the blessings are predicated can they possibly be received. SO HAS GOD SPOKEN!

And so have I been commanded to testify!

CHAPTER XXI

MAJESTY BECOMES DIVINITY

When one lives and thinks upon the earthly plane he is existing fully and completely on the mortal level. He is a grubby mortal. He is abiding in a *"lone and dreary world"* no matter how he may try to glamorize it to hide the impermanence of its imagined joys and its counterfeit novelties of evils.

When one is wrapped, even for a moment, in the sublime ecstasy of spiritual inspiration he is lifted back into the Garden of Eden Estate. This realm of contact with the holy, divine, vibrating wonder of the peace and power of God's enfolding love is that realm out of which man was cast, because of transgression.

When one's mind is wholly centered upon the things of this earth he becomes, as the scriptures declare, a being "carnal, sensual and devilish!" "Carnal" is when one's thoughts are centered upon the things of the flesh and of the world and are completely earthy. "Sensual" is when one is ruled and governed by the lusts of the senses as he permits himself to be enslaved and ruled by his mortal, physical sensations. He yields himself to become the slave instead of being the divine master and ruler of his own realm or kingdom.

As one begins to develop that sublime, eternal, powerful gift of love he will find himself more and more lifted into a higher vibratory realm of joyous, ecstatic splendor.

254

He will finally know fully that "The Fruit of the Tree of Life IS the LOVE of God which is shed forth through the hearts of the children of men!"

The "Fruit of the Tree of Life" is in reality the full essence of perfect, divine love. It is the enfolding fulness of God's protection and approval and joyous ecstasy as it is expressed in the heart of man. It is the essence of everlasting life. It is the perfection of all that is.

When man was cast out of the ancient Garden of Paradise, because of transgressions, "Cherubim, with his flaming sword, was placed at the entrance to guard the way to the Tree of Life, lest man put forth his hand and partake of the Fruit thereof and live forever in his sins." Sin is the cause of sickness, suffering and—death.

If man had been permitted to partake of the sacred Tree of Life, without OVERCOMING his sins and his inclinations to sin he would have heaped upon himself all the miseries of suffering and physical anguish and mortal decay and the unendurable agonies to which the flesh can be subject and still have gone on living without any possible release. And so it was that death was permitted as a way of escape. And the "Wages of Sin IS DEATH!" And the wages of sin is also the suffering and the pain and the illnesses of mortality.

Christ explained it thus when He healed those who came to Him for healing: "Go thy way and SIN NO MORE *lest a worse thing befall thee!*" This statement is more far-reaching than anyone realizes. Only in OVERCOMING can the evils of mortal life be eliminated. And only in the divine OVERCOMING can the hold of death be released for "The last enemy to be overcome is death." But the enemies that must be conquered before death is overcome are the evils and the ills of life and the decrepitudes of old age and the weaknesses and flaws of character.

And there are those who make no effort to overcome yet desire and expect the rewards of all righteousness. They would not change themselves for all the glories of heaven, they are so completely satisfied with themselves just as they are. These are usually the self-righteous, self-deceived ones who are also the great deceivers who work tirelessly upon others instead of upon themselves. They are "the blind, leaders of the blind," who stand at the entrance to that "broad, open Way that leads to destruction" or death, insisting that all whom they contact must enter that unholy path, which they are treading — the Path of death! For they will die! And those who follow them will likewise die. The centuries before them prove the error of their teachings, but they see not. The leaders they have followed have all died. And they, too, will die.

This entrance back into the Edenic Estate is one that must be EARNED. Desiring or believing one has received its gifts of life eternal is a condition of self-deception brought on by that feeling of self-righteousness, which is an impossible condition to cope with by the messengers of Light.

One must live the laws. He must perfect the gift of love right within himself before the "Love of God can be shed forth through his heart," which is the gift of LIFE. One must work upon himself — NOT SO MUCH UPON OTHERS. And when he has purified and perfected himself and sanctified himself, then only can others behold his Light and be healed by the love that will pour forth from his being. And this will be a power so silent and so love-filled no words will be needed to testify of it—or of God. "For my Kingdom is not in *word* but in *power,* saith the Lord."

The self-righteous ones are not only deceived but they are evil. They refuse to enter that Straight and Narrow Path that leads to Life Eternal, glorified in love and filled with Light. They so fully believe they are already perfect they make no effort to OVERCOME. But, being blinded by their self-righteousness, they hang onto their old beliefs, their old doctrines and dogmas as they usher all who will listen to them into that pathway of their own dark principles of destruction.

Paul's admonition to "leave even the principles and the doctrine of Christ, and *go on to perfection,*" is ignored. They drag the stairway He left for the ungodly along with them and the Straight and Narrow Pathway of Perfection is never entered at all, though they may deceive themselves into believing that they are the very road to Light.

And all such will continue to hammer their old doctrines and to preach their old principles until old age and illness finally silences them and they, too, go shamefully into the grave as their ancestors and leaders before them have gone.

Generations of false preachers have died and will continue to die as they have lived "by the letter of the law." "THE LETTER KILLETH!" And it will continue to kill! Only the SPIRIT GIVETH LIFE! And the Spirit is manifest as the literal, living contact with God. *It is the* LOVE OF GOD made manifest in a human soul as he steps forth into that Straight and Narrow Path—the Path of perfection—The Path of glory—The Path of Jesus Christ —The Path of OVERCOMING! This is the only possible Path that can "OVERCOME THE EVILS OF ONE'S LIFE," the aches and the pains and the physical handicaps and the mortal miseries and the weaknesses and the self-righteousness and the sins.

And he who travels this Straight and Narrow Path is traveling that glorified Road of self-purification as he works upon himself instead of upon others.

And there are truly "Those who do! And those who do not! And those who undo!" And these latter are the most deadly of all as they close the gate of glory to those who would enter, by holding forth their own dogmatic insistence of the perfections of that broad, dismal, darkness of the way that leads only to destruction! Such can not possibly re-enter Paradise. Neither can those who follow their teachings.

There are those who shout about the need to receive the "baptism of the Spirit" as they call it. And they ignore completely Christ's glorious information, shared with Nicodemus and left for anyone who will, to take hold of and fulfill. This divine power to be "BORN OF THE SPIRIT" is the divine reality of true fulfilling and of fulfillment. "The baptism of the spirit," of which these fanatical ones shout, is a condition understood not at all. It is but the touch of the Holy Spirit upon one, seeking to awaken him or to prepare him for the fulness of the "BIRTH OF THE SPIRIT." It is but the small quickening touch of life within that developing infant body still held enfolded in its mother's womb.

To believe that this momentary touch of inspiration, this tiny quickening of the life impulse is the whole meaning and purpose of life is a deadly fallacy. It is like claiming that the first quickening of that life force in the infant's body enfolded within the mother's womb is the fulness of birth and of life itself.

This touch of the Spirit is so misunderstood and so exaggerated into the whole purpose and meaning of existence the powers of life which were meant to be awakened to prepare one for the fulness of the real BIRTH are squandered and dissipated and that child may yet come forth still-born. That quickening touch of life within that infant body *is not birth* nor the fulfillment of life. It is but a quickening to testify that there is a greater fulfillment to come.

There are those who have had this touch of the first quickening of that life force who become so wildly hysterical in their abandonment of ungodly behavior they have forfeited all right to the fulness of the Spirit in their shouting, screaming misbehavior as it becomes the desecrating noise of sounding brass and clanging cymbals, which profiteth them nothing.

"That the Gentiles, which followed not after righteousness, have attained to righteousness, even the righteousness which is of faith.

"But Israel, which followed after the law of righteousness, hath not attained to the law of righteousness.

"Wherefore? Because they sought it not by faith, but as it were by the works of the law. For they stumbled at that stumblingstone;

"As it is written, Behold, I lay in Zion a stumbling stone and rock of offence; but whosoever believeth on him shall not be ashamed." (Romans 9:30-33).

And so the stumblingstone remains to lull into a carnal state of security those who are not weaned from the breasts or drawn from the milk and who are satisfied with the clanging cymbals and the noisy demonstrations of sounding brass emptiness.

It must be understood that only as one is truly "BORN OF THE SPIRIT" can he have the power to go forth in the full service of perfection. Such only will have the Spirit bear witness of him as he is sent forth to serve even with the full ability to "Come and go as the wind" to whatsoever assignment is awaiting him, under the hand of God. And such "will speak no word save God commands it and perform no act save God reveals it." And such will only act and speak in majesty and power.

"God is not the author of confusion, but of peace." (I Cor. 14:33). God is never the author of wild, noisy, babbling demonstrations but of divine and holy majesty.

And the "sounding brass and the clanging cymbals" spoken of in first Corinthians, the thirteenth chapter, is but the loud, uncontrolled demonstrations of those who go forth and perform all the mightiest miracles under heaven, but without perfect love. Perfect love never behaves itself unseemly. It is never puffed up but is always humble and gracious and majestic as it is manifested under perfect control.

"He that hath no rule over his own spirit is like a city that is broken down, and without walls." (Pr. 25:28).

"He that is slow to anger is better than the mighty; and he that RULETH HIS SPIRIT than he that taketh a city. (Pr. 16:32).

In order that the final SEAL, given by the Lord, Jesus Christ, can be placed at the end of this record, this information must be stressed. Always complete control and divine majesty must be the manifested quality of each progressing soul. Each individual must be prepared and instructed in the strict discipline of himself. He must understand the necessity of majestic, perfect control and use the power within himself to rule over his own spirit at all times. Otherwise, his works will profit him nothing for they are but "sounding brass and clanging cymbals," which is but an unholy noise.

Only in this divine control can the SEAL of life be placed upon one's brow. Only as one learns to control his emotions can he travel the Pathway of the Gods. Only in exerted majestic control can one master the divine qualities within himself necessary to become god-like as he works for the fulfillment of perfection in the attainment of divinity.

And now, if you are prepared, I place this sacred SEAL of Jesus Christ in your hands, that you yourselves might receive, in time, the seal of divinity upon your foreheads. The knowledge must first be placed within your conscious minds before it can appear upon your brows.

And only those who have perfect love and true humility and a degree of majesty can possibly do the works which Christ did—WHICH WORKS ONLY ARE ACCEPTABLE BEFORE GOD, for these are the only works that are profitable. And only such could possibly be prepared to do the GREATER WORKS, WHICH ARE DONE IN SILENCE and under the full-flowing of God's holy vibrations and power, under perfect control. This is LOVE made manifest, which love is completely self-less.

Preachers and teachers and even some professing prophets have been going forth for years as "they preach for hire and divine for money," according to Micah, the third chapter and eleventh verse. They take upon themselves the authority and calling of being ambassadors of the Lord, Jesus Christ. Yet in Hebrews, chapter five and verse four, it states plainly: "And no man taketh this honor unto himself, but he that IS called of God, as was Aaron." And Aaron was called by the direct voice of God.

This same scripture goes on to state that even Christ did not glorify himself to be made a high priest, but God called Him to that office as "he said unto him, Thou art my Son, today have I begotten thee." (Heb. 5:4-5).

Christ spent the first thirty years of His life in preparing Himself for such a divine calling. He spent those years working upon Himself, *not upon others*. And when He was prepared, God The Father acknowledged it and Christ was called by God.

And so it was that He was prepared to speak no word save God commanded it and perform no act (or miracle) save God revealed it. And so it must be understood that each person must first prepare himself, purify himself, sanctify himself, and perfect himself before he is prepared to work upon others. This inner training cannot be obtained in any college or school of divinity or monastery as one crams his mind with facts and formulas while his soul remains empty and unglorified. Neither can such authority be assumed by any individual with the mere desire to become a servant in the hands of God. One must first learn to LIVE the laws Christ gave. And Christ alone is the Teacher and the one who issues the sanction of approval upon those who enter His employ.

Thousands, yes, tens of thousands have gone forth with a tiny shred of knowledge to work upon others as they have fulfilled none of the requirements within themselves that are so necessary to be an accepted ambassador of the Lord, Jesus Christ. These usurpers of divine authority are always working upon others as they block the way to Light and to God with their insignificant opinions and dogmas and creeds and doctrines and their pet passages of scripture. And they understand not that "The letter killeth" — and has continued to kill, for generations of them have died — and their leaders before them.

It is the "Spirit that giveth life!" "For the law made nothing perfect, but the bringing in of a better hope did, by which we draw nigh unto God." (Heb. 8:19). And even more so in our day, have many assumed to demonstrate the power of the Spirit, seeking His approval as they blasphemed against God with their ungodly demonstrations, which "profiteth them nothing!" And many of those who take upon themselves the authority to be representatives of Jesus Christ know not that every employer chooses his employees. Christ's words to His Apostles were, "Ye have not chosen me! But I have chosen you — and ordained you!" And those who assume to take His approval upon themselves usually become the recipients of various afflictions and illnesses.

And just to listen to the boastings of these usurpers of authority, as they repeatedly proclaim their mighty spiritual accomplishment, which occurred during their rare moments of inspiration, is like listening to a doctor's instrument boasting how it saved lives and how it performed many mighty works. What has an instrument to boast of in the hands of the Physician?

As one works upon himself, instead of upon others, seeking to perfect the gift of love within himself, he truly begins to "evolve from the man kingdom into the God Kingdom!" As one's heart is generated by love his being begins to change. His heart becomes softened and melted and opens wide to the great inflowing love of God. Then it is that he is offering to God the only approved sacrifice — The sacrifice of a broken or OPEN HEART and a contrite (humble) spirit. This is the only sacrifice acceptable since the supreme one of the Son of God upon the cross. As one thus opens his heart he is preparing himself to be taught of God. "And they are called Gods unto whom the word of God comes!" These are the ones God is able to teach! This is the divine, holy contact with the Almighty, which is achieved only by learning to LOVE GOD WITH ALL THE HEART!

As one loves with all his soul, the physical being is renovated, cleansed, purified, renewed and spiritualized — every living cell, organ, nerve, sinew and atom of it. And one begins to feel not only an assurance of royalty within himself, but of majesty! And there is no person on this earth who can be so lowly and obscure and insignificant and friendless that he cannot evolve from that condition of negative worthlessness as love is generated through his entire being. His body becomes quickened and renewed — and ageless — and deathless!

As one loves with all his mind, his mind has to be "Single To The Glory of God!" It is automatic. It is as natural as existence itself. And — IT IS SO! And there can be no argument.

And no one can fully worship and praise God with ALL his mind who does it through the gift of tongues, as so many claim. If one is to give praise and to love God with ALL his mind then his conscious mind must be a part of that adoration. For, unless he understands with his conscious mind, the power and the magnitude of his love and adoration and the expression of it, he is not loving with ALL his mind. He must be fully aware of every word of love expressed, of praise offered, and of devotion released through his intelligence.

There is no one in existence who will send out love and not be loved. He will not need to seek out or cling to others to give him their small crumbs of acceptance or love to relieve his loneliness. He will be a dispenser of love, a being radiant, beautiful and attractive as he attracts others to him.

Then as one "loves with all his strength," until he establishes that divine vibration right within himself (and it does not take long to accomplish this), he will realize suddenly that he is a part of this great love. This very loving with all one's strength is but the "asking with all the energy of heart to be possessed of this love." "And he who asks shall receive — for everyone who asks receives!" And it is so! And as this love fills one's being he will realize suddenly that he IS this LOVE! Love! Pure! Perfect and divine! Then that one realizes that he truly evolved from grubby mortality into royalty, which is a condition of assurance and honorable self-respect, in which all the inferior traits, along with self-deception, are eliminated. This is when one has not only applied but literally fulfilled the "law of the angels!" Then from this state of royal awareness one next advances or evolves into the understanding and application of majesty. And from majesty one progresses into divinity.

It is then the fifteen virtues, or perfect jewels, of "Charity," listed in that most famous chapter of First Corinthians, chapter thirteen, are glorified and made manifest right in that individual. AND THOSE VIRTUES OR JEWELS ARE HIS! AND HE IS THEM! All the faults of the sounding brass and of the clanging cymbals of self-display are understood as being the "puffed-up," "unseemly behavior" of those who take it upon themselves to be the ministers of righteousness without first having fulfilled the principles of righteousness within themselves. So it is but the noise of those "Seeking their own" or their rewards of credits and attention as they "vaunt themselves" in an unholy display of acclaim, which is completely "profitless" "for it profiteth them nothing!"

This is the great "iniquity" which Christ will reject and condemn, as well as those who encourage their emotions to go out of control. Emotions out of control IS "iniquity!" And "iniquity" is the lack of "inner quiet" in which one loses all contact with God. Such cannot possibly be directed by Him. The command is: "BE STILL (or quiet) AND KNOW THAT I AM GOD!" In this inner *stillness* is "The Peace that passeth understanding!" It is when and how and where the power of God is released "TO DO THE WORKS!" "Iniquity," or lack of emotional control, is always a lack of the divine contact with God. And those who work "iniquity" are those who not only keep their own emotions and spirits stirred up, but the emotions of others, in an hysterical display of outward show.

When the Spirit of the Lord is poured out in its fulness only those can be benefited and enlightened who have acquired the majesty of control displayed always by the Lord, Jesus Christ.

Those who give way to hysterical abandon often become temporarily possessed by foreign spirits who speak through them, like the medium who is taken over by some departed or evil spirit.

The noisy ones, with their sounding brass and their clanging cymbals have never learned the divine majesty of spiritual control or emotional stability in which "ALL THINGS BECOME SUBJECT UNTO THEM — The Life and the Light and THE SPIRIT — and finally the "POWER" when they have proved themselves qualified and worthy to handle it. Those who go out of control have never learned to love for love itself is the fundamental element of divine control. They may profess their great love but it is only words, for their very fruits deny their claim. "And by their fruits shall you know them!" Not by their display of gifts — or words — or demonstrations. The fruits are plainly manifest and the nature of them as the pure, UNFEIGN-ED love of Christ is manifested in their lives. This love must be real! It must be beautiful and enduring, changing not with every mood or varying condition or situation one is called to face.

Without this divine, perfected degree of love one may perform all the mightiest miracles possible and it will "PROFIT HIM NOTHING!" For "HE IS NOTHING!" (I Cor. 13:2). These are the ones who will stand before Christ, demanding His acknowledgement and He will answer: "Depart from me, ye that work iniquity; I know ye not!"

As love is generated it becomes the fulfilling power of all things. It is the everlasting reality. "It endureth for-ever!" It is man's glorified robes of divinity. It is perfection — "EVEN AS THE FATHER IN HEAVEN IS PERFECT!"

And he who desires this love until he automatically is praying "with all the energy of heart, or strength, he will become possessed or filled with it — "AND IT WILL BE WELL WITH HIM!"

And thus, with this love brought forth and perfected right within the individual, he is prepared.to "BE BORN OF THE SPIRIT!" This is how so great an accomplishment is achieved. And in no other way!

Christ did not explain the method to Nicodemus. No! It has never before been revealed just how one may attain unto this divine "BIRTH OF THE SPIRIT, so that he can come and go as the wind, and no one will know whence he came or whither he goeth!" (John chapter 3).

But here are the keys — and here is the method by which one may use those keys. And the door itself is before you! "For you are the door to everything!" (Odes of Solomon 17:10). And only in and through the perfecting of love within you can that door within you be opened.

And so I make an end of the works which I have been instructed to share. And Christ Himself will place the final SEAL upon these records.

And so I bid you all a loving, gracious farewell until we are privileged to meet.

Amen!

And the blessings of God be multiplied upon you divine, evolving Sons and Daughters of glory!

Chapter XXII

THE KEYS OF EVERLASTING POWER

Many individuals limit their goals by limiting their knowledge and their desires. They pursue the same humdrum path of ordinary mortality every day of their lives without ever realizing that their lives could be glorious and triumphantly wonderful if they would only make the effort to climb out of the deep rut in which they exist, and will continue to exist, unless they lift themselves up to get a higher vision and a comprehension of the full purpose and meaning of life.

Man was created to have dominion over the earth and over everything upon it. And you may be assured that that first dominion was to be over himself. He was created to be a ruler of majesty as he learned to contact and control the powers latent within himself.

The method of achievement is quite simple when one begins to visualize the goal he wishes to attain. It is always up to each individual to set his own goals. But many of the wicked, degenerate ones of this day and age think that the only dominion of any value is to dominate and control others as they bring them into abject servitude, such as Hitler accomplished. And like Hitler, all such will find their own goals crushing them completely as they are destroyed by their own selfishness and greeds.

The purpose of this work is to reveal the everlasting glory of true victory as one evolves into the full potentialities of his true, righteous, powerful dominion.

It is a well-known scientific fact that, if one thinks of something long enough and hard enough, it will tend to realize itself. This is one of the eternal laws of dominion and of PROMISE.

Every successful individual has visualized himself or herself as successful long before it became a reality. The actor dreams of being a star, the intern sees himself as a noted physician, and each player in the field of sports was obsessed with his ambitions for fame and success before he ever achieved his goal. The ambition tends, indeed, to realize itself AFTER the individual has paid the price — or fulfilled the laws required for such victory.

The price required is a dedicated desire that holds one's attention constantly upon the goal he yearns to reach. This concentration or dedication is the pattern of fulfillment. It is the very seed that must grow and fulfill the thought pattern or desire held forth. Every desire is a living seed with the full potentials of complete realization when held as a vision in the mind of an individual.

"Without vision the people perish!" (Prov. 29:18)

Those without vision will truly perish. They are traveling "that broad, open path that leads to destruction" — or death.

Vision embraces a goal, a desiring, a hope, an ideal, a pattern which one sets for himself to fulfill. Without such a pattern there is no fulfillment. One merely exists.

And now, to return to the full function of the Holy Helper, the Divine Comforter, that is given to abide in man. The abode of this glorious Helper is within the subconscious domain of man's mind. It is this Holy Helper that makes all achievements possible. It gives one the help to master any project, become proficient in any undertaking, or to achieve success in any field of endeavor. Proficiency is Its gift or divine legacy to man. In operating a typewriter, an adding machine, driving a car or flying an airplane or in manipulating any piece of machinery or in becoming a great artist or an inspired musician, or just learning the perfection of self-control is Its function to perfect as It brings one to mastery. But man's cooperation is quite necessary for such perfecting.

As the subconscious is renovated and cleansed through the sustained exercise of learning to love God with ALL the mind, the wondrous Helper is released from all negative, crowded, cramped, discordant functioning as Its powers are opened up for the use and perfecting of the individual.

The powers of the Holy Helper are so limitless only miracles are released into the life of him who learns to draw upon Its fabulous functioning. It never sleeps! It never tires! It never grows impatient! With Its solicitous alertness It seeks to fulfill every desire of man as it LEADS INTO ALL TRUTH — solves every problem and enlightens the mind to "*comprehend all things!*" And It is also the source of everlasting joy and glorious achievement. It is the great perfectionist as it assists one to become perfect in every undertaking as he lives the law of the angels.

The Holy Helper releases power and joy unspeakable as one learns to associate with this wonderful Spirit of Truth, this Holy Spirit of Promise, this Divine Comforter, this dedicated, dynamic Helper, which God has given to abide in us. It is joy and glory beyond imagining.

"For it is given to abide in you, the record of heaven, THE COMFORTER, the Truth of all things, that which quickeneth all things; and maketh alive all things; that which KNOWETH ALL THINGS and hath ALL POWER!"

Through this divine Helper is established the contact with Almighty God. This contact is established and made manifest through the Holy Ghost or divine Comforter, or that all-knowing, inner guide. It acts, at first, as the "voice of conscience" either in giving counsel or rebuke for errors, or for that thrilling, satisfying, glorifying touch of divine approval as one is patted on the back and embraced by the very love of heaven over some noble act well done.

And there are those unfortunate ones who "sear that voice of conscience with a red hot iron" as they reject It emphatically. And by this method It can be forever silenced by any human being as It finally pleads with God for permission to withdraw from that individual. And then is that man left unto himself and his way becomes ever more dark and unholy. These become the most desolate of all men for they have cut themselves off from the Promises of God completely. They become what is known as "LOST SOULS!" And there are many of them walking the earth today. They dwell in darkness as the powers of evil take over their lives, leading them into ever greater evils and wickedness.

As the voice of conscience is appreciated and encouraged one begins to follow that divine invitation of the Almighty Father to "*Walk with me!*" Or "*Abide in me and I will abide in you!*" This contact with the Holy Helper is man's guide into glory. And it is released and contacted through fulfilling that First and Great Commandment of living LOVE, released to God.

As one loves God with ALL his mind, that glorious, All-powerful, All-knowing, Divine Helper or Comforter is released from within Its realm to be a constant, living Com-

panion of unspeakable worth. It is an "ever ready Help in
time of need!" And at all times It is there to give assistance,
courage and understanding upon any problem. It comforts
and heals the heart in times of sorrow or distress. It brings
all things past to one's remembrance as that one's mind becomes ever more alert and youthful. Such a one cannot
possibly become forgetful, senile or inadequate. It is the
quickening power that is given to abide in man. It not only
has the power "To quicken, but to make alive all things!"

With such fellowship one need never grow old or ugly.
And if he is already old It can gradually help to quicken
and to renew the cells of the body as old age and ugliness
and death are OVERCOME and banished. This Holy Helper is the Divine Assistant of God sent to man by the Lord
Jesus Christ. It never fails except when man rejects it. But
there are thousands who, in their blind ignorance, love and
nourish and keep alive their sorrows in a defiling cesspool
of self-pity. Such individuals would not relinquish one moment of their defiling negative attitudes for all the joy in
heaven. Their very misery is their joy. And thus they reject
the Comforter. Yet It is always there, until utterly rejected,
seeking to give Comfort for every real or imagined moment
of loneliness or desolation. In Its very tenderness and merciful understanding it can help to compensate for any loss,
for any sorrow. And in accepting such proffered help the
individual will be lifted completely above the evils of his
life into a person of majesty and power.

This Holy Helper also has the power to enlighten the
mind upon all problems, regardless of how impossible they
seem. "IT LEADS INTO ALL TRUTH" so that one eventually "becomes filled with Light and comprehends all
things!" This glorious, unfailing condition has been PROM-

ISED BY GOD HIMSELF to those "Whose eyes become single to His glory!" These advancing ones also "become filled with Light and understanding so that there can be no darkness in them." And to such the Promise is: "God will unveil His face to them" — and they will actually KNOW GOD, not just know about Him! "And this is life eternal, to KNOW Thee, the only true and Living God, and Jesus Christ, whom Thou hast sent." And it is the Holy Helper, the divine Comforter, the Holy Spirit that is assigned to lead one into ALL TRUTH, ALL POWER and ALL JOY AND ACHIEVEMENT as It is accepted and released to perform Its full functioning.

As the Holy Helper or the Holy Spirit of Promise is contacted and accepted It does lead one into All-Truth. And in this contact one cannot possibly be deceived by darkness or error or by the rattling brass or clanging cymbals of those seeking to glorify themselves with their self-acclamations and unrighteous pretentions.

As one learns to open up first his mind, then his whole being, to this glorious companionship with this most gracious, Divine Helper, his joy increases until he grows into the "Fulness of Joy!" And there is no possible way to describe this glorious condition. One can only know and understand its breath-taking wonder who prepares himself to experience it.

With the subconscious mind renovated and cleansed and purified *through loving God with All the mind,* The Holy Comforter is released from Its tomb or sepulcher right within man. And with Its release It becomes man's perfecting, success, glorifying, joyous fulfilling mechanism of everlasting power. And Its Power is limitless! It is boundless! It is eternal!

Through the companionship of the Holy Helper or Spirit one can accomplish every noble task, achieve success in any and every undertaking as he himself becomes glorious in a singing vibration of breathtaking gratitude and joyous ecstasy.

"Without vision the people perish!" Yes! They do perish. They all go down into death and the grave.

It is only through the gift of vision that one can possibly take hold of the divine Promises of Almighty God!

One must begin to contact the Holy Comforter or Helper through his own gift of vision and his power to believe. This does not mean that he will necessarily behold the Holy Comforter with his physical eyes. This is not the pattern or plan of contact because this contact must be made through FAITH rather than through sight. The real contact, at first, is just that glorious allover feeling of all-knowing joyous ecstasy.

And this contact is made by visualizing the goal one wishes to achieve or attain. As one holds his desire forth, by the mental design of the conscious mind, it is accepted by the Holy Helper or Holy Spirit of Promise and is deposited into the realm of the subconscious mind. There it is the Power of the Holy Helper, within, this personal contact with Almighty God that does the works. It is infallible! It is All-Powerful! It is glorious and unfailing! It is wonderful beyond thought! And it is man's to use and to associate with at all times! It is the great and "*wonderful* Counselor" promised to man from the beginning. And it is man's to use, for "ALL that the Father has is yours!" To use! To enjoy! and to glorify!

One may advance until he has a mild mental vision of these divine higher goals but, until he begins to visualize himself as fulfilling them, he is seeing the Promises "afar off" and not preparing himself for full accomplishment.

In the eleventh chapter of Hebrews we are told how faith worked in the lives of the ancients, how Enoch was translated so that death could not touch him; how Noah built the ark through his faith in the Promises given to him; how Abraham also lived by the Promises that were opened to him, as also to Sarah.

In the thirteenth to the fifteenth verses of that eleventh chapter it states how all these Patriarchs, that is, except Enoch, died in faith, not having received the Promises, but having seen them "AFAR OFF: and were persuaded of them, and embraced them, and confessed that they were strangers and pilgrims on the earth, for they that say such things declare plainly that they seek a country.

"And truly, if they had been mindful of that country from whence they came out, THEY WOULD HAVE HAD OPPORTUNITY TO HAVE RETURNED." If they had beheld the PROMISES as being literal and real and placed them in the present they would not have looked at them in the *"afar off"* and could have fulfilled them in their day, and in their fulness.

This scripture of the "afar off" is tremendous. None of the Patriarchs of old or any living soul since, who has beheld the Holy Promises of God, needed to have died. Those, like the ancient Patriarchs who have been privileged to glimpse the higher Promises, have failed because they have placed them "AFAR OFF;" because of their lack of vision as they have been satisfied with the *hearing* instead of with the DOING! The Patriarchs could have each and everyone OVERCOME and reached the greater land, beyond death, had they but brought it into their present vision instead of beholding it always as being "AFAR OFF!"

The vision of the Promises is exactly where each man places it. It can remain in the "AFAR OFF" or it can be fulfilled in the great eternal NOW!

This is why each one must visualize himself as fulfilling the PROMISES in the NOW! LIVE ALWAYS AS THOUGH YOU HAD ALREADY FULFILLED THE DYNAMIC PROMISES OF ALMIGHTY GOD! Live them and you will KNOW and BE these Promises. This *IS* THE LAW OF FULFILLMENT!

This is *the "exercising of great and mighty faith!"* In this practice the doubts and fears are automatically eliminated as one begins to find the power and the strength of the Holy Helper and grows into Its constant fellowship. This sacred companionship becomes so real and so exalting and so glorious that life has no meaning without it. It is joy and ecstasy and enlightenment and the unfolding of the powers of Almighty God in the life of that individual. This very companionship is the divine contact with God the Father. And this contact and this constant awareness is the rightful heritage of everyone who will only learn to BELIEVE and accept it.

The way of contact is the great love as one renovates his mind by the singing glory of inner praise and loving devotion to God for the continual assistance of this divine Comforter or Holy Helper. And with one's mind thus cleansed by the great love he truly loves his neighbor for no one could love God with all his mind and hold evil, resentful, hateful thoughts in his mind against anyone. He truly thinks only the most beautiful things possible as his mind and lips lose the power to hurt and wound. And he, himself becomes as dynamically beautiful as his thoughts for, "As a man thinketh in his heart, so is he!" In this renovating of the subconscious mind through LOVE the Comforter or Helper is released to assist and to bring Its unspeakable powers of all fulfillment into the life of that individual.

This must be thoroughly understood, that no idea or desire could possibly form in a human mind in the first place if it were not possible. "Anything a man can think is possible else he could not think it!" To the one who doubts, nothing IS possible, for the doubter himself has decreed it so. And so it is — for him. He has damned his own progress and enlightenment by his own unbelief.

This sacred, divine Holy Helper brings to fruition and completion all righteous desires as they are held forth in the great eternal NOW! As one makes the best possible use of his gift of imagination the desires of his soul are rayed or reflected out for fulfilling and "God shall reward him openly" or bring into open manifestation the fulfilling of those righteous desires. In the using of this powerful law of manifestation those divine elements, of which the entire universe is filled, are gathered into form, this divine and holy "substance of things hoped for!" This very substance is but waiting to "BECOME". By learning to use the gift of visualization, which is HOPE itself in action, one begins to enter the ranks of the great ones where doubts and negation are forever banished.

In Ephesians, chapter three, verses nineteen and twenty is given this powerful information: "And to know the love of Christ, which passeth knowledge (which means it goes beyond conscious thought into the vibrational realm of true reality), that ye might be filled with the fulness of God.

"NOW UNTO HIM THAT IS ABLE TO DO EXCEED-INGLY ABUNDANTLY ABOVE ALL THAT WE ASK OR THINK, ACCORDING TO THE POWER THAT WORKETH IN US!" Or according to the power which we permit It to use as It works in us.

In learning to associate with this divine, Holy Helper or Comforter one can "learn to talk with It as one man talks with another." Then, after one gives thanks and praise and rejoices in that sacred fellowship, he can make his desires and hopes known and he will be given the assurance of their fulfillment as he learns to LISTEN. It is in the learning to LISTEN that one will be directed into all happiness and master every undertaking and fulfill every PROMISE. It, the divine Assistant, will unfold the way to master every requirement for complete and magnificent accomplishment. The very association with this powerful source of glory is a joy forever.

"The Light of Christ is given to abide in every man who cometh into the world. And he who rejects that Light is under condemnation." This Light of Christ is the voice of conscience. And It is given to abide in every man who cometh into the world, until it is totally rejected and one's "conscience becomes seared with a red hot iron." After such drastic rejection that Holy Spirit or Comforter, or guiding voice or Holy Helper, upon request is permitted to leave that individual unto himself—and from there on his wickedness and his evils and wanton disregard for either God or his fellowman truly brings him into a state of total rejection. This divine Light of Christ, this glorious, wonderful voice of Conscience, this Wondrous Comforter is the greatest most glorious gift God could give to man. And It does lead one into ALL TRUTH and All Joy and All

Perfection, when accepted. And man himself can help direct It.

Imagination, love and suggestions are natural forces used in gaining the complete assistance of this glorious Assistant which helps accomplish All fulfillment. The only prerequisite in using suggestion is the genuine desire to attain the goal one sets for himself along that joyous road of anticipation and magnificent achievement. The released vibration of joyous ecstasy is the sunshine necessary for fulfilling the accomplishment as the Holy Helper brings forth into the open the request held out from within "the Secret closet" of true prayer or divine contact.

This "Secret Place of the Most High," this sacred "Holy of Holies," is the place of divine everlasting peace and fulfillment "For he who dwells in the Secret Place of the Most High abides under the shadow of the Almighty" where no evil or danger of disappointments or distresses or disasters can possibly touch him.

The Holy Helper is also the Revealer or source of hunches. His hunches are sometimes so compellingly powerful they would almost transform the very stones or the individual who has seemingly become petrified in his own orthodoxed unbelief.

Every individual on the earth has had hunches at some time or another just as everyone has had that voice of conscience bear witness of the good or the bad things he has done. Those who have learned to obey their hunches, however, usually take credit to themselves for those great moments of minute instruction. So very few acknowledge such hunches with a thought or a word of "Thanks" to that Higher Source whence they came.

This divine power of cooperation with the Holy Helper quickly becomes apparent when It is coupled with joyous enthusiasm and gratitude. With man's released thanks It then becomes a tremendous, undeniable force of triumphant, glorious Help.

As one contacts that Holy Helper or that Divine Light of Christ and works with It, knowingly, It begins to reveal Truths and facts beyond mere hunches. And with that comprehensive contact it becomes a simple matter to instill into the subconscious mind a positive success pattern as one applies his intelligence and energies to work with the divine Powers of God. The pattern one selects to be fulfilled will not be brought into the realm of reality by any half-hearted measures. And so trying the divine technique for only a few days cannot accomplish the fulfilling of the great Promise of Its eternal companionship in an ever present awareness. This divine contact and fellowship must be a constant, growing, fulfilling accomplishment of ever-increasing satisfaction. Results are as sure to come as the sun is to rise on the morrow if one but practices the technique of using the imagination to hold forth that desired request in minute detail and with loving confidence. As one holds forth his holy desires in this manner, without reservation or doubts and in all righteousness, they must be fulfilled. THIS IS THE PROMISE — And it cannot fail!

Anyone who works for this glorious accomplishment of constant contact with the Divine for any selfish or ulterior motives will find himself a leader of the ungodly, bereft of light and truth and LIFE — and rejected. He becomes but a clanger of cymbals and a rattler of noisy, brass implements of confusion. And it will all be vain and empty and will avail him nothing.

Only in and through learning to love God with all the heart, soul, and mind can anyone possibly contact the Divine and KNOW of the glory and the Power of the PROMISES and receive of their fulfilling as "The Love of God is shed forth through his heart as the fountains of living water!"

This procedure is infallible. It must work! "There is a law irrevocably decreed in heaven, before the foundations of the world, upon which all blessings are predicated; and if we obtain any blessing from God it is by obedience to the law upon which it is predicated."

And the foundation of the law is based on a sincere desiring along with a belief in the Promises of God. Then the perfect pattern or goal must be held forth WITHOUT DOUBTING! This is the method of all fulfillment.

"And he who asks anything of the Lord and DOES NOT DOUBT IN HIS HEART, HE SHALL HAVE WHATSOEVER HE ASKS!" And "Everyone who asks receives!"

There are two methods by which one can use this divine and holy law of fulfillment and no one can apply either without being benefited and eventually "quickened." One way is to "go into your secret closet, (or closing the door or conscious mind to all outside activities and distractions) talk to the Father Who seeth in secret, and He will reward you openly"—or bring into tangible, undeniable reality the answer to your request. This is one way.

The other way is to be used as one goes to sleep at night. As the mind changes shifts from the conscious to the unconscious, between waking and sleeping, the conscious messages can best be relayed to the Divine Helper. This is the best method that can be used by a beginner or until that divine companionship is fully established. In this brief period of transition from waking to sleeping it is most easy to transplant the desires through mental visioning into the subconscious, or into the fulfilling power of the Divine, Holy Helper, for He doeth the works and will work out the glory of Its full manifestation. These two methods are in reality one and the same thing. The only requisite is that the desiring or request must be sincere and all haggling and all doubting must be absent.

This brings about the true contact with God. Not just for an exalting, fleeting moment! Not for a day only! Not just for the fulfilling of one small request or for a moment of self-satisfying demonstration, but for one's entire life as he moves into the realm of All-Power!

First, make a mental blueprint of your goal and be sure it is a worthwhile, worthy aim, otherwise you are cheating yourself and belittling the powers of Almighty God!

The most glorious and powerful of all desires is to request that the gift of PERFECT LOVE become completely established in you—EVEN THAT YOU MIGHT BECOME THAT DIVINE, HOLY LOVE OF MERCY AND COM-PASSION AND HEALING, PERFECTING GLORY! With this gift established "ALL ELSE WILL BE ADDED!" This is the fulness of that Kingdom of Heaven within! And when one actually becomes that love he will auto-matically be "BORN OF THE SPIRIT", which alone holds the keys and powers of full service and eternal joy, along with the power to be able to do THE GREATER WORKS. Within this gift of perfect love is the power to *overcome all things*— EVEN DEATH! It also contains the glorious accomplishment to be ordained of God so that all things will become subject unto that individual. "And all things will become subject unto him, both in heaven and on earth; the Life and the Light; the Spirit and the Power!" etc.

Eph. 3:19-20: "And to know the love of Christ which passeth knowledge, that ye might be filled with the fulness of God.

"NOW UNTO HIM THAT IS ABLE TO DO EXCEEDINGLY ABUNDANTLY ABOVE ALL THAT WE ASK OR THINK, ACCORDING TO THE POWER THAT WORKETH IN US!"

The power that worketh in us is the power of glory and of fulfillment, even the powers of God as we ourselves permit them to work in us. Our own desiring and our own degree of believing, even our own awareness and opened understanding, is the gauge by which these Powers are permitted to work in us. A sealed mind or an unbelieving heart cannot possibly receive of these higher blessings in their fulness.

Take for instance, this glorious information: "KNOW THE TRUTH AND THE TRUTH WILL MAKE YOU FREE! AND HE WHO IS FREE SHALL BE FREE INDEED!"

And for centuries upon centuries this divine promise has lain dormant and unfulfilled in the lives of mortals on this earth.

How does one go about learning to KNOW THE TRUTH? Each church and denomination has declared in words of pounded thunder that it alone has the TRUTH even while its members have had no freedom from the ills of life. They have grown old and miserable and have perished. None have ever been released from their earthly problems and vicissitudes and evils and ignorance and fears and negation—and DEATH! Worries and darkness have cluttered their lives as they have remained in complete bondage to the full evils and frustrations of mortal life.

Then ask the question, which Christ was asked so long ago and could not explain because none at that time were prepared to understand, "What *is* TRUTH?"

If the divine Comforter has been given to abide in man— and if It is also the "Spirit of Truth" or the Light of Christ and "leads into ALL TRUTH," then the answer and the fulfilling of that sacred Promise lies in receiving the divine contact with the most Wonderful Comforter, that Holy Spirit of Promise, the Divine Helper. IT KNOWS TRUTH! Its mission is to lead man into ALL-TRUTH! And this could not possibly be fulfilled or brought to pass without man also KNOWING THE TRUTH! The full TRUTH! Not just a small portion of it! And with that KNOWING one becomes FREE, even that "he will be born of the Spirit and will be able to come and go as the wind and no one will know from whence he came or whither he goeth!"

And this degree of Truth and Perfection can only be accomplished by living the First and Great Commandment. It holds the keys to all perfection and all fulfillment. Only in the LIVING of this law can one advance above the laws of mortality and become forever dynamically, gloriously free. Only by the fulfilling of this great love does one have the power to be so freed and exalted that no mortal laws can ever again possibly restrict or hold him in their bondage. And he ascends above the promises and the prophecies and the teachings of the Prophets, for he is "no longer under the laws (or mortality) or the Prophets." He is henceforth taught of God! "And they shall all be taught of God!" "They shall no longer teach each man his neighbor for God Himself shall be their Teacher."

And now, another thought or two I am required to give before this record is closed.

Each individual is to be "tested and tried in all things!" But be not dismayed or afraid! Each testing is a glory and brings its own rewards. The testings are only the gauge to verify your own glorious advancement. And because one person was given a certain type of testing does not mean yours will be the same. When you can hold every vibration in exulting praise and rejoicing, no matter what comes or goes in your life, you have achieved the perfect control so that no negative, doubtful vibrations can possibly be dropped into your subconscious realm, then you have become a MASTER.

And since it is within that subconscious mind that is the abode or cradle of that beloved Comforter, the divine Helper, "THAT LITTLE CHILD" that must be loved with such tender, careful consideration and care in order for it to grow and mature until one's being is filled with Its Power and Glory, it must be guarded. It is to be forever protected from the refuse and swill of one's evil, discordant, negative vibrations of wrath and jealousies and doubts and fears and evil reactions. It must be held in love and surrounded always in joy and gladness and faith and confidence and such infinite tenderness. Yes! "It must be loved as a little child!" It must be guarded from all evils even as a little child is guarded. It must be protected from every mortal vibration and every negative thought. And as that "small voice of conscience" is listened to and welcomed and obeyed that voice will grow in volume and grandeur and power. And Its divine love and approval will give power and strength and enlightenment to that noble, courageous one who learns to tune his ears to LISTENING and learns to follow. And then only can "IT LEAD INTO ALL TRUTH and REVEAL ALL RIGHTEOUSNESS AND BESTOW ALL POWER!"

As the subconscious mind is cleansed and renovated through learning to "Love God with all the mind" that Holy Helper, that divine Holy Spirit of Promise, that glorious Comforter, that Pure Light of Christ, can be released to reveal ALL TRUTH. And only then can one possibly be prepared to *comprehend* all truth!

And then it is that the *conscious* mind is freed from the negation of selfish, negative thinking and will truly have lost the power to "HURT OR WOUND." And then will that individual's voice be heard among the Gods. And then is when one will have completely fulfilled the law of the angels and will advance above that law into the higher laws of divinity.

And when the conscious mind has been opened to become the dynamic instrument for sending out only love, the subconscious will be purified and cleansed and perfected and the "LITTLE CHILD" will have matured until It fills the entire being of man.

Then, as the conscious mind sends out only love, without doubts or negation or any antagonistic, discordant thoughts of jealousy or wrath or resentment, one is automatically able to open the doors to that divine, Superconscious mind.

This superconscious mind is the "SACRED CORNERSTONE which was rejected by the builders." It contains the complete contact with God. This most holy truth is indeed sacred and has been carefully guarded down the ages.

The Great Pyramid of Egypt contains this hidden knowledge. The Great Pyramid of Gizeh was constructed under the minute instruction of the Almighty. And under the Spirit of inspiration that Pyramid was selected to glorify the seal of the United States of America. This seal, in its fulness, displays the great cornerstone that was rejected by the builders as it is exalted above the Pyramid itself. And upon this capstone or chief cornerstone is displayed the great ALL-SEEING EYE of all wisdom and knowledge. This sacred emblem is also placed upon every slip of paper money issued by the government of the United States.

The divine Truth so beautifully portrayed in this sacred symbol has existed for centuries and everlasting ages as it reveals the hidden secret of the rejected powers contained right within man. Each man has been the builder of himself. And each man has rejected the truth of his own inherent divinity and divine powers. And in that rejection man has truly rejected the things of Light and power and glory for within that sacred capstone, the superconscious mind, is contained the Great All-Seeing Eye of All-Knowing. And even to this day it is still rejected as man is left to remain in a dormant inactive, mediocre state of mere mortality. This is of his own doing and choice, "as he has rejected that divine Light of Christ which was given to abide in every man who cometh into the world!"

This great "ALL-SEEING EYE, right within man, is locked within the sacred superconscious realm and when that realm is opened through the perfecting of LOVE that realm will become a living part of man's divine heritage. And as that "ALL-SEEING, ALL-KNOWING EYE IS OPENED AND USED, one will fulfill that glorious PROMISE That he shall comprehend all things!" And God will unveil His face unto Him. This is man's true legacy. Yet it can only be received as one prepares himself for so divine a gift and power by living that First and Great Commandment as one learns to love God with ALL HIS MIND. Then is the supreme mind opened and its unspeakable powers of Light and Truth bestowed in their fulness. Then is one truly filled with Light and there can be no darkness in him. And only LOVE can release It and bring Its divine powers into activity within man as It is no longer rejected by the builders of the physical temple of man—himself.

Beyond this I cannot take you! Only you can travel this Path from here on into the realm of full KNOWING as you yourselves prepare to experience the glory of the KNOWLEDGE OF GOD—and of ETERNAL LIFE!"

And God bless you forever and forever—With all my love! Amen!

Annalee Skarin

Chapter XXIII

THE MATURITY OF THE SOUL

Returning again to First Corinthians, chapter thirteen, verses eight to eleven and verse thirteen, it states that "Charity never faileth; but whether there be prophecies, they shall fail; whether there be tongues, they shall cease; whether there be knowledge, it shall vanish away.

"For we know in part, and we prophesy in part.

"But WHEN THAT WHICH IS PERFECT IS COME, then that which is in part shall be done away.

"When I was a child, I spake as a child, I understood as a child, I thought (and acted) as a child, but WHEN I BECAME A MAN (a son of God), I PUT AWAY CHILD-ISH THINGS.

"And now abideth FAITH, HOPE, CHARITY, THESE THREE: but the greatest of these is charity," or the pure, divine, Christ-like LOVE. And only when the childish demonstrations are put aside can that which is PERFECT be brought forth. For that which is PERFECT IS LOVE, and it does not need to demonstrate. It just IS! LOVE is the continual outflowing of PERFECTION. This LOVE or PERFECTION is the power of God made manifest in the divine FRUITS, not in the noisy gifts put on display.

"The law made nothing perfect, but the bringing of a BETTER HOPE DID!" (Heb. 7:19). This marvelous wonder of HOPE, which cannot be acclaimed or demonstrated, reveals the patterns of PERFECTION—"Even as the Father in heaven is PERFECT!"

"Enthusiasm doesn't consist of raising your voice, of turning handsprings or of jumping and yelling. Enthusiasm is knowledge on fire." (Bill Wood, from Case and Comment).

As Paul explained these tremendous gifts of almost unspeakable power, he pointed out that all these powers were a worthless and empty display, without value, unless they were accompanied by that divine and holy attribute of LOVE. And when the perfect LOVE is brought forth then that which is PERFECT IS COME and all the other things, or demonstrations, will be done away. The gifts availeth nothing in themselves, and he that only possesses them is NOTHING without true love. "And though I have the gift of prophecy, and understand all mysteries, and all knowledge; and though I have all faith, so that I could remove mountains, and have not charity, I AM NOTHING. And *though I bestow all my goods to feed the poor, and though I give my body to be burned,* and have not charity (or the pure love of Christ), it PROFITETH ME NOTHING!" (Verses 3-4)

The most tremendous, powerful gifts under heaven availeth nothing without LOVE. Yes, all the greatest gifts in existence are but a total loss without that which is PERFECT! And the only thing that is PERFECT IS LOVE! The gifts are only a PART of or a small portion of the fulness of the perfection which God holds out to His children. These designated gifts are but the toys of infancy. And any who are satisfied with the playthings of childhood can never move on into that which is PERFECT.

It is most clearly stated that when that which is PER-FECT is come then that which is only in part shall be done away. The undignified, childish behavior, the romping and shouting will be done away as completely and thoroughly as the dolls and the toys of childhood. The follies and foibles of "make-believe" will be an amusing or even an embarrassing memory as one moves on into the reality of the three glorious attributes of FAITH, HOPE and CHARITY, in a full possession of the divine majesty which must accompany them.

In this maturity one naturally perfects FAITH in order to fulfill the divine HOPE, or vision, which is revealed to his soul through that glorious "SPIRIT OF PROMISE:" which PROMISE always includes the PERFECTION OF THE PURE CHRIST-LIKE LOVE!

All the childish ideas, the immature behavior, the ungodly self-acclaim and displays will be understood to be but the noisy brass and the clanging cymbals used to keep one entertained or occupied with the worthless amusements of childhood, in the crib that is so short one's attention must be held upon outside rattles and foolish demonstrations in order to restrain and hold his attention. While his discomfort in the tiny, outgrown bed of unprogressiveness, with the covering that is too narrow for comfort, becomes increasingly unacceptable if he becomes STILL and takes time to observe.

The ancient cry of God is heard at the present time to counteract the increasing noise and confusion of those without knowledge, as it is echoed and re-echoed around the world: "To whom can He (God) teach knowledge? And whom shall he make to understand doctrine? Them that are weaned from the milk and drawn from the breasts." (Isa. 28)

Added to this record of Isaiah is the one in Hebrews, chapter five, verses twelve to fourteen, which states that those who are fed by others, or who accept whatever is given to them are only receiving the diet of milk. Those not drawn from the breasts accept whatsoever their leaders offer them, even as an infant accepts the milk without question or resistance. In this attitude of complete acceptance or infantile satisfaction they remain immature. They continue to be numbered among "Such as have need of milk, and not of strong meat.

"For everyone that useth milk is unskillful in the word of righteousness; for he is a babe.

"But strong meat (the food of maturity) belongeth to them that are full of age, even those by reason of use have their senses exercised to discern both good and evil." And, because of their exercised intelligence, they can make a choice of that which they desire to accept, without FEAR. Those who are still infants, accepting only what their selected leaders offer, are often fed only on a diet of FEAR and are, therefore, afraid to look in order to see what is really good or evil. These are truly held in an unprogressive, infantile state. The FEARFUL are the first on the list who will experience the "SECOND DEATH," according to Revelations, chapter twenty and verse eight. The FEARFUL are already damned because they are afraid to investigate or even look. Therefore, their progress and knowledge cease. Paul admonishd the believers in Jesus Christ to PROVE ALL THINGS—and to *hold fast to that which is GOOD!* Those who seek only to *disprove* all new things are only condemning themselves into the realms of those who have relinquished their right of progress and who are, therefore, damned. Damnation is a state of complete unprogressiveness where all growth and progress is stopped.

This quotation must be included here, from the great Herbert Spencer, a true thinker: "There is a principle which is a bar against all information, which is proof against all argument, and which cannot fail to keep a man in everlasting ignorance. That principle is condemnation before investigation."

Another jewel of truth comes from the Rev. Arthur Ford:

> "From the cowardice that fears new truth,
> From the laziness that accepts half truths,
> From the arrogance that knows all truth,
> O Lord, deliver us!"

"A thirst for knowledge is just as important as the acquisition and the application of knowledge." (J. O. Brisbin. —Business Fundamental World. 12-68)

Only those searching souls who are *"hungering and thirsting after righteousness"* are truly prepared to KNOW TRUTH. "KNOW THE TRUTH AND THE TRUTH WILL MAKE YOU FREE." It is then that the half truths, the partial truths and the untruths become inadequate. To KNOW the TRUTH one must "HUNGER AND THIRST" after a complete knowledge of God, not just be willing to verify what he has already accepted or espoused. Only the full truth can appease the awakened hungering of the soul— which TRUTH IS PERFECTION! "For those whose eyes become single to the glory of God will be filled with Light and there will be no darkness in them, and THEY WILL COMPREHEND ALL THINGS!" In other words, "THEY WILL KNOW THE TRUTH!" These are the ones whose eyes are truly single to the glory of God and are not upon their own imagined importance or on half-truths—or perhaps untruths.

Those who are no longer satisfied or willing to accept anything and everything that is fed to them by their "blind leaders" will reach beyond the crib of infancy and the childish methods of entertainment. They will no longer "TRUST IN THE ARM OF FLESH" but with their own souls alerted they will go on to God to ask for a KNOWL-EDGE OF THE TRUTH. They will seek diligently. They will seek HIM early—AND THEY WILL FIND HIM! These awakening, progressing ones are fulfilling that merciful invitation to "ask, to seek and to knock." And God's promise is that "EVERYONE", regardless of his background, mistakes, race, color or creed, "SHALL RECEIVE!". "EVERYONE who asks receives! And he who seeks shall find (TRUTH), and unto him who knocks it shall be opened!" So stands the eternal, everlasting PROMISE of Almighty God! And those who go to men for their information and answers, instead of to God, are trusting in the arm of flesh. "Woe be to him that trusteth in the arm of flesh, or maketh flesh his arm!"

As one is weaned from the milk and drawn from the breasts, or from "trusting in the arm of flesh," which is symbolical of the restraining arms with which an infant is held, he will develop his own tastes and choices and judgment. And as he humbles himself to "ask, to seek and to knock," to KNOW TRUTH as it is revealed to him personally, *from God,* instead of from the blind leaders, he will "Grow and wax strong" in the process of a glorious maturing into sonhood.

"And they who are led by the Spirit of God they are the

Sons of God. The Spirit itself beareth witness with our spirit that we are the children of God; and if children, then heirs; heirs of God, joint-heirs with Christ." (Romans 8:14, 16, 17).

In Galatians, chapter five, verse eighteen, it also states: "And they who are led by the Spirit of God (not men) they are the sons of God."

Or, according to the 82nd Psalm, verse six, and verified by Jesus Christ, in the record given in John 10:34-36, as follows: "Is it not written in your law, I said ye are Gods: And if he called them Gods, unto whom the word of God came, *and the scriptures cannot be broken;* say ye of Him, whom the Father hath sanctified, and sent into the world, Thou blasphemest; because I said, I am the son of God?"

John 6:45, quoting from the Prophets, which prophetic records are not included in our present scriptures: *"It is written in the Prophets,* and they shall all be taught of God. Every man therefore that hath heard, and hath learned of the Father, cometh unto me," (Christ).

Then Christ gave this information: "But the Comforter, which is the Holy Ghost, whom the Father will send, in my name, he shall teach you all things, and bring all things to your remembrance, whatsoever I have said unto you." (John 14:26).

In Hebrews 7:19, it states so clearly that "The law made nothing PERFECT, but the bringing of a better HOPE DID." This *"Better hope"* which is to be brought forth through FAITH is the PROMISE of awareness that every blessing ever given by the prophets and by Jesus Christ can literally be fulfilled in us. This is the "BETTER HOPE" which reaches beyond the laws and the prophets into that which IS PERFECT — which divine Perfection is to be fulfilled in us. And this PERFECTION is brought forth through the developing and use of LOVE. The whole pattern is revealed in that sacred, holy Sermon given by Christ upon the Mount.

This ability to grow into the status of a son of God demands that one leave the trappings of babyhood, the childish crib, the toys and playthings of infancy behind and grow into sonhood.

As one's physical, infant body is formed in the womb, it is fed through the umbilical cord until the body is full fashioned; then the baby body, completely prepared, is BORN into this physical, mortal world.

And so it is also as one develops the spiritual body that it might "BE BORN OF THE SPIRIT." The same process of growth is necessary. The need for spiritual food is the meaning of the Lord's Prayer, which states: "Our Father, which art in heaven, hallowed be Thy Name * * * GIVE US THIS DAY OUR DAILY BREAD—" etc. This prayer is not for the physical food, the potatoes and meat of the flesh, or of mortality. This request, which Christ placed in the hands of man, is for the divine food by which the spiritual growth can be fully accomplished This holy prayer of the Lord has a far deeper meaning than for mere earthly needs. It contains the eternal request of the soul for an awakened awareness and "Hungering" by which it might "Partake of the food which mortal men know not of."

This is the food of which both John the Baptist and Christ partook. "And they grew and waxed strong" (in spirit).

The spiritual food that goes beyond the milk of infancy into the food of manhood, the meat of which only the strong, maturing man can partake, is the request for the daily supply needed for spiritual growth, for the perfecting of the soul. It is the food that will appease the "hungering and thirsting" of the soul for complete fulfillment.

Those who are no longer content with their infant conformity and their inadequate, childish crib, their baby toys and who awake to throw off the swaddling clothes of an outgrown covering, the noisy brass jangling of empty demonstrations, the clanging of cymbals and the undignified entertainment and confusion of childhood will automatically begin to "hunger and thirst" for the divine diet of Almighty God, the meat of the Father. And it is this development, this "hungering and thirsting after righteousness," which starts the development into manhood or sonship.

Truly is it stated: "Blessed is he who hungers and thirsts after righteousness," "For he shall be filled with the fulness of God", according to the complete revelation of this scripture, which was left out of the Bible.

Only as one "hungers and thirsts after righteousness" or the true spiritual knowledge, that he might "KNOW THE TRUTH," can his full maturing take place. The very "hungering and thirsting" is the opening contact between God the Father and the individual as he begins to develop and to use the spiritual umbilical cord that furnishes that which is necessary for his spiritual growth. Only those who "hunger and thirst" can be fed with the bread of life so that eventually they might be prepared to "BE BORN OF THE SPIRIT!"

There are thousands who have claimed and who do claim that they have received that sacred BIRTH, who know nothing about it. They are but tiny children rattling their toys in the childish game of "make-believe," even while vomiting up the spiritual food intended for them to use for their own growth and development.

They who have received momentary nourishment as they have been touched by inspiration, as God has fed them a small serving of His Holy Spirit, hoping to prepare them for the fulness of LIFE so that they could, in time, mature into their own perfection and "BE BORN OF THE SPIRIT," have so often failed to use that divine nourishment righteously. Instead of using that glorious portion of spiritual ecstasy as the divine substance on which they could grow into perfection, they have failed to assimilate its power and have immediately spewed it out in "UNSEEMLY BEHAVIOR" as they have "defiled the banquet tables of the Lord with their vomit," as Isaiah proclaimed.

Whenever anyone has received a touch of the Spirit of Almighty God it was intended for his own divine growth into majesty and honor and perfection. It was never intended to be spewed out in "Unseemly Behavior" of defilement. That holy, glorious touch of inspiration or Spirit was given to be used for spiritual growth and not intended to be spewed out and squandered. It was meant to be held in silence and digested as the entire being of that individual absorbed and fed upon its hallowed perfection of majestic development and everlasting power. Those who have squandered that divine, holy nourishment and Spirit of God thus will never grow into the glory of maturity *to be born of the Spirit*. They will remain infants, living upon milk, instead of the meat of the Father. And they will continue to vomit up that milk in "UNSEEMLY" displays.

————

"He who knows not God always tells it. He who knows God tells it not." This is the ancient truth spoken by the Great Ones. And it is so! This knowledge of God is too sacred to speak, too glorious to share except with those who

already KNOW GOD — and then there is no need to discuss it or explain. This knowledge is held in that sacred depths of the soul as it continually blesses and heals and enlightens.

And anyone who actually KNOWS God has the gift of eternal life and need not die.

In this day and age the whole earth is defiled under the constant bombardment of false statements concerning God. In the very bigotry and ignorance of man God's holiness is defiled.

When Christ prayed that his Apostles might be One, even as He and the Father were One, feeble-minded ones have assumed that they were one identical, amalgamated being. And even that in time all mankind would be amalgamated into that being, losing their own identity, their personalities and the purpose and the meaning of existence. And this is Devil's doctrine.

God, in the beginning, when performing that first marriage, proclaimed that "Man and His wife are ONE." He did not mean that they would amalgamate into one glob, losing their individuality. He meant they would be united in purpose and aim as helpmates to each other.

The false idea and teaching that God and Christ are one identical being is disproved by the scriptures in so many different passages·

Matt. 3:16-17: "And Jesus, when he was baptized, went up straightway out of the water: and lo, the heavens opened unto him, and he saw the Spirit of God descending like a dove, and lighting upon him.

"AND LO A VOICE FROM HEAVEN SAYING, THIS IS MY BELOVED SON, IN WHOM I AM WELL PLEASED." (See also Mark I:II and Matt. 17:5)

"While he (Peter on the Mount) yet spake, behold, a bright cloud overshadowed them: and behold A VOICE OUT OF THE CLOUD, which said, This is my Beloved Son, in whom I am well pleased, hear ye him." (Mark 9:7 and Luke 9:35).

In II Peter 1:16-19 is given this information: "For we have not followed cunningly devised fables, when we made known unto you the power and coming of our Lord Jesus Christ, but were eye witnesses of his majesty.

"For HE RECEIVED FROM GOD THE FATHER honor and glory, when there came such a voice to him FROM THE EXCELLENT GLORY, THIS IS MY BELOVED SON, IN WHOM I AM WELL PLEASED.

"AND THIS VOICE WHICH CAME FROM HEAVEN WE HEARD WHEN WE WERE WITH HIM IN THE HOLY MOUNT.

"We have also a more sure word of Prophecy; whereunto ye do well that ye take heed, as unto a light that shineth in a dark place, until the day dawn, and the day star arise in your heart." It is true that one might see with his eyes and be deceived. He might hear with his ears and not fully comprehend. But that "more sure word of prophecy" is that inner witness of God which cannot lie or possibly be misunderstood. This is that seat of contact right within man which cannot be duplicated. When this is developed one receives that most sacred of all gifts — THE GIFT OF DISCERNMENT!

This sacred Gift of discernment is a guarantee against false doctrine, false witnesses and evil pretenders. It is also a guarantee as the true witness to truth. This most sacred, holy gift is the only one which can place one among the "ELECT"! It is true that the powers of darkness are raging up and down on the earth as Satan is working double time to put across his false doctrines and beliefs. And so great and so subtle are his methods that he "WILL DECEIVE THE VERY ELECT, IF POSSIBLE!" But it is impossible to deceive the ELECT because "they have that more sure Word of Prophecy," which has been brought forth from within, as unto a light that shineth in a dark place." And those who take heed to it will have that "DAY STAR" of inner revelation arise in their hearts, for then will the day of light and understanding dawn — AND THEY WILL KNOW THE TRUTH. And none can deceive them.

This gift of discernment is most holy and pure. It is developed as one begins to turn inward to the very depths of his own soul to ascertain truth. This is the "SECRET PLACE OF THE MOST HIGH!" It is that sacred "HOLY OF HOLIES!" It is the place of contact with God. And it is there that the Holy Spirit bears witness to all things which are true. As one learns "TO TAKE HEED TO THIS MORE SURE WITNESS OF TRUTH" he ceases to judge doctrines or beliefs of others by his own mental capacity, but rather turns to that "MORE SURE WORD OF PROPHECY" or KNOWING, which goes beyond sight or hearing or even of human thinking.

As one begins to take heed unto that glorious witness which abides as a Light which shineth in a dark place, the very inner depths of one's being, the day of complete comprehension will dawn and that day of revelation in all personal matters and of the full comprehension of TRUTH will arise in his heart. And he will receive the "more sure word of Prophecy." HE WILL KNOW THE TRUTH of all things. And none will be able to deceive Him. (There will be more given on this later).

In returning to this false doctrine about God, which is sweeping the earth at the present time, that gift of discernment is most urgently needed.

As you study the following passages of scripture, turn to that inner witness, that more sure word of prophecy and demand to KNOW the Truth.

Now, concerning the greater evidence of Jesus Christ being the *Son* of God, *not God*, let us turn for a moment to the histories of Europe, to the records of the martyrs which numbered into the hundreds. Most of them bear witness as they were being consumed by flames that they could see Christ standing on the right hand of God. They were giving their lives for a witness for Him and He bore witness to their greatness and the acceptance of their sacrifice by appearing before them in the company of His Father. There were always the two individuals who were thus seen.

Mark 16:19: "So then after the Lord had spoken unto them, he was received up into heaven, AND SAT ON THE RIGHT HAND OF GOD."

Romans 8:34: "Who is he that condemneth? It is Christ that died, yea, rather, that is risen again, who is even at THE RIGHT HAND OF GOD!"

Col. 3:1: "If ye then be risen with Christ, seek those things which are above, where CHRIST SITTETH ON THE RIGHT HAND OF GOD."

Acts. 2:33: "Therefore being by the RIGHT HAND OF GOD exalted, and having received of the Father the promise of the Holy Ghost"— etc.

Acts 7:55-56: In regard to Stephen's dying as he was stoned to death is added this glorious witness from the scriptures. "But he (Stephen), being full of the Holy Ghost, looked up steadfastly into heaven, and saw the glory of God, and JESUS STANDING ON THE RIGHT HAND OF GOD,

"And said, Behold, I see the heavens opened, and THE SON OF MAN STANDING ON THE RIGHT HAND OF GOD."

If Christ and God were one it would be a rather stupid, awkward position to see HIM sitting on his own right hand. Or according to the above quotation it would be even more idiotic to be standing on his own right hand. Try it and see.

Then Peter gives this testimony of Christ "Who is gone into heaven, and is ON THE RIGHT HAND OF GOD: Angels and authorities and powers being made subject unto him." (I Peter 3:22)

Heb. 10:12: "But this man (Jesus), after he had offered one sacrifice for sins for ever, sat down ON THE RIGHT HAND OF GOD."

"AND SO DO I BEAR WITNESS ALSO."

Now in Luke 22:69 are the words of Jesus Christ Himself concerning this dynamic truth of two individual personalities: "HENCEFORTH SHALL THE SON OF MAN SIT ON THE RIGHT HAND OF THE POWER OF GOD."

There is nothing in all the scriptures to verify the erroneous belief that man is God. "They were called *Gods,* unto whom the WORD OF GOD CAME." This scripture does not say that they WERE GOD. However, there is the record which states: "As man is God once was, and as God is man may become." Which is no more than saying that the infant in its crib can become a man even as his father is a man. It does not state that the infant will become his father.

"Man and his wife are one," This assuredly does not state that they blend into a bunglesome, uncoordinated, awkward single being. It does not mean that either or both give up their status as individuals or lose their own identity.

Isa. 14:12-15: "HOW ART THOU FALLEN FROM HEAVEN, O LUCIFER, SON OF THE MORNING! HOW ART THOU CUT DOWN TO THE GROUND, WHICH DIDST WEAKEN THE NATIONS!

"FOR THOU HAST SAID IN THINE HEART, I WILL ASCEND INTO HEAVEN, I WILL EXALT MY THRONE ABOVE THE STARS OF GOD: I WILL SIT ALSO UPON THE MOUNT OF THE CONGREGATION, IN THE SIDES OF THE NORTH:

"I WILL ASCEND ABOVE THE HEIGHTS OF THE CLOUDS: *I WILL BE LIKE THE MOST HIGH!*

"Yet thou shalt be brought down to hell, to the sides of the pit."

––––––––

Christ often bore witness of the Father within. He was speaking of "the Great God who standeth in the congregation of the Mighty who judgeth among the Gods." He was speaking of the God of Whom it is said, "For in Him we live and move and have our being." But remember this, before the infant is born or matured enough to be born into this world it lives and moves and has its being in the mother. But that does not make it the mother. So it is that man, seeking to fulfill his spiritual development, lives and moves and literally has his being in his Holy completeness and essence and love which is the reality of the God who does sit in the congregation of the mighty and who judges among the Gods — for there are Lords many and there are Gods many. And this earth is the school for Gods for all those who take advantage of the opportunity so exquisitely divine.

However, regardless of the many times in which Christ bore witness to the Father within, Who doeth the works, when Mary went to throw herself down at his feet in adoration and worshipping devotion he restrained her, saying, "Touch me not, for I have not yet ascended to my Father which is in Heaven. This is our Father, Who art In Heaven. He is the one with whom we dwelt before we ever came to this earth to accept the responsibility of taking upon us the training of mortality. He was the One Who assigned us to our various nationalities and even to our family assignments.

And even as Christ was chosen from the foundations of the world to be the Redeemer, then let it be here known that He was an individual and there were others to choose from else He could not possibly have been *chosen.* There cannot be a CHOICE unless there is more than one to choose from.

And it was Christ who engraved those names upon that most Holy of all Scrolls, that "Sacred Lamb's Book of Life." To have one's name thus entered upon that record was one of the greatest possible honors to receive. And those whose names were engraved upon that divine document had earned that right through personal achievements. They were individuals then — and would always be distinct with personalities all their own. Through the eons of existence, before the foundations of the earth were laid, each individual who was to have the privilege of eventually inhabiting this world had progressed according to his own desiring and choice. And, according to the many passages of scripture which testify of that Sacred Scroll, those only who were worthy had their names thus written into that Secred Book. And, according to the scriptures, there were those whose names were not written in that "Lamb's Book of Life."

Thus, for ages and eons, each individual developed his own personality and identity and worthiness or his own unworthiness. And to think that there are those who actually try to teach that those ageless eternities of development are to be blotted out as man is, according to their erroneous interpretation, be canceled as man is absorbed back into NOTHING, is wicked, even blasphemous, and an insult to both God and man.

That we existed as individuals is verified in numerous passages of scripture; in the calling of Jeremiah the prophet; in the record of Job, who so bewailed the day of his birth into this world, and to whom God spoke out of the whirlwind, demanding, "Job, gird up now thy loins like a man, for I will demand of thee, and answer thou me, Where wast thou when I laid the foundations of the earth and ALL THE SONS OF GOD SHOUTED FOR JOY — AND THE MORNING STARS SANG TOGETHER?"

Remember also, as Christ was dying on the cross, He uttered these everlasting words of eternal truth: "Father, into thy hands I commend my Spirit." (Luke 23:46). At that moment he certainly was not attempting to put across a falsehood to deceive the world. He was speaking the dynamic words of everlasting truth.

Christ did testify that he and his Father were ONE. He also prayed that his apostles would become One even as he and the Father were ONE. This ONENESS did not mean a mass amalgamation of all, but a unity of love and purpose and agreement and individual perfection.

"THERE IS NOTHING IN SCRIPTURES THAT ONE'S LIFE IS TO PREPARE HIM TO GO SLOPPING

ABOUT THE COSMOS WITH NO IDENTITY." (Michael Drury, of Cedar Crest College.)

————

Those who are teaching that all men are going to be amalgamated into one great being — God — are teaching Devil Doctrine.

The condemnation which Lucifer and his followers will receive, along with all those they are able to deceive, is that they shall receive the "Second Death."

The Second Death is reserved for those who failed to fulfill their own inborn goodness and who were unworthy to have any part in the great promises of fulfillment. The Second Death is also for those who have been orthodoxed into a state of fear so that they dare not search for TRUTH, but live by the dead doctrines and creeds of their ancestors and pastors. They are dead and withered branches that are fit only to be burned. The FEARFUL are the ones who head the list of those to receive that Second Death. Those who follow are "the *unbelieving*, and the abominable, and murderers, and whoremongers and sorcerers, and idolaters and all liars." (Rev· 21:8)

The completion of that Second Death is the death of the soul as it is required to relinquish the personality as the essence and energies it consists of are drawn back into the great source of energy from which it came. And that essence no longer has an identity or a personality. It is no longer a being — a living soul. It is NO-THING!

Lucifer knows this is the great condemnation and the judgment that is awaiting him. He knows he cannot escape it, but proud and haughty as ever he is seeking at this time to try to make it appear as the most glamorous condition possible to receive, in hopes that he can take the blind, unsuspecting ones along with him. His entire existence has been a flaming desire to destroy, to torture, to afflict and to torment man and to control him as a puppet on a string. He has sought always to produce great dictatorships upon this earth in order that he could dominate all mankind. He demands that all obey him as he seeks to control even their thinking — and to absorb their personalities.

And now that Lucifer's reign is nearing its close he is seeking even more desperately to deceive and to glamorize that Second Death which awaits him and his followers and those who have yielded themselves to his false teachings and his sway. And so has the false, evil doctrine of being ABSORBED back into God as nonentities been spread-ing and expanding until it has become a stench to cover the earth. It seeks to give a glamor of importance to those without understanding and who KNOW NOT THE TRUTH.

And many of those who are without comprehension, and who are so weak in soul and erring in judgment they do not desire to face the responsibility of their own frauds and failures, are proclaiming that they will be absorbed back into God, or declare in outrageous blasphemy that they are God. And thus they are deceiving themselves as they seek to deceive others who are willing to become Satan's instruments in endeavoring to glamorize that most hideous judgment, the SECOND DEATH.

Those who, in humility and loving devotion, seek to KNOW TRUTH will not be deceived by such evil, defiled teachings. They will have the ability to discern between the truth and the error, abiding wholly in the Secret Place of the Most High or in direct contact with that "Light that shineth in a dark place." And they will be taught of God, and will need no man to teach them.

This glorious Spirit of Discernment is one of the most Sacred, powerful, holy gifts possible to receive. It is not a gift to be put on display or boasted about. It is a gift to prepare one to DO THE GREATER WORKS. Those who love God with all their hearts, minds and souls will naturally grow into the living wonder and marvel of this most divine, powerful gift of DISCERNMENT.

The holy ones, for such they are, who have this sacred gift of discernment *are* THE ELECT. And their very election is to be called to associate with that glorious, chosen group of the ELECT, WHICH CANNOT BE DECEIVED, because it is impossible to deceive them. Their eyes being single to the glory of God, instead of being centered upon their own imagined importance and their false concepts, is proof against deception, for there shall be no darkness in them. They will be filled with Light — and comprehend all things. These will be able to discern between TRUTH and error. And no man will be able to deceive them. No! Not even Lucifer himself. FOR THEY WILL KNOW THE TRUTH! To them the guiles of Satan and all the clever, powerful doctrines of falsehood which he has so cleverly disguised and fostered are as nothing.

And so, as Lucifer goes down into that Second Death and his legions of demon followers with him, his one consuming desire will be to take the whole human race with him. And so it is he is trying so desperately to make the yielding up of personality of each individual as something very desirable. And his teachings are a lie! And he is the Father of lies! And to have to relinquish that divine personality which has taken such long ages and eons to develop is an abhorrent condition, not a thing desirable nor righteous. He is seeking to make it appear as the very ultimate in all existence. And to him and to his followers it is indeed the ultimate — THE VERY END!

Pray for the gift of discernment, that you be not deceived. Pray to be taught of God. Pray for the gift of perfect love. And know that deep desiring or intensity automatically draws attention from the worlds beyond. This is the blessed "Hungering and Thirsting After Righteousness." This very intensity or deep desiring is the most urgent, dynamic form of ASKING possible to generate. This is the "Praying with all the energy of heart" required for fulfillment.

An Appendix to the Preceding Chapter

"Know the TRUTH and the TRUTH will make you free!" Accept falsehood and you are forever in bondage.

"My sheep hear my voice and they know me, and a stranger they will not follow!" Christ's voice is the voice of TRUTH and those who *know Truth* will never be deceived.

'And when ye shall receive these things (or anything for that matter), I would exhort you that ye ask God, the Eternal Father, in the name of Jesus Christ if these things are not true; and IF YE SHALL ASK WITH A SINCERE HEART, WITH REAL INTENT (or desire), having faith in Christ, he will manifest the TRUTH UNTO YOU BY THE POWER OF THE HOLY GHOST.

"And by the power of the Holy Ghost ye may know the TRUTH of all things." (the ancient prophet, Moroni).

In the center of the soul is where one abides under the shadow of the Almighty, "in the secret Place of the Most

High." And when one goes inward with his questions, to this place of divine contact, he cannot possibly be deceived. Only *truth* can abide here and only TRUTH will be revealed here.

As one goes thus within he will be exalted into the status of the ELECT! These holy ones who have faith enough to PROVE ALL THINGS will learn to trust not in their own understandings but will go to that more sure word of Prophecy. This is the realm of the *Elect* and it is impossible to deceive them.

Some are born with that most sacred, holy gift of DISCERNMENT. But all may develop it. It is for those who trust in God and walk with God, not leaning to their own understanding. These are the ones whose hearts and minds are open, that they might be taught of God· These follow not every foolish "wind of doctrine" devised by man or instigated by Lucifer.

The 38th Ode of Solomon is beautiful indeed on the power of TRUTH. "I went up to the light of truth as if into a chariot;

"And the Truth took me and led me; and carried me across pits and gulleys; and from the rocks and the waves it preserved me;

"And it became to me a heaven of Salvation; and set me on the arms of immortal life:

"And it went with me and made me rest, and suffered me not to wander, because it was the TRUTH;

"And I ran no risk, because I walked with Him;

"And I did not make an error in anything, because I obeyed the Truth.

"For error flees away from it, and meets it not; but the Truth proceeds in the right path, and

"Whatever I did not know, it made clear to me, all the poisons of error, AND THE PLAGUES OF DEATH WHICH THEY THINK TO BE SWEETNESS."

Come, Beloved! Come! Join those sacred, holy ones, the ELECT, and the power of the deceiver will never be able to touch you with the falsehoods of error and destruction. "Ask God the Eternal Father" to KNOW *truth* — and the Truth will be revealed to you by the power of the Holy Ghost! Amen!

CHAPTER XXIV

"THEY WERE CALLED GODS UNTO
WHOM THE WORD OF GOD CAME!"

To be "Born of the Spirit" is the true fulfilling of this phase of existence. "For everyone who is born of the Spirit will have the power to come and go as the wind and no one will know from whence they came or whither they goeth" in their service of Sonhood and they step forth to "DO THE GREATER WORKS."

In Isaiah 40:28-31, is given this dynamic information: "Hast thou not known? Has thou not heard, that the everlasting God, the Lord, the Creator of the ends of the earth, fainteth not, neither is weary, there is no searching of his understanding.

"He giveth power to the faint; and to them that hath no might he increaseth strength. Even the youths shall faint and be weary, and the young men shall utterly fall.

"But *they that wait upon the Lord* (or who patiently partake of the divine nourishment of the Almighty through that spiritual, umbilical cord or direct channel into heaven, until they grow into maturity) *shall renew their strength; they shall* MOUNT UP WITH WINGS AS EAGLES; *they shall run and not be weary; and shall walk and not faint."* And in the fulness of this holy promise of God is given this added scripture from other sources than the Bible: "They shall receive treasures of knowledge, even hidden treasures. They shall receive HEALTH IN THEIR NAVEL

314

and marrow in their bones, strength in their loins and in their sinews.

"And I, the Lord, give unto them a promise that the destroying angel shall pass them by as the children of Israel, and not slay them."

This is the fulness of the PROMISE given to those who "LIVE BY EVERY WORD OF GOD." "For they will be called Gods unto whom the WORD OF GOD comes." They will as surely advance into divinity and righteousness as the oak tree grows from the acorn, the cat from the kitten, the chick from the egg.

In the promise that the destroying angel shall pass them by is the promise that they will be immune from death, so that no one can take their lives from them, except they permit it. This is the promise of being able to do all the works which Christ did. And this promise is given to those who OVERCOME as they "Hunger and thirst after righteousness."

The health in the navel is the most remarkable part of this divine revelation. The navel is where the umbilical cord of the infant was or is attached to the body in its prenatal state. To go back to this promise of "health in the navel" years after that physical need is over is most amazing. The promise that those who fulfill the laws of righteousness, will "RECEIVE HEALTH IN THEIR NAVEL" is the promise of the SPIRITUAL DEVELOPMENT as the divine, heavenly sustenance is supplied to the maturing, spiritual body within. And unless there is health in the developing infant's navel it cannot possibly grow or even exist. So it is in the spiritual growth required. There must be "health in the navel" to mature spiritually.

It is as the infant begins its growth that the umbilical cord is formed. At first it is not much more than a tiny thread. However this cord is enlarged as the tiny body develops and the demands are increased. The supply is expanded according to the increasing needs or the degree of nourishment must be continually increased to supply the growing needs of the infant. So it is with each individual as he travels this spiritual pathway of fulfilling.

"That which is born of the flesh is flesh:" said Christ to the questioning Nicodemus, long ago: "But that which is born of the Spirit IS Spirit!" With the powers to "come and go" in the calling of a divine service that fulfills the promise of being able to qualify to not only do all the works which Christ did but "TO DO EVEN THE GREATER WORKS."

Again, only if there is *health in the navel* can that contact with the divine supplier of spiritual food, the meat from the Father, be drawn into the being of man as he is nourished and prepared to "BE BORN OF THE SPIRIT." As one learns to "hunger and thirst after righteousness" the supply of increasing nourishment is also increased as the soul's full maturity takes place. And it is during this holy process of "WAITING UPON THE LORD," as Isaiah said, that one receives the renewal of his physical body and the power also to mount up with wings, as eagles, or to "BE BORN OF THE SPIRIT!"

And as the umbilical cord, supplying the pre-natal needs of the forming infant, waiting upon the development of its own tiny body, was or is attached to the very center of its being, so also is that area of the navel still the location of this heavenly supply. "The Secret Place of the Most High" is the spiritual navel right within man. "And he who abides in the "Secret Place of the Most High, dwelleth under the shadow of the Almighty," as he *"waits upon the Lord,"* for his own maturing. This "Secret Place of the Most High" is the divine "HOLY OF HOLIES," the inner-most chamber of the temple of man as the individual appointed to the assignment learns to become holy enough to enter and to finally abide in that most Holy Spot of divine contact with God as his spirit is nourished, developed and prepared to "Be Born of God." And as this is being accomplished one is truly "WAITING UPON THE LORD!" He is also *"dwelling under the shadow of the Almighty,"* or within or under God's loving, protecting embrace and continuing supply of assistance.

This is also the spot into which one can take any new doctrine and, holding it forth in prayer, will KNOW whether it is truth or not. No evil influence or falsehood can be accepted into this holy of holies, the point of contact with God.

And the divine offering, the only acceptable sacrifice that God will acknowledge from any child upon this earth, is, as He proclaimed, not the giving of all one's goods to feed the poor, or even his body to be burned, or the giving of all his time and talents in service, but only the "SACRI-FICE OF A BROKEN (or open) HEART AND A CON-TRITE SPIRIT." And it is only this ordained, *appointed sacrifice* that can open up the heart center, the navel and its connection with that glorious umbilical cord, which is the only open channel for inflowing nourishment direct from the throne of God. And as one opens this channel, that through his own "hungering and thirsting" he begins to draw upon that supply, can it be given. This is the method of spiritual maturity and sonship.

As this is accomplished, this opening of the heart center, from the navel on upward, as it is offered to God, "with a humble, contrite spirit," that individual's "hungering and thirsting after righteousness" begins and he becomes "BLESSED" indeed. And it is this "hungering and thirsting," this urgent longing of the developing soul that pumps or draws that holy essence of spiritual supply into his being. And this supply is joy and LOVE. It is also known as "THE WORD OF GOD!" It is that inner, personal instruction and assurance that lifts one slowly and surely above the status of mere mortality. "And they were called Gods unto whom the WORD OF GOD CAME!

This HOLY Place of the Most High, this spiritual navel, this contact point with the umbilical cord, is the condition or accomplishment where one receives the benediction and the blessing of that Holy Spirit of Promise, as It promises that the PERFECTION desired and the complete fulfillment, for which the soul so earnestly yearns, will be reached. It is also the place where one is enfolded in "The Peace that passeth understanding" or which goes beyond the physical, mortal mind to comprehend, as that individual develops into a Prince of Peace.

"And those who are born of love are born of God," so testified John the Beloved. These are the true sons of God and they will need none to teach them for God Himself will be their teacher." And when they have fulfilled their assigned period of "WAITING UPON THE LORD" their full development will have been accomplished. They, having fulfilled all the laws of righteousness, even the "hungering and thirsting" necessary to keep the spiritual food flowing from the Almighty, will "BE BORN OF THE SPIRIT!"

Contained within this holy accomplishment, all the laws of earth and mortality and of heaven and eternity are fulfilled. "He who keeps that First and Great Commandment has fulfilled all the laws and the prophets." Every breathtaking promise of the scriptures and of the prophets and of the angels and of Jesus Christ and of Almighty God Himself will be fulfilled. And henceforth "All things will be subject unto him, both in heaven and on earth, the Light and the Life; the Spirit and the Power, sent forth by the will of the Father, through Jesus Christ His Son." And they become co-heirs and joint heirs with the Lord Jesus Christ for they will have OVERCOME all things, even as He OVERCAME!

As one opens up his living heart center (not just the physical heart organ), his whole inner being will be prepared to receive the nourishment through the healthy navel or spiritual point of equipment. That supply of celestial food, the nourishment of pure perfection is drawn into man's being through his "hungering and thirsting after righteousness" and he literally begins to partake of THE FRUIT OF THE TREE OF LIFE. This holy "hungering" and the degree and intensity of it gauges the amount of nourishment bestowed and even the speed of one's growth. And according to the individual supply is one's growth measured. This food of the spirit is truly "LIFE EVERLASTING—even the food of LIFE ETERNAL." As one continues to make use of the supply so is it increased, as one receives his "daily bread" or food from the "Father which art in heaven."

This is what Christ was explaining when He called Himself the vine and described man as the branches. Christ IS the vine. He is, shall we say, the umbilical cord? He is the connecting or directing power of that holy supply of nourishment to each individual, according to their developed capacities to receive. And it is measured to each one according to the degree of his "hungering and his thirsting." The majority of mankind, however, have sealed themselves against receiving any spiritual food whatsoever. In other words, they have no "HEALTH IN THEIR NAVEL" for that living Christ center has never been contacted because they have been so satisfied with "the letter of the law"—that little written letter of the meager passages of scripture contained in those incomplete verses of our Bible. Anyone who believes that God knows nothing more and can reveal nothing more than what is contained in those books is mocking God and his very thoughts are blasphemy.

"Christ is the vine" while God, the Father is the Husbandman, the Supplier. This opening or contact with the sacred umbilical cord, this "sacred Place of the Most High," this contact with the spiritual navel, brings "the life more abundant," the great spiritual Life, which Christ came to give. "I came that ye might have Life and have it more abundantly." This abundant life goes beyond any physical imaging or desiring. This is that which IS PERFECT!

It is from this "Secret Place of the Most High" that one learns to open and to contact or develop the umbilical cord, or that sacred channel into heaven. And Christ IS the source of Its establishment, the tender Director of its forming and its perfecting. The knowledge and humble use of this glorious privilege of being able to receive continual nourishment or enlightenment from God, the Father, is a glory beyond words. It is "THE BREAD OF LIFE!" It is the contact with the realm of jeweled glory, the Place of divine ecstasy! It is the realm of those things "Which man's mortal eyes have never beheld, nor his ears ever heard, nor yet has entered into his heart." "These are the things which God has prepared for those who LOVE Him!"

And mankind has foolishly believed that all of this is something to be revealed and bestowed upon the righteous AFTER DEATH. And they have held to this blind belief because of the precepts of men. These dynamic blessings were ordained and intended for this life. They were intended for every individual who would prepare himself to receive them, while in the flesh. Just as Christ challenged Nicodemus with this question, after explaining the purpose and power of "Being Born of the Spirit!" "If I have told you *earthly* things and you believed not, how can you believe if I told you heavenly things?" And to this day no one has accepted or believed that glorious promise Christ gave of "BEING BORN OF THE SPIRIT, WITH THE POWER TO COME AND TO GO AS THE WIND . . ." etc.

These great and almost unspeakable blessings are *earthly* things because they must be comprehended and fulfilled while on this earth. Then only can one be prepared to advance into those heavenly truths and glories beyond this mortal realm. And those things which are beyond are only hinted at, not fully mentioned. For instance, "They were called Gods, or would become gods unto whom the Word of God came, or to whom that sacred supply of the continued, LIVING WORD of God comes." And again, in accepting of this higher, divine way of instruction, "LET NO MAN DECEIVE YOU!" Give ear to God alone for "He will be your teacher and you will need none to teach you!"

These dynamic blessings of KNOWING THE TRUTH,

of BEING BORN OF THE SPIRIT, of COMPREHEND-
ING THE THINGS WHICH MORTAL EYES HAVE
NEVER BEFORE SEEN, NOR EARS HEARD, NOR
HEART CONTEMPLATED" are all blessings which can
be received and enjoyed as one accepts them, fulfills them
and moves on into their realms of everlasting power. These
blessings are for the great eternal NOW, as man opens his
heart to believe and his mind to accept through developing
that "hungering and thirsting after righteousness," which
alone can make one "BLESSED!" Yes! "KNOW THE
TRUTH AND THE TRUTH WILL MAKE YOU FREE!"
"KNOW GOD AND YOU WILL HAVE LIFE ETER-
NAL, FOR THIS IS LIFE ETERNAL TO KNOW THEE,
THE ONLY TRUE AND LIVING GOD AND JESUS
CHRIST WHOM YOU HAVE SENT!" "Those who know
not God are always talking about it. Those who KNOW
God tell it not!"

As one practices diligently and sincerely that First and
Great Commandment, working upon his heart and soul,
as he exercises his mind, with all his strength, will most
assuredly have revealed to him those wondrous glories
which God has reserved "FOR THOSE WHO LOVE HIM."
"And God will unveil His Face to those who Love Him!"
Remember this, "And if you love me you will keep my
commandments." Anyone who truly loves God will assuredly seek to fulfill and to perfect that First and Great Commandment of complete devotion. This is the love that has
nothing to do with the teaching of men, or with the fears
that man's inadequate teachings have fostered. This is the
love that is complete, the love that has put aside "self"
and its proud, hypocritical, outside services of display, lip
service and emotionalism. This is the love that desires only

to give, instead of seeking only to receive credits and honors. This is the type of love that can glorify God in all conditions, tribulations and hazards. It is the love that is not seeking for a "sugar daddy" to listen to its whimpering complaints, selfish demands or unreasonable requests, which individuals have not prepared themselves to receive. Those filled with perfected love are the ones who can rejoice in all things; in pain, in seeming misfortunes, in anguish or sorrow, and relinquishing these harassments unto the Lord, glorify His Name and rejoice forevermore as they themselves become glorified. These are the ones who can truly transmute any condition in existence by their attitude of praising gratitude. And in fulfilling this powerful privilege they themselves will become translated beings, "BORN OF THE SPIRIT!"

"Behold, I stand at the door and knock; if any man will open the door, I will come in and sup with him and he with me." This is when that holy, divine food is shared with the individual who truly "hungers and thirsts" for something beyond grubby, mortal existence. And this door, at which Christ is waiting, is the opening to that inner channel through which one can receive continual instruction from God. This door has always been within man, waiting for him to awaken and answer that call within his own longing, hungering soul. This very entrance is the door into "THAT KINGDOM OF RIGHTEOUSNESS WITHIN, *in which all else is added.*" This is the realm in which each individual can receive personal instruction from Almighty God.

Those who believe that everything God knows, or has thought, or has spoken, or will speak, is contained in that one volume, The Bible, are degrading and belittling the intelligence of God, and denying His power. They are seeking to bring God down to their own cramped level of thinking and being. They are, with their own ignorance and bigotry and impiety, commanding God to be silent forever more. They are placing a gag upon the mouth of God by their own warped, narrow minds. They are proclaiming that God has had His say and can never speak again. The very absurdity of such an idea is sheer blasphemy.

God Himself declared, "I will do nothing except I reveal my mind and will unto my servants, the prophets."

In the last verse recorded in the testimony of beloved Saint John is given this wonderful bit of information: "And there are also many other things which Jesus did, and which, if they should be written every one, I suppose that even the world itself could not contain the books that should be written. Amen." So testified Christ's most beloved apostle, the one dearest to His heart.

In the fifteenth chapter of Saint John is stressed several times the glorious truth that Christ Himself is the vine and that without that contact with the vine man can produce no fruit, or accomplish no good, but is destined to become withered and useless and worthy only to be cut off and cast into the fire.

Also, on that last night Christ spent with his apostles, he informed them that there were many more things which he desired to share with them but that they were not prepared to receive them."

Then is given this glorious information, in John 16:12, as follows: "Howbeit when he, the Spirit of Truth is come, he will guide you into all truth, for he shall not speak of himself; but whatsoever he shall hear that shall he speak; and he will show you things to come." Here again is the promise of that divine, eternal contact and the information of continued instruction from Almighty God.

"And no man receiveth a fulness unless he keepeth His commandments." "And if he keeps that First and Great Commandment he has fulfilled ALL THE LAWS AND THE COMMANDMENTS AND THE PROPHETS." And to continue with that first sentence of this paragraph: "He that keepeth His commandments RECEIVETH TRUTH AND LIGHT, UNTIL HE IS GLORIFIED IN TRUTH AND KNOWETH ALL THINGS." Such is the promise of Almighty God.

"And this is the confidence that we have in him, that, if we ask anything according to his will, he heareth us:

"And if we know that He hear us; whatsoever we ask, we know that we have the petitions that we desired of him!" (I John 5:14-15). No one can enter that "Kingdom of Heaven within" and ask for anything amiss, for in that holy Place of the Most High his requests and his desires are purified and cleansed of selfishness and self-seeking and become wholly single to the glory of God.

"For the word (or that inner instruction) of the Lord *is* TRUTH, and whatsoever is truth is Light, and whatsoever is Light is Spirit, even the Spirit of Jesus Christ, and the Spirit giveth Light to EVERY MAN that cometh into the world; and the Spirit enlighteneth EVERY MAN through the world, that harkeneth to the voice of the Spirit. And EVERYONE that harkeneth to the voice of the Spirit cometh unto God, even the Father." Nothing could be plainer than this and there is nothing more beautiful or more gratifying to the soul.

"For man is spirit. The elements are eternal, and Spirit and element, inseparably connected (or when man is born

of the Spirit), receiveth a fulness of joy. And when separated (by death) cannot receive a fulness of joy."

"And great shall be their reward, and eternal shall be their
glory.

"And to them I will reveal all the mysteries, yea, all the
hidden mysteries of my Kingdom from days of old, and for
ages to come, will I make known unto them the good
pleasure of my will concerning all things.

"Yea, even the wonders of eternity shall they know, and
things to come will I show them, even the things of many
generations.

"And *their wisdom shall be great,* AND THEIR UN-
DERSTANDING REACH INTO HEAVEN, and *before
them the wisdom of the wise shall perish and the understanding of the prudent shall come to naught.*

*"For by my Spirit will I enlighten them and by my
power will* I make known unto them the secrets of my will
—yea—even those things which eye hath not seen, nor ear
heard; nor yet has entered into the heart of man!" These
are the promises and the blessings which God has prepared
for those who LOVE HIM, or who fulfill that First and
Great Commandment, for only they will prove their LOVE.
It is most assuredly true that only those who do fulfill that
First and Great Commandment of perfecting their LOVE
FOR GOD, will be prepared to receive that great, unspeakable Promise in its fulness. They alone will be prepared
to behold and to hear and to fully comprehend those great,
dynamic blessings which God has hid up from the foundations of the world for those who LOVE HIM! These are
the great and mighty things which He has hid up because
of the hardness of men's hearts, and the blindness of their
minds and because of the great wickedness of unbelief."

If anyone desires to know if God LIVES and if He will or can fulfill His PROMISES, has only to "PROVE ME NOW HEREWITH!" by LIVING THE LAWS THAT HAVE BEEN GIVEN.

God also PROMISES that to those "Who purify themselves before Him, will He grant the PRIVILEGE OF SEEING AND KNOWING FOR THEMSELVES. That through the power and manifestation of the Spirit WHILE IN THE FLESH they will comprehend all things!" They will truly "Be born of the Spirit and be prepared to enter the world of glory!" Such are the PROMISES OF GOD as He waits for man to fulfill the laws pertaining to them.

The great key and the lock and the DOOR have always been right within the reach of every man's hand. It has been as close to him as his navel and as unnoticed. This holy contact with the divine supply of continual spiritual nourishment is given freely, until that which is PERFECT IS COME, or is developed and brought forth. This glory and fulfillment are awaiting those who realize they do not already KNOW everything, or possess all knowledge, or have all power, and through this acknowledgment grow humble so that they can begin to "Ask, to seek and to knock" so that they can be taught of God, in a new child-like humility.

In this very turning to God their maturing commences as they leave their childish vestures and swaddling blankets behind. This higher way is only for those who begin to "hunger and thirst after righteousness." And it is only those who are willing to leave their dependence on the "arm of flesh" and their noisy, jangling of their brass toys and their clanging cymbals and their babyish rattles behind. It is for those who have outgrown the infant crib, of which Isaiah so clearly spoke. It is for those who have developed the "hungering and the thirsting after righteousness" instead of showy "self-righteousness" with which they have permitted themselves to be held in unprogressiveness or who have themselves sought to awe the minds of men by their own childish, show-off antics and display.

It is as one seeks that holy "Kingdom of God" or divine contact with God, within, that his faith turns into KNOWING and his KNOWING turns into POWER. It is in this contact or center, this "Kingdom of heaven within" that one learns to fulfill all the laws of righteousness. He learns to be STILL and to actually KNOW GOD.

In this contact only can one receive the "fulness of joy, which belongs to the saints alone." This "Holy Place of the Most High" is the "Holy of Holies" or that seat of contact with God, or the point of instruction or revelation as one begins to associate with God. It is the place of contact with the great, outflowing glory of divine ecstasy and inner instruction. This ecstasy is at first given in just small measured portions. This is how and why one only receives those ecstatic, spiritual thrills occasionally at first, that is, until he learns to control them and to hold himself in holy majesty.

It must be noted here the boundless effort that is required to learn to control and to manipulate a small, infant body. It takes two full years, plus childhood, and often all the years of adolescence to learn to master the physical body. The spiritual body, as it develops, requires time also to be brought into perfect control as one learns to glorify the emotional system. It takes time and desiring to bring the spiritual, emotional being into the maturity of divine majestic, regal nobility of glorious mastery.

It is as one matures or grows, through his continued "hungering and thirsting" for an ever increasing supply of this divine, spiritual nourishment that the glory of divine ecstasy and joy and LOVE increases until it becomes a steady, permanent current of living, vibrating, effulgent fulfillment. Only by this method can one possibly "evolve from the man kingdom into the God Kingdom," or into the fulness of sonship as he is prepared to "Be Born of the Spirit!"

That inner center within man's own soul is the "secret closet" in which one can close the door to all outside negation and discords and disturbances and actually converse with God—AND RECEIVE ANSWERS! This has been known "as walking with God!" It is the developed ability to associate with the Divine. And those who learn to make this contact have truly found "THE KINGDOM OF HEAVEN WITHIN, in which all else is added." As one makes this contact all negation and evils and anguish and mortal worries and turmoils are left behind. They are dissolved by the Light and the glory of God!

"And whatsoever you ask when you pray, believe that you receive it, and you shall have it." This is the point where the Holy Spirit of Promise bears witness that your prayers have been heard—AND WILL BE FULFILLED! This is when you know that God has heard them. This is also the point Enoch reached when he received "this assurance from God, before he was translated, that he pleased God." "And if we KNOW that He heareth us; then we KNOW that WE SHALL RECEIVE WHATSOEVER WE ASK."

"He who asketh in Spirit asketh according to the Will of God, and he shall have whatsoever he asketh." "He who asketh in Spirit" IS asking according to the Will of God because in that Holy, inner contact all one's desires become glorified, according to God's Holy Will, because one becomes so in tune with the Almighty his very desires become spiritualized and exquisitely beautiful! And one could not possibly "ASK AMISS" in such a realm of Holy Peace and Divine assurance. He could not even think of self-centered, mediocre requests. His desires are exalted into glorious visions of beauty and perfection, according to the will of God! "And he shall have whatsoever he asks." In this holy center, or inner contact, as one associates or walks with God, there is always that assurance that "the Father will reward him openly" or bring to pass or accomplish the completion of the desire out in the open, or make it a tangible accomplishment. And he shall assuredly have whatsoever he asketh. And then one can, with complete assurance, "Lay hold of the best gifts," as Paul admonished. The little, skimpy, selfish, commonplace or ordinary requests melt away as the hoar frost before the morning sun.

Remember this always: "They draw near to me with their lips and with their tongues they honor me, but they have removed their hearts far from me. Their fear toward me (and toward new truth) is taught by the precepts of men." This fallacious method of pretending to worship God is as empty and void and meaningless as it is possible to imagine. The LOVE toward God is not taught by the precepts of men. This divine, perfect LOVE is taught by the Spirit of God as individuals lift up their hearts to worship and adore. It is brought forth as one learns to sing THAT NEW SONG, of praise and LOVE and gratitude, which none but the righteous can learn. This song will open the doors to that "Kingdom of Heaven within." It will lead one to the complete fulfilling of that First and Great Commandment.

It is in this yielding and adoring and gratitude and praise

that one evolves into the point of full KNOWING. He is then prepared to be "wrapped in the power and glory of His Maker and will be caught up to dwell with Him," or become a translated being. In this accomplishment one becomes an actual bearer of these holy, living vibrations of eternal light and glorious ecstasy, filled with the full, comprehensive knowledge of God. He never again descends into the old ways of mortal fears and evils and negative thinking and living and existing, but remains in that higher realm of Spiritual attainment and "needs go no more out, into the lone and dreary world." And though he may choose to serve upon this earth, as *a translated being,* he will be able henceforth "to come and go as the wind," from one glorious assignment to another as he performs THE GREATER WORKS!

It is through the spiritual umbilical cord that the "substance of THINGS HOPED FOR" are brought into being as the Father fulfills the requests, or rewards that individual "openly" as his innermost hopes and desires are brought forth into complete fulfillment. One has but to hold forth his HOPES, without doubting, and FAITH will fashion the plan or pattern for their PERFECT FULFILLING. This is the "BETTER HOPE" that cannot be made perfect through the law or mortal ideas or beliefs. This is why FAITH, HOPE and CHARITY, which is the perfect Christ LOVE, are the only attributes or gifts of lasting virtue or worth. And the greatest of these three is LOVE!

Always the great and marvelous PROMISES are reserved for THOSE WHO LOVE GOD. "All things work together for good to those WHO LOVE GOD!" And the great and unspeakable things, which have been hid up from the foundation of the world, those things which mortal eyes have never seen, nor mortal ears ever heard, neither has entered into the heart of man, are the things which God has prepared for THOSE WHO LOVE HIM!" (Not in lip service but from their hearts.)

This LOVE is the greatest glory, the greatest joy, the greatest ecstatic wonder ever held out to man. God does not need such love as we can offer. It is man who needs to give that LOVE that his soul may grow into the fulfillment of all the great and breath-taking PROMISES OF ALMIGHTY GOD!

Concentrate on loving God with all your heart, and as you hold to this practice you will naturally begin to love Him with all your soul and with all your mind—and you will love your neighbor as yourself, for you cannot have eyes single to the glory of God and carry around petty dislikes and agonizing hates for any man. The precious writer of the "ODES OF SOLOMON" wrote: "No way is hard where there is a simple heart. Nor is there any wound where the thoughts are upright. Nor is there any storm in the depth of the illuminated thought."

As the desire for this most wonderful, divine, powerful gift of PERFECT LOVE grows and is intensified within one the great unfolding or fulfillment will be accomplished. And he who loves thus will "BE BORN OF THE SPIRIT" and God will reveal those great, unspeakable things which "eyes have never before beheld, nor mortal ears heard, neither has entered into the heart of man." This is the PROMISE to those who LOVE GOD. And it was meant to be accomplished *while in this life*. And there is also that unforgettable PROMISE that God will unveil His face unto those who LOVE thus.

In this Living Love one's mind and lips lose the power

to hurt and wound, and his voice will be heard among the Gods, for he will be prepared to associate with Divinity.

Glorious one, this is your heritage! This is the PROMISE! And, as the constant awareness of this sacred contact or continual realization of the TRUTH of God's PROMISES are made manifest, your hold upon that divine, sacred, umbilical cord will become assured until you "Fulfill all righteousness" and are fully prepared to "BE BORN OF THE SPIRIT!" A son of the Living God! A true son of divine, everlasting majesty and power! "These are the PROMISES!"

Peter unveiled briefly this method of divine instruction from God in these words: "For we have not followed cunningly devised fables, when we made known unto you the power and glory of our Lord, Jesus Christ, *but were eye witnesses of his majesty.* For he received from God the Father honor and glory, when there came a voice to him from the excellent glory. This is my Beloved Son in whom I am well pleased. *And this voice which came from heaven* WE HEARD when we were with him in the holy mount. *But we have also a more sure word of prophecy* (than either seeing or hearing); whereunto ye do well that ye take heed as unto a light that shineth in a dark place, *until the day dawn, and the day star arise in your heart.*" This is the instruction that promises the complete contact with God in which the full KNOWING IS ACCOMPLISHED. (2 Peter 1:16-19).

"The Spirit of Revelation is in connection with these blessings. A person may profit by noticing the first intimation of the Spirit of Revelation; for instance, when you feel pure intelligence flowing into you, it may give you sudden strokes of ideas, so that by noticing it, you find it fulfilled the same day or soon; (i.e.) those things that were pre-

sented unto your minds by the Spirit of God, WILL COME
TO PASS: and thus by learning the Spirit of God and understanding it, you may grow into the principle of revelation, until you BECOME PERFECT IN CHRIST JESUS."

This very Spirit of Revelation is the ability to receive the
Word of God as it is given to you personally from the Almighty. As one grows into this marvel of revealing does not
necessarily entitle him to the right to go out shouting it to
the world, such behavior, when encouraged or uncontrolled,
often leads one into false prophesying and exhibitionism
and evil. And this will close securely that channel of increasing direction from the Heavenly Father. One's growth
and perfecting ends with his own yielding to his inclination
to display the "self."

When the Spirit of Revelation does come it is but the
witness of that contact and association with God. And it is
for one's own personal growth, at first. In time that individual may be called to share such holy messages or
teachings, but only after he is ordained of God and SENT
FORTH to become the humble servant, even the very least
in the hands of the Almighty, with the "self" completely
crucified or put aside.

"These are the mysteries of Godliness!" They contain the
mystery and the method of becoming God-like or the plan
or pattern of growing into the principle of revelation until
one becomes "PERFECT IN CHRIST JESUS." This is how
one receives the word of God and so advances into divinity.

Truly, "The law made nothing PERFECT, but the bringing of a better Hope did!" And that which is PERFECT
is the dynamic, pure perfection of LOVE ITSELF. And it
can be brought forth only through the "hungering and
thirsting" as HOPE IS ESTABLISHED WITHIN. And it

is in this very "hungering and thirsting" that one learns to "SING THAT NEW SONG OF PRAISE AND LOVE AND GRATITUDE!"

This is how HOPE in the PROMISES is established and accomplished as FAITH FASHIONS AND FULFILLS THE PATTERN OF THE HOPE OR DESIRE HELD FORTH, through a hungering heart. This is why, of all the gifts mentioned, only FAITH, HOPE and CHARITY are eternal and lasting. Perfect these gifts and you will become PERFECT. This is how the method and the unfolding of that WHICH IS PERFECT WILL COME or be brought forth. And the command is that you "BECOME PERFECT EVEN AS THE FATHER IN HEAVEN IS PERFECT!"

But this must be remembered also: "He who says he is perfect is a liar and the truth is not in him!" If one has reached the stage where he has *overcome* all things he would be the last person on earth to tell it. Such boasting would instantly cancel his claim and turn it into vainglorious self-righteousness and the very laws of such perfection would be annulled. Such a one, having broken the very laws of perfection or "righteousness," would be left unto himself, to boast perhaps in his empty memories, a weak vain individual without power or contact or light. He would be NOTHING and would assuredly be a liar! And so it is true that none who is perfect could ever speak about it without degrading himself and closing the halls of glory and fulfillment to his soul.

And now, I ask that you live these laws of "righteousness" which have been unfolded in this record and you will KNOW whether I have spoken of myself or whether they are of God.

So be it—forever and forever—Amen!

THE SEAL!

"Eye hath not seen, nor ear heard, neither hath it entered into the heart of man the things which God hath prepared for those who love him." (Isa. 64:4 and I Cor. 2:9).

Just a small glimpse of these great and mighty things, which have been hid up from the foundations of the world, "am I now about to open unto the understandings of those who LOVE Me.

Behold, I am Jesus Christ, Son of the Living God, and there is none other Name given under heaven whereby man can be saved." (Acts 4:12).

I hereby place my seal upon this work that you may know it is of me—and none other. And according to your understandings and your love and your power to believe will these things be comprehended by you. "For the natural man receiveth not the things of the Spirit of God: for they are foolish unto him: neither can he know them, because they are spiritually discerned." (I Cor. 2:14).

In this record is given the meaning of the name "ELOHIM" or the ancient Hebrew name of God. It is a masculine plural of a feminine noun, meaning God and His Mate—for "We shall make man in our own image, MALE AND FEMALE." To whom was he speaking? It had to be Someone of female form else where would be the pattern? This very Name Elohim enfolds the full potential of man's divine destiny as he OVERCOMES—and "evolves from the man kingdom into the God Kingdom."

336

This earth is the "School for Gods!" And "AS man is, God once was and, as God is, man may become!" Not all will attain unto this glorious fulfillment because of the greeds and hatreds and evils and wickedness they have generated within their own beings. And the greatest wickedness of all is UNBELIEF! Within this word, *"unbelief,"* are all the evils of men generated.

As you, my holy, advancing ones, filled with love and a belief in the PROMISES, evolve, you will eventually be called upon to use the powers of your own perfection in the process of creation. You too will give forth that all-powerful command: "LET THERE BE LIGHT!" Else why would this information be imparted unto you right from the beginning of man's sojourn on earth?

And from the LIGHT, which you have learned to generate in your own beings, as you have progressed in your schooling of preparation, will the atoms be formed to create worlds—and all that they contain: "FOR ALL THAT THE FATHER HAS IS YOURS!"

After your graduation into Godhood is finished you will be called to create first a world. And you will be the Elohim or the Gods over it. And you will people it with your own Spiritual offspring. And you, as their heavenly parents, will be solicitous of their every need and righteous desires as they will call upon you for help and understanding, for love will be yours in its fulness.

Your spiritual children, in turn, will advance into those same powers of creation as they, too, progress. And thus you will be lifted and exalted into rulers of solar systems. As their spiritual children advance so will you advance and be exalted into the rulers of galaxies—and eventually universes.

And thus, "God standeth in the congregation of the Mighty. He judgeth among the Gods!" And I, Jesus Christ, will be exalted also and advanced as you advance in the progressing spiral of eternal glory and divine achievement. For the Father has said, "This is my work and my glory, to bring to pass the immortality and the eternal life of man!" And so the Heavenly Father will be exalted to a higher degree of glory by each progressing generation of Gods evolving under Him.

Thus one advances into Godhood as he, too, uses the Light and knowledge he has accumulated in his eons of schooling and progress, to rule first over a world, then a solar system—a galaxy and finally a universe—and on and on—into infinitude. This is the pattern and this is the plan and this is the purpose and the meaning of all that is and all that has been and all that will be. PERFECTION! GLORY! EXALTATION! ACHIEVEMENT! AND ETERNAL PROGRESS! And this has been the divine procedure that has been taking place from the very beginning of eternity! And "There is no beginning—and no end!" Thus it is and ever has been and will continue to be forever and forever!

And now, I must give you a reminder of the things that "Were given to abide in you, THE RECORD OF HEAVEN," which is a memory of the pre-existent estate when you earned the right to have your name written in the "Lamb's Book of Life." And know fully that your name was written there because you had earned the right to have it engraved upon that sacred scroll of honor before the foundations of the world, according to your own righteousness and holy desires and your great love.

In that day, so long ago, you were existing in a realm of peace and beauty and happiness as you were abiding in the realms of heaven and in the Presence of God and with a full knowledge of your relationship to Him as your Heavenly or Spiritual Father. And this record of memory is given to abide in you.

"Furthermore, we have had fathers of our flesh which corrected us, and we gave them reverence; shall we not much rather be in subjection unto the Father of Spirits, and live?"

You do—and did have a Father of your Spirits and you did have fathers of your mortal bodies. But they are not the same. And it is given, "Call no man your Father upon the earth: for one is your Father, which is in heaven." (Matt. 23:19)·

"Oh God, the God of the Spirits of all flesh . . ." (Num. 16:22).

"Then shall the dust return to the earth as it was: and the Spirit shall RETURN unto God who gave it." (Ecc. 12:7). But the flesh only returns to the earth if it has remained unglorified and earthy. It is *in* and *with* the flesh that death must be OVERCOME.

Your spirits are eternal! You are not mere mortal beings, as you have supposed. You are from the race and the lineage of Gods — Gods endless — generations of Them — reaching above this world and this planetary system and this galaxy and this universe — and on — and on — a lineage so great and so divine and so endless that if you could but glimpse the fulness of your Heavenly Father you might be given a faint understanding of His Father before Him— and His Father before Him—and so, on—and on! The generations of Gods are endless and they comprise your Spiritual ancestry. And if, for only one moment, you would open your hearts to understand, you will begin to be prepared to *Comprehend all things* and to receive all power.

And the invitation is and has always been: "Come and partake of the Fountains of Life freely!" Yes! Come! That you might KNOW THE TRUTH, that you might be eternally FREE! Free from the bondage of mortality and ignorance and small, half-truths and all men's bigotry and all self-righteousness. Yes! Come! And walk with God! "And be ye perfect, even as your Father in heaven is perfect!"

———————

And now, Blessed Ones, it is true that "Perfect love never fails; but whether there be prophecies, they shall fail; whether there be tongues, they shall cease; whether there be knowledge, it shall vanish away.

"For now, you know in part, and you prophesy in part.

"But when that which IS PERFECT is come, then that which is in part shall be done away.

"Now abideth (or continueth) Faith, Hope and Charity (which is the pure, divine, glorious LOVE), these three; and the greatest, the most perfect, the most sublime, eternal attribute is CHARITY or the unlimited power of LOVE! LOVE is that which is PERFECT. And when that which is PERFECT is come or is developed or brought forth then the gifts, or that which is only in part, shall be done away. And *the fruits of the Spirit* alone will remain. And it is by their FRUITS that they will be known, not by their gifts. And those FRUITS will consist of the divine attributes of *Perfected* LOVE, namely mercy, compassion, gentleness, longsuffering, humility, joy, divine ecstasy and eternal gladness! And these will be their treasures in heaven, which no power can corrupt or take from them."

As long as there are those who display only the GIFTS OF THE SPIRIT and none of the FRUITS, then you may know with a sure knowing that LOVE has not yet been made perfect in their lives. When LOVE is made perfect, then the gifts, or that which is only in part, or the outward show, will be done away or transformed into the GREATER works, of silent, powerful, dynamic witnessing of God as to the worthiness of that individual. Man uses the gifts unintentionally perhaps, to bear witness of himself, though in his blindness he believes he is bearing witness of God. But the gifts used thus will profit him nothing.

It is the FRUITS which contain the power of divinity and of true service. The FRUITS are the inward power of fulfillment. And it is by their FRUITS only that anyone will be acknowledged or accepted in the higher realms. It is the gifts which are displayed as the sounding brass and the clanging cymbals. And it is to this group that I will profess that I have never known them, for when the gifts are used without the perfected LOVE, they are unacceptable and void and profiteth them nothing

My Beloved Ones, open up your minds to understand and your hearts to receive and so shall the fulness of the PROMISES become established unto you. And *you will be filled with Light and comprehend all things,*—Not just glimpse them in part, through a glass dimly, but you will truly be able to comprehend ALL things—"AND ALL THINGS WILL BECOME SUBJECT UNTO YOU, BOTH IN HEAVEN AND ON EARTH; THE LIFE AND THE LIGHT, THE SPIRIT AND THE POWER, sent forth by the will of the Father, through me, Jesus Christ, His Son."

The First and Great Commandment contains all perfection as one LIVES it. One who fulfills it is no longer under mortal laws or the shadow or burden of them. This LOVE is the very Fountains of Living Water, which I promised to you centuries ago.

Come, My Beloved Ones, and partake of the Rivers of Life freely for the draft is now held out to you that you, partaking of it, will never need to thirst again. Nor will you ever need to die!

And by the great LOVE, or by the FRUITS thereof, shall you be known, for LOVE only brings the fulfillment of that which is PERFECT! When LOVE is perfected in any individual he will truly "BE BORN OF THE SPIRIT!" And He will comprehend all things, fully and completely—not just in part.

And so is My SEAL placed upon this work! And no man can remove this SEAL, for the power which is over the SEAL is greater than they! And the Name of the Father is upon it! And my Name is upon it, even the Name of Jesus Christ, your Redeemer, the Son of the Living God! And the Name of the Holy Ghost is upon it!

And it shall stand as long as the earth shall stand!

FOR I HAVE SPOKEN! AND I LIE NOT!

SO BE IT! Amen!